Artificial Bear Optimization (ABO): A New Approach of Metaheuristic Algorithm for Business Intelligence

Dr.P. Mary Jeyanthi

Faculty in Institute of Management Technology,

Nagpur, Maharashtra.

Email: pmjeyanthi@imtnag.ac.in / dr.maryprem@gmail.com

Published by

Artificial Bear Optimization (ABO): A New Approach of Metaheuristic Algorithm for Business Intelligence

ISBN 978-93-87862-654

Author

Dr.P. Mary Jeyanthi

Bonfring

309, 2nd Floor, 5th Street Extension, Gandhipuram,

Coimbatore-641 012.

Tamilnadu, India.

E-mail: info@bonfring.org

Website: www.bonfring.org

Phone: 0422 4213231

Author Details

Dr.P. Mary Jeyanthi is working as a faculty at the Institute of Management Technology, Nagpur, Maharashtra. She had one decade of industry experience in HDFC Bank Ltd, Business Intelligence Unit, Chennai, Tamil Nadu. She had the hands full of expertise in Business Intelligence and forecasting analytics. She had done her research in "A New Implementation of Mathematical Models with metaheuristic Algorithms for Business Intelligence". Business Intelligence & Analytics initiatives on High Net Worth (HNW) Portfolio and She will be responsible for the creation and execution of strategies.

Besides that, she had published a number of research papers in various national and international reputed journals. Conducted several workshops on Research Methodology and Business Intelligence. With 10+ years of experience in Information Technology professional in Banking Sector with extensive skills and experience in Business Intelligence with Metaheuristics algorithm and Passion in teaching to enrich the environment with knowledge and Self-discipline. Being an Entrepreneur, intensive knowledge in the research field. She will be invited as a Chief Guest in Inter college symposium and Summit across India. She is the Resource Person by many colleges regarding soft skill training and workshops related to research paper writing. She had contributed many articles in magazines related the Building up the Human Capital and Business Analytics. She is expertise in novelty approach of writing and managing the analytics with real-time scenarios. Her research interest in Business Intelligence and Analytics, Artificial Intelligence, Big data analytics, Management Information Systems, Data Analysis, and Business models.

In this book, Dr.P. Mary Jeyanthi innovated nature inspired metaheuristic algorithm. She inspired the functionality of Bear smelling sense and implement in the way of optimization. She developed the algorithm inspired by Bear Smelling sense; the name of the algorithm is Artificial Bear Optimization (ABO). In this book provides the insights of metaheuristic algorithms and its limitations and how ABO will help for Business Intelligence problems.

"I thank Almighty Lord Jesus Christ & my lovable husband Prem, My little angels Eva & Jael for their wonderful support & sacrifice"

CHAPTER 1

Fundamental of Business Intelligence

1.1. Introduction

Organisation today faces enormous costs pressure and changing business requirement. In specific, the business world has many complex processes, potential investment is highly risky and accurate data for optimization efforts are sometimes lacking. On the other hand, Information Technology (IT) has been altering the nature of the processes, products, industries, companies and even competition itself (Porter & Millar, 1985).In order to succeed today's organizations must understand how this technology can create substantial and sustainable competitive advantages. IT has not only affected the individual process orany activities performed, but it has been enhancing the company's ability to exploit linkages between activities, both inside and outside the company (Porter & Millar, 1985, p. 152) through new information flow.

In this generation of continuous technological advancements, the available tools in solving business problems and handling huge amounts of data are constantly increasing. A few years ago, the problems which were considered impossible are now easily solved using desktops and laptops. Although the fundamentals of mathematics and statistics do not change, the availability of sophisticated computer software has changed the way the problems have been approached. Adapting the low-cost massive data -storage technologies and the wide availability of internet connections have made available large amounts of data that have been collected and accumulated by the various organizations over the years. Today's knowledge economy, it is no longer sufficient for only key individuals in any organization to have all the information. Competition is shortening business-cycles, forcing businesses to be more agile and thus pushing more decision-making responsibility to not just strategists and analysts, but all tactical and operational decision-makers. Indeed, these are some of the main reasons why Business Intelligence (BI) initiatives continue to be front and center for most enterprises, and BI-related activities keep on rising.

Business Intelligence (BI) refers to a variety of software applications, enables the organizations' raw data for intelligent decision making. These BI's are formed with some related performance, which includes online analytical processing, data mining, querying and reporting along with the techniques that include multidimensional analyses modeling, mathematical projection, ad-hoc queries, and 'canned' reporting.

The fact-based decision making is the main concept of BI that results in a single version of the truth. The BI system provides the decision maker, the tools and methodologies which result in effective and timely decisions. Decisions can be classified in terms of methods such as stagnant Decision making and dynamic decision making. Traditionally, the mathematical models and algorithms are used to analyze a largenumber of alternative actions, which helps to attain more exact conclusions and achieve efficient and timely decisions. By implementing the BI system, it would be concluded that that decision-making process is amplified efficiently.

1.2. Background of the Study

1.2.1. Business Intelligence (BI): Usage and Future

According to Gartner's report in the year, 2009 predicted the following in BI market development. Through 2012, it was expected that 35 percent or more companies which are placed in the top 5,000, due to lack of information, tools, and processes, regularly fail in futuristic decision-making in order to bring significant changes in their markets and business. By 2012, it was expected that around 40 percent of the total budget would be controlled by Business Intelligence in the business unit. Again, by the year 2012, it was assessed that coarse-grained application mash-ups delivered one-third of the analysis applications which were applied to business processes.

The top Business Intelligence trends were reported by the special report from the *information management* in the year 2009 as "green computing, social networking, data visualization, mobile BI, predictive analytics, composite applications, cloud computing, and multi-touch" (Claudia, 2006). Aberdeen group's study provided insights about the Software-as-a-Service (SaaS) business intelligence creating an interest in an increasing trend when compared to the past years with doubling of deployment approach by the organizations - 15% in 2009 when compared to 2008 it was 7%. Chris Kanarcus, InfoWorld, pointed out in his article that IDC, a research firm, growth data reports also similarly show that an increase in the SaaS BI market could be experienced about 22 percent in the year 2013 due to the increased sophistication for the product, strained IT budgets, including other factors (Rao, 2003).

Nowadays, BI is becoming popular and used by more and more organizations for better decision-making in business, which is proved by Gartner's research report (Gartner Research, 2009). The report said, *"For the fourth year in a row, BI applications have been ranked the top technology priority in the 2009 Gartner Executive programs survey of more than 1,500 Chief Information Officers (CIOs) around the world."*

Further, in India, the market for business intelligence (BI) software is forecasted to reach $81.5 million in 2012 which is an increase of 15.6% from 2011, according to Gartner Inc. Despite the economic slowdown, the report predicted that due to its smarter, more agile and efficient business, the usage has been increased within the organization. The report also said that "the BI market has remained strong because the dominant vendors continue to put BI, analytics and performance management at the centre of their messaging, while end-user organizations largely continue their BI projects, hoping that resulting transparency and insights will enable them to cut costs and enhance productivity and agility down the line" (Singh, 2011). Table 1.1 below shows the business Intelligence total software revenue (in Million of US dollars).

Table 1.1: Business Intelligence Total Software Revenue (in millions of US dollars) by Companies

Company	2013 Revenue	2013 Market Share (%)	2012 Revenue	2012-2013 Growth (%)
SAP	3,057.0	21.3	2,902.0	5.3
Oracle	1,994.0	13.9	1,952.0	2.1
IBM	1,820.0	12.7	1,735.0	4.9
SAS Institute	1,696.0	11.8	1,600.0	6.0
Microsoft	1,379.0	9.6	1,190.0	15.9
Others	4,422.0	30.8	3,932.0	12.5
Total	**14,368.0**	**100.0**	**13,311.0**	**7.9**

Source: Adapted from Gartner (2014)

Further, Table1.2 shows different software usage and their market share. BI platform occupied 59.5% followed by CPM suites.

Table 1.2: Business Intelligence and Analytics Software by Segment, Worldwide (in millions of US dollars) by Companies

Sub-segment	2013 Revenue	2013 Market Share (%)	2012 Revenue	2012-2013 Growth (%)
Analytic Applications and Performance Management	2,001	13.9	1,890	5.8
BI Platforms	8,550	59.5	7,857	8.8
CPM Suites	2,735	19.0	2,602	5.1
Advanced Analytics	1,082	7.5	962	12.5
Total	**14,368**	**100.0**	**13,311**	**7.9**

Source: Adapted from Gartner (2014)

Being a time as well as resource consuming process, BI implementation is also expensive. Mostly, with no expected results or not fulfilling the vaguely defined expectations as in the past, it failed to provide as expected results within the given time and budget.

This is important to improve the performance of business thus by satisfying the BI project sponsors. In this book, various critical success factors in BI implementation would be studied using secondary data (**Literature review, Chapter II**). Based on the identified critical success factors and a new algorithm would be developed and compared with the previously developed algorithms. **The following section briefly discussed the importance of decision making and the need for BI for such decision-making system.**

1.2.2. *Role of Decision Making System in Organization*

Decision-making is a core activity of organizational life. Poor or bad decisions have huge consequences for organizations, many times even threatening their existence. However, it was not, until Simon (1947) wrote his book 'Administrative Behaviour' that decision making was introduced as a focal point for studying organizations. Since then, the study of decision making has become an important research topic in organizational theory and has made many contributions, contributing to some extent, to the status that organizational theory enjoys today (Hodgkinson & Starbuck 2008). In the decision-making literature, decisions have been classified according to decision types such as structured and unstructured decisions or as introduced by Simon (1977), between programmed and non-programmed decisions. Simon (1977) stated that "Decisions are programmed to the extent that they are repetitive and routine, to the extent that a definite procedure has been worked out for handling them so that they don't have to be treated from scratch each time they occur" (p. 46). On the other hand, decisions are non-programmed "to the extent that they are novel, unstructured and unusually consequential" (ibid., p. 46). Programmed or structured decisions incorporate measurable, well-defined, and compatible criteria were as non-programmed or unstructured decisions come under the heading of "problem-solving" (Simon 1977, pp. 64-65). Operational decisions are structured, and strategic decisions are unstructured (Simon 1977). In particular, Mintzberg et al. (1976) define strategic to those decisions that are "important in terms of actions taken, the resources committed, or the precedents set" (p.246) and those are usually made under uncertainty and, which does have a programmed solution.

Hence, the objective of decision analysis is to provide managers with useful information for understanding various managerial aspects of a problem and to choose the best solution among many alternatives. On purpose of this research is to develop and implement effective marketing programs to fully utilizing a customer database in a very specific decision analysis paradigm. As a result of growing interest in micromarketing, it is important for many firms especially banks devote considerable resources to identify potential customers that may be open to targeted marketing messages.

Due to the easy availability of data warehouses combining demographics, psychographics, and behavioral information, it became more critical. Various database approaches for direct marketing is followed by both the marketing (Bult and Wansbeek, 1995; Gonul and Shi, 1998; Persma and Jonker, 2000) and data mining communities (Bhattacharaya, 1998; Piatetsky-Shapiro and Masand, 1999; Kim et al., 2001; Domingos and Richarson, 2001). Direct marketing uses the traditional method of optimal selection of mailing targets and it is considered as important factors for direct marketing to be successful. This model aims in identifying the customer who will respond to a specific solicitation campaign letter which is based on the customer's estimated probability of responding to marketing programs. The market managers make the strategic marketing plan with the decision support from customer targeting model which an often neglected functionality. For example, while recovering the operational costs of a specific campaign if marketers want to know how many customers should be targeted to maximize the expected net profit or increase market share. To obtain these goals, a sensitivity analysis is done by market managers that shows how the value of the objective function (e.g. the expected net profit from the campaign) changes as campaign parameters vary (e.g. the campaign scope measured by a number of customers targeted). These issues become even more problematic when the interpretability of the model is important. It is necessary for the managers to understand the key drivers of consumer response, in database marketing applications. 'Black Box' is a predictive model which is not useful for developing comprehensive marketing strategies. From this research, using data mining optimization techniques, a new algorithm is developed.

1.2.3. Data Mining

In the industrial implementation of data mining methods, CRM is used rapidly (Ngai, et al., 2009). With the help of advanced algorithms such as Statistics, Artificial Intelligence, and Machine Learning, data mining methods uncover hidden knowledge and patterns in large amounts of data and provide both evidence and support for decision makers (Turbanet al., 2007, p. 305). More importantly, predictive data mining methods can forecast customers' behavior and answer questions that are difficult or time-consuming than traditional approaches such as, Online Analytical Processing (OLAP), spreadsheets, and statistics (Rygielski, et al., 2002). Data mining is one of the steps in a larger framework: Knowledge Discovery in Databases (KDD) (Fayyadet al., 1996) is a process of extracting knowledge from data in the context of large databases. The most popular data mining task is Clustering. It attempts to divide data into groups, such that the differences among clusters are maximized and the variations within each are minimized.

Therefore, the capability of clustering algorithms to reveal natural groupings of data makes it a widely used technique for conducting customer segmentation.

The process of searching and analyzing data in order to find implicit but potentially useful information is called as Data mining. This process involves selecting, exploring and modeling large amounts of data to uncover previously unknown patterns, and ultimately comprehensible information, from the large database. The methods followed by Data mining include Statistical Analysis, Decision Tree, Neural Networks rules induction and refinement, and graphic visualization. Even though tools of Data mining have been available for a long time, the advances in computer hardware and software, particularly exploratory tools, data visualization,and neural network, have made data mining more attractive and practical. The typical data mining process consists of the following steps.

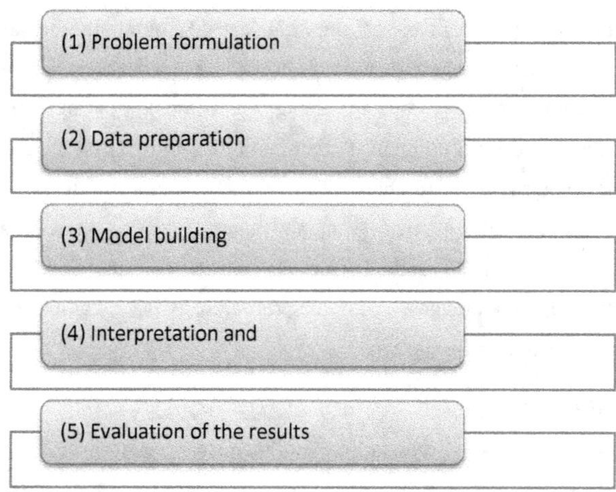

Figure 1.1: The Typical Data Mining Process

The main component of Data mining is pattern extraction, and it deals with the relationship between subsets of data. Definition of the pattern is **(4):** a statement S in L that describes relationships among subsets of facts F_s of a given set of facts, F, with some certainty C, such as that S is simpler than the enumeration of all facts in F_s. The task of Data mining is to extract patterns from large data sets. The task of data mining is classifiedintofive categories as summarized in Figure 1.1. Even though it supports other data mining tasks, taxonomy reflects the entering role of data visualization as a separate data mining task. Validation of the results is also a data mining task. By the fact that the validation supports the other data mining tasks and is always necessary within research, these tasks were not mentioned as a separate one.

According to the type of knowledge extracted by the tasks these data mining tasks are grouped. The first step to gain useful marketing insights and marking critical marketing decisions is identifying the patterns in a large data set. The data mining tasks are developed as an assortment of customer and market knowledge which forms the core of knowledge management process.

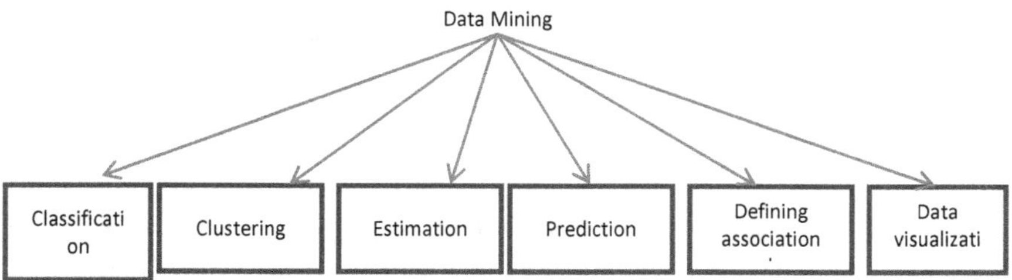

Figure 1.2: A taxonomy of Data mining Tasks (Source: Adopted from Rygielskietal, 2002)

1.2.4. Optimization Techniques

1.2.4.1. Nature Inspired Intelligence (NII)

Artificial Intelligence (AI) corresponds to nature-inspired techniques and methodologies that are based on how biological systems and natural networks deal with real-world situations in nature (Vassiliadis & Dounias, 2007). These methodologies are used in research papers related to different subjects such as General Optimization problems, Industrial applications, and Data processing. These techniques are considered to be very efficient in finding near-optimum solutions to problems.

- Becausethere are enclosed with some unique characteristics and properties. For example, in Ant Colony Optimization (ACO) and Particle Swarm Optimization (PSO) algorithms, special cooperation among members of the population takes place, as well as effective and advantageous information feedback mechanisms
- In artificial immune systems, DNA computing and membrane computing do not have as many applications like the aforementioned methods at the moment, still, they imitate some of the unique functions of the human nature that gives them great potential for future implementation

1.3. Previous Work

Customer segmentation is one of the most significant methods used in studies of traditional marketing.

From these studies, the existing customer segmentation is classified into the methodology and application-oriented approaches. The methodology oriented studies applied mathematical methodologies. For instance, these methodologies apply genetic algorithms, neural network, statistical works, and Fuzzy set to identify the optimized segmented from homogenous group (Hu & Sheub, 2003; Hwang, Jung, & Suh, 2004; Jiao & Zhang, 2005; Jonker et al., 2004; Kim, Jung, Suh, & Hwang, 2006; Kim & Street, 2004; Kim et al., 2005; Tsai & Chiu, 2004; Vellido, Lisboa, & Meehan, 1999). However, in the case of application-oriented approaches, in specific applications, the researcher must search for the optimum method. In such applications, previous studies combined multiple methods to solve customer segmentation issues.

Even though both customer and market segmentation have similarity in the literature, the availability of their clustering mechanisms is different. The goal of market segmentation is to acquire new customers, and this is the first step of CRM, while customer acquisition using socio-demographic data. Using both socio-demographic and transactional data, customer segmentation works at all the steps of CRM. To achieve more accurate clusters or segment's methodology-driven studies are used, these segmentation modified some data clustering techniques such as Self-Organizing Map (SOM), or use a combination of two or more data mining (such as Lee et al. 2004; Jedid-Jah et al., 2004 and Kim et al., 2008). "On the other hand, application-oriented researches must search for the optimum method for solving segmentation problems in specific applications" (Chan, 2008). Mostly, they define and create new variable for clustering procedure or use different variables in sequential clustering steps (Such as Hwang et al., 2004; Kim et al., 2006; Hsieh 2004; Chang et al., 2007; Chan 2008; McCarty & Hastak, 2007; Lee & Park, 2005; Cheng & Chen, 2009 and Seog et al., 2005). Lifetime Value (LTV) has an important role in the current literature on customer segmentation.

For example, the LTV model from Hwang et al(2004), includes past profit contribution, potential benefit, and defection probability of a customer for wireless telecommunication customers segmentation is suggested. In Kim et al. (2006), based on analyzing customer value and customer segmentation, a framework is proposed. Through a case study on a wireless telecommunication company, the strategies that are offered to customer segments are illustrated. Reference Forward Model (RFM) is a major input for customer segmentation. Hsieh (2004), identify groups of customers in a self-organizing map neural network, which is based on repayment behavior and recency, frequency, and monetary behavioral scoring predictors. The bank customers are classified into three major profitable groups of customers. The customer's attributes that are determined using an Apriori association rule inducer are the resulting groups of the customer profile.

Using two different datasets, McCarty and Hastak (2007), RFM, CHAID, and logistic regression are investigated as analytical methods for direct marketing segmentation.

As a result of Cheng and Chen (2009) a new procedure, joining the quantitative value of RFM attributes and K-means algorithm into Rough Set theory (RS theory), is proposed to extract meaning rules. Other than the combination of above -mentioned input variables, these are also utilized by researchers. For example, Chan (2008), present campaign strategies that combine customer targeting and customer segmentation. From this research customer behavior is identified using an RFM model and then uses an LTV model to evaluate proposed segmented customers. To cluster customers, some authors use a combination of other different variables and measures. For example, Lee and Park (2005) aimed at profitable customer's segmentation by providing an easy, efficient, and more practical alternative approach based on the customer satisfaction survey.

The multi agent-based system is presented by the author, called the survey-based profitable customers segmentation system that executes the customer satisfaction survey and conducts the mining of the customer satisfaction survey, socio-demographic and accounting database through the integrated uses of business intelligence tools such as DEA (Data Envelopment Analysis), Self-Organizing Map (SOM) neural network, and C4.5 for the profitable customers segmentation. In Chang and Hung (2007), a potential model for customers in purchasing behavior is proposed. This model is obtained from past purchasing behavior of loyal customers and the web server log files of loyal and potential customers by means of clustering analysis and association rules analysis. In the same year, Stone et al. (2006) developed a framework based on data mining for customer segmentation and constructed a new customer segmentation method based on survival character. The new customer segmentation method consists of two-steps. The step consists of K-means clustering arithmetic; customers are clustered into different segments by similar survival characters (i.e. churn trend). And the second step includes each cluster's survival/hazard function is predicted by survival analyzing, then the validity of clustering is tested and customer churns trend is identified. Sheu et al. (2005), investigated the integrating data mining and experiential marketing to segment online game customers.

The outcome can help the firms to predict and understand the new consumers' purchase behavior. In accordance with the authors, an increase in the purchase for the new different attributes' consumers, the online game's manufacturers could draw up the different market strategies.

In Seog et al. (2005), groups of retail customers were determined and characterized, based on their perception of commitment to the retailer and the degree of use of its technological equipment. Similarly, as mentioned before, some authors have focused on the segmentation procedure from a technical point of view. For example, in Lee et al. (2004), using cross-national market segmentation, a new methodology is developed. The authors introduced a Two-Phase Approach (TPA) integrating statistical and data mining methods. The first phase statistical method conducts (MCFA: Multi-Group Confirmatory Factor analysis) by testing the difference between national clustering factors. The Data mining method conducted the second phase (a two-level SOM) to develop the actual clusters within each nation. In Huang et al. (2007), Support Vector Clustering (SVC) for marketing segmentation was used. In Kim et al (2008), based on novel clustering algorithms a Genetic Algorithms is proposed (GAs) to effectively segment the online shopping market. Even, in Hung and Tsai (2008), a novel market segmentation approach that was proposed for market segmentation of real-world multimedia on demand in Taiwan with the Hierarchical self-organizing segmentation model (HSOS),

Application-oriented researches must search for the optimum method for solving segmentation problems in specific applications (Chan, 2005; Chung, Oh, Kim, & Han, 2004; Jones, Easley, & Koehler, 2006; Kuo, An, Wang, and Chung, 2006; Shin & Sohn, 2004; Woo, Bae, & Park, 2005). By implementing these studies, sometimes they combine multiple methods to solve the customer segmentation problem for specific individual applications (Chung et al., 2004; Kim & Street 2004; Kim et al., 2005; Kuo et al., 2006; Shin & Sohn, 2004). Using artificial neural network practices in market segmentation methodology was proposed are relatively fewer articles with the Meta-Heuristic, ART2, data mining, Genetic Algorithm,and fuzzy algorithms. Even though it does not mean the application of artificial neural network in this aspect, the fewer number of articles related to the above category of artificial neural network application to market segmentation is less mature than in the others.

From the results, it is suggested that more research can be conducted in the market segmentation domain. In order to maximize an organization's profits through segmentation, strategists have to segment the market and thus increase the profitability of the organization. In addition to the real-life problem based by the marketers, previous studies to our knowledge only attempted to explain the purpose of Business Intelligence and proposed to explain the theoretical methodology of BI such as Predictive analysis, Forecasting analysis, Supply chain management, Scorecards,andDashboards. However, none of the research had focused on a standard methodology that would be applicable for enterprise-wide BI methodologies.

Even the existing methodologies, failed to provide a high level of interactive and Adhoc reporting requirements as still, enterprises tend to use only excel and spreadsheet functions. For instance, in a 1958 article, IBM researcher Hans Peter Luhn used the phrase business intelligence. He stated intelligence as: "the ability to apprehend the interrelationships of presented facts in such a way as to guide action towards a desired goal". Business intelligence as it is unstated today is supposed to have developed from the Decision Support Systems which began in the 1960s and developed all through the mid-80s.

To conclude, the study of the survey has been conducted for current BI methodologies and its limitations and expectations. Since it will be reputable with the new methodology to overcome the limitations of the existing methodology and fulfill the expectations. In the existing dissertation, there is no consistent enterprise-wide BI Methodologies. Still, now the business analysts are using Excel and spreadsheet functions. Existing BI tools suffer from a lack of analysis and visualization capabilities. Daily raising the data volume is the biggest hectic to manage the big data set. Only 10% of BI users are sophisticated enough to utilize a BI Tool. The inconsistency of the response produced by more than one advanced user is also known as multiple versions of the truth. Given this background, the present dissertation attempted to propose that exploit the desirable characteristics of Genetic Algorithms (GAs) and Artificial Neural Network (ANNs).

1.4.　Problem Identification

The managers often find it challenging even to obtain basic business information such as pending orders, stock levels, sales trends, and the history of individual customers. In most of the cases, even the key account managers take hours or even days to answer these questions, because they might be in different systems, for example, to retrieve the information about orders that are stored in a system for 'orders and sales processing', payment data in the 'accounting system' and information on past and 'planned activities' and contacts with individual customers in the 'Customer Relationship Management' (CRM) system. The exchange of information between these systems is impossible for the average users because these are designed separately and moreover involves complicated processes. Moreover, it is not easy for a non-technical user to obtain the desired information quickly.

The co-operation of employees from the IT department is requested to make complex queries from the database to provide the requisite data. In the end, the necessary information (usually in the form of different reports) must be obtained from various departments and employees.

A few rare cases take even several days or even weeks to collect such a piece of information, in which case the information may become too old, but still, they would be useful. It remarks that even though the organizations are rich in data, but they seem to be poor in information that is completely inappropriate. The challenge is how to transform data into useful information (Carver & Ritacco, 2006, p. 3). Over the last few years, it has become important to obtain useful information in real time, as it is the factor of success for companies. The time a manager who makes the business decision has been reduced drastically. Due to the competitive pressures in businesses, the intelligent decisions are made based on their incoming business data, and these decisions must be made quickly (Business Intelligence and Data Warehousing, 2005, p. 5). The main problem is that the huge amount of data must be converted into useful information in a timely manner in order to provide the manager with solid information for their decision. By converting the non-transparent data into useful information in real time, could contribute a significant competitive advantage for the company. Thus the business intelligence is the tool that enables the manager to make the decision. In the organization, this system had become the most indispensable part of the success. Business intelligence helps the managers to effectively detect the important trends, facilitate expedient decision making and analyze the behavior of customers.

Before

Figure 1.3: Decision Making without a Business Intelligence Tool

After

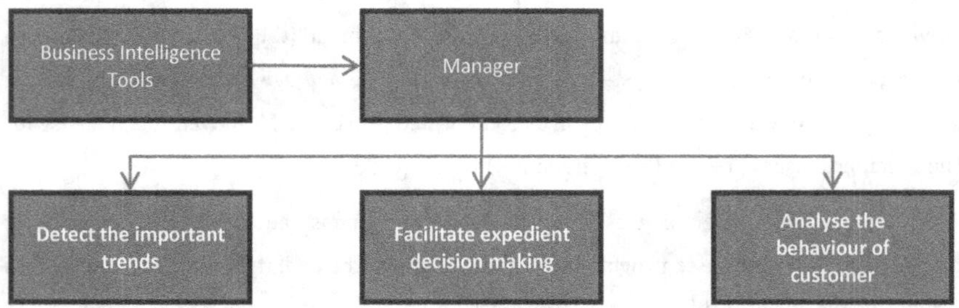

Figure 1.4: Decision Making with Business Intelligence Tool

In retail banks and commercial banks, especially in India in order to identify optional customer banks generally depend on traditional segmentation approaches. Their segmentation method enables banks to target their marketing campaigns by offering various products and services. It appeared that that segmentation only provides overview client behavior and intends to challenging and identify the optional customer. Moreover to retrieve data banks generally depend on both demographic and accounting database from a CRM (Lee & Park,2005) The traditional segmentation of clients in retail and commercial banking are methods used in banks. To various customer segments, these banks' products and offers are created. These traditional segmentation techniques can blur a view to real client behavior and they are used for analysis of customer behavioral features.

For the successful segmentation of profitable customers, the data from the socio-demographic and accounting database jointly with customer satisfaction surveys data obtained from a CRM system is used (Lee & Park, 2005). The first step is to identify the problem correctly. In order to formulate hypotheses for the investigation, the examined critical symptoms must be analyzed and interpreted. After analyzing and identifying the problem, effort should be directed towards defining an appropriate mathematical model to represent the system. Since the identified problem is from the huge set of customers, we need to identify the best optimal customer. The customer must be valid and trustworthy to avoid the risk in the market. The other way of saying is to find the valid optimal population (Customer or Candidate) from different sectors such as banking, Recruitment Board and any industry to explore the optimization.

1.5. Motivation for this Book

This research tackles this challenging problem by developing a framework to provide direction and decision in evaluating and selecting a data mining tool for an organization' s sector and background. In particular, the research will look in depth at evaluating visualization data mining tools. Previous work at evaluating software, data mining and visualization tools will be investigated and used to create a visual data mining framework. However, no studies to the knowledge of this author have looked at combining these different methodologies into a single unified framework.

After the framework has been developed it will be applied to several visual data mining tools to evaluate and compare the tools using a number of criteria from the framework for marking the evaluating the visual data mining tool. The research will propose a new algorithm considering the limitations of existing ANN and genetic models.

In addition, the study also evaluates existing algorithms in terms of its benefits and drawbacks of each and how best to find the most suitable algorithm. This will not be a comprehensive review of commercial tools but instead provides a method for evaluating tools and as a point of reference for selecting the best BI tool for the particular problem. The aim of the research project is to create an evaluation framework, for knowledge management advisers and business users to provide criteria on choosing a suitable for BI tool for an organization and compare with the existing framework.

1.6.   Research Objectives

Given the above challenges and gap, behind the Business intelligence to achieve the fact-based and single version of the truth, the present study proposed a new algorithm based on the selecting the right combination of people, processes, and technology with the Metaheuristics algorithm.

To analyze the potential growth of customer profitability and reduce risk exposure through more accurate financial credit scoring of their customers. The goal of this book is to design and develop the new algorithm and at the same time to find the optimal customer from the huge set of customers in the current industry.

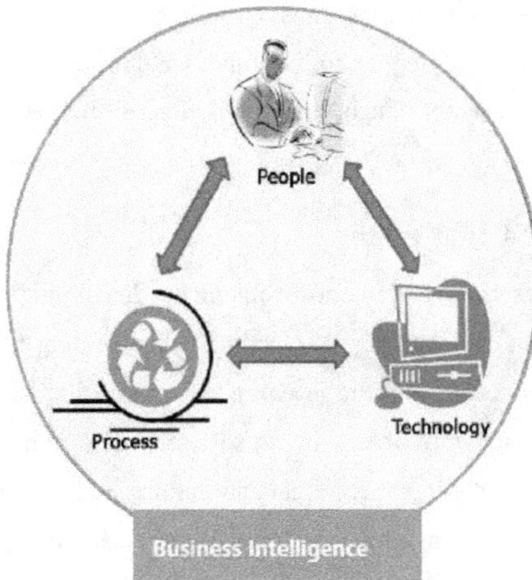

Figure 1.5: BI Using People, Process, Technology to Enable Value

To overcome the challenges behind Business intelligence is that to achieve the facts based and the single version of the truth in decision making. The optimal customer must be valued and trustworthy to avoid the risk in the market.

In this book, to accomplish the optimal customer the following five stages were adopted: Database preparation and Normalize the data in the first stage, Applying the existing Meta-heuristics algorithms individually is the second stage, Applying the proposed new algorithms in the third stage, Compare and analysis with the existing Meta-heuristics algorithms with the new algorithms is in the fourth stage and Intelligence concept is implemented with Backpropagation algorithm in the fifth stage (See Figure 1.6 for the proposed model). The following are the specific objectives developed for the present book

- To evaluate the applicability of existing algorithms to find optimal customers
- To design and develop the meta-heuristic algorithm to solve the business intelligence problem, with the particular focus on identification of optimal customer from the huge set of customer.
- To evaluate the newly proposed Meta-heuristic algorithm with the existing algorithms (Genetic Algorithm (GA), Ant Colony Optimization (ACO) and Artificial Bee Colony Algorithm (ABA).
- To implement the proposed algorithm using the back propagation method.

1.7. Scope of the Research

The scope of the work is to restrict implement the new optimization techniques to overcome the limitations of existing optimization techniques and lacking the understanding behind in the meta-heuristic algorithms. The key motivation behind this study was to perform the analysis of popular meta-heuristic algorithms and comparative studywas made with existing versus new algorithm and validating with Receiver Operating Characteristics (ROC) curve. At the same time, the intelligence concept is implemented with Back Propagation algorithm for forecasting the customer performance.

1.8. Methodology

In the industrial market, through the Direct Sales Team (DST), we have availed the open market customer database. The availability of data sets is a huge number in the industry. We have considered randomly 1,000 populations for this research investigation. From these populations, to attain the valued optimal population through the Optimization techniques or Meta-heuristic algorithms which are inspired by nature will facilitate to construct the application or tool to attain the optimal state in decision making. To overcome the limitations in the existing algorithms, the new proposed algorithm, Artificial Bear Optimization (ABO) is designed and implemented, and the performance is evaluated by Area Under the Curve (AUC) using ROC curve.

1.9.   Proposed Algorithms for Business Intelligence Problems

To overcome the real-life problems with the complex or irrelevant functionality of existing algorithm and to avoid manual decision making in the industry, the present study to implement the new algorithm with the impression of BEAR smells sense.

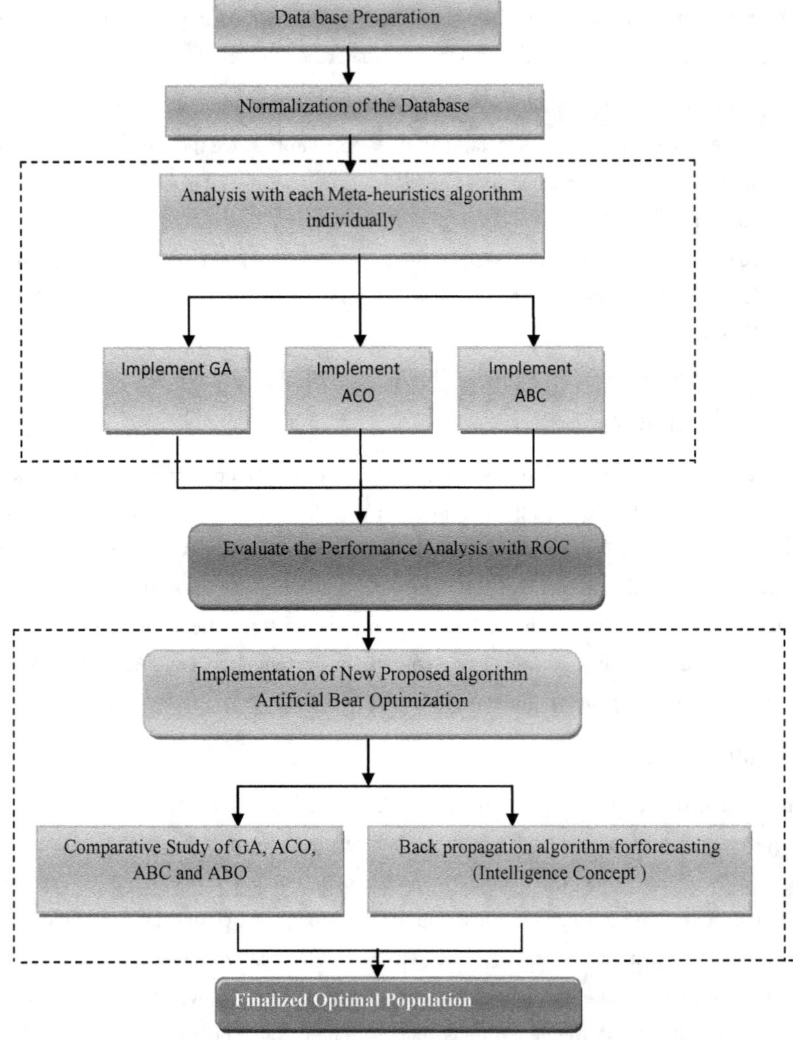

Figure 1.6: Flow Chart of Overall Proposed Application

Figure 1.6 represents the overall application that has beenproposed to find the optimal population.

Genetic Algorithm (GA), Ant Colony Optimization (ACO) and Artificial Bee Colony (ABC) algorithms are implemented and find the resulting database to set and evaluate the performance with Receiver Operating Characteristic (ROC) curve.

1.10. Framework of the Book

In this research, the new proposed ABO algorithm is implemented in the application and for forecasting Back Propagation Algorithm is implemented. The book is designed into seven Chapters. The first chapter is introductory, and the chapters discuss the proposed techniques in detail. In addition, this chapter also introduces the key terms and main concepts BI and current problems faced by banks during customer segmentation. A further brief overview of BI and its importance in decision-making methodologies and previous work on different tools adopted for decision making would be analyzed in this section. Based on the analysis, the chapter would frame the objectives and present a brief methodology.

Chapter 2 would be a literature review where

Methodical overviews of the existing techniques for Business intelligence in optimization techniques are summarized in this chapter. The architecture of discovery and composition of the new framework developed for the analysis of gene expression data along with the architectural diagram are discussed. The three models are presented, namely, the semi-supervisedtwo-dimensional hierarchical data clustering technique, two-dimensional hierarchical clustering (2-DHC) with the hybrid similarity measure, and the fast quadtree. In particular, existing papers are discussed elaborately with their limitations. Further, the review identifies limitations in the existing models and provides the gap for the present study through which the research objectives are developed. The motivation for this research work is also explained.

Chapter 3

Elaborately discusses the optimal state problem in Business intelligence and provides the limitations of BI and defines the proposed solution using the existing studies.

Chapter 4: Normalization and Optimization

This chapter talks about Database preparation and the implementation of normalization and its importance.

Chapter 5: Meta-heuristics algorithms and proposed algorithms with forecasting analysis

In this chapter, tracking the optimized customer from the huge set of the customer from GA, ACO, ABC algorithm is discussed. A detailed explanation of the proposed algorithm and to forecast the customer, implementation of Back-Propagation Algorithm is provided.

Chapter 6: Performance Evaluation

In this chapter, ROC analysis is drafted to evaluate the optimal customer for GA, ACO, ABC and ABO algorithms.

Chapter 7: Conclusion

The Book is finished with key findings and recommendations.

CHAPTER 2

Literature Review

2.1. Introduction

The present chapter critically analyses the previous studies on Business Intelligence both from its benefits and challenges, and the review of various algorithms developed till the date to support business decision-making. The literature presented within this survey maybe is not exhaustive, but it could be considered as a representative picture of the existing trends in the area of business intelligence. The papers selected were mainly taken from web databases such as the ScienceDirect, the Citeseer, the Emerald Library, and the IEEE. Specifically, the keywords which guided our search were the following, matched properly in meaningful combinations of two or three, with an appropriate use of AND/OR logical connectors: {Business Intelligence Platform AND Decision Making System AND [Intelligence OR Intelligent]} OR {Data Mining AND Optimization techniques AND Algorithms} OR {Ant AND Colony AND Optimization} OR {Genetic AND Algorithm AND Optimization} OR {Artificial AND Bee AND Colony AND Algorithm} OR {[Customer OR Selection] AND Optimization}.This section specifically discussed under the following sub-headings. Section I discusses the concept and definition of business intelligence, the critical success and failure factors to be considered during implementation of business intelligence, the critical success and failure factors to be considered during implementation of business intelligence and focused on previous studies that had developed different algorithms for business intelligence. Following this Section-II focused discusses the Rationality and problem solving, Characteristics of DSS, components of DSS, Quality of Decision Making, Types of the decision, Decision Making Methods, previous work.Section III briefly highlight the importance of gathering related data in order to assist managerial decision making. This section further describes the major task of data mining such as dependencies modeling, classification, the clustering and the associations (sequential patterns). These algorithms will be reviewed to identify the gaps existing. The following section briefly discusses the business intelligence.

2.2. Business Intelligence

2.2.1. Concept and Definition of Business Intelligence

In the year 1989, the Gartner group invented the term 'Business Intelligence' (e.g., Lawton, 2006).

In the past, it is always considered that the BI was confined to users who are technologically advanced and aware of writing their own database queries or able to develop their self-prediction models etc., The software was mainly created by the collection of their improved capabilities, which made them easy to use and provide effective decision making for the organization. The combination of data warehouse and BI was firmly held (e.g. Watson and Wixom, 2007). However, a semantic model was developed, which was designed to aggregate or store data on behalf of a data warehouse. Based on these results, it doesn't surprise since few researchers (e.g., Eckerson, 2007) suggested a maturity model in BI, which is progressive from data warehousing to BI services *"BI is a poorly defined term and its industry origin means that different software vendors and consulting organizations have defined it to suit their products; some even use 'BI' for the entire range of decision support approaches."* as per the argument placed by Arnott and Pervan (2005, p71). The following section defines BI and for more definitions refer to **Appendix 2.**

Business Intelligence according to Foley and Manon (2010) is 'Business Intelligence (BI) is a combination of processes, policies, culture, and technologies for gathering, manipulating, storing, and analyzing data collected from internal and external sources, in order to communicate information, create knowledge, and inform decision making' while a more narrow-down definition which focused on BI's technological aspects is proposed by Watson and Wixom (2010) as follows, 'umbrella term that are commonly used to describe the technologies, applications and processes for gathering, storing, accessing and analyzing data to help users make better' based on the above definitions, it is understood that no single definition can be given to Business Intelligence as it is a broad and complex initiative which was discussed by several authors who include Arnott and Pervan (2005), Trkman, McCormack, de Oliveira, and Ladeira (2010) and Howson (2007). It is also understood that Human factor is important in BI because there is no such thing called BI if there are no people to interpret its meaning and act according to the significant information retrieved (English, 2005).Finnish research (Hannula & Pirttimaki, 2003) findings are also consistent with this statement, in which the BI's key aspects are considered to be content and humane approaches by 75% of the interviewees. So the definition provided by English (op. cit.) is as follows "the ability of an enterprise to act effectively through the exploitation of its human and information resources." It is accepted that technology component is important because it adds quality to the information obtained that eases the business users to analyze the past, present and predict the future of business operations.

This definition is followed by the description for BI as *'Special Purpose Information System'* since its' key role in decision making support. A similar definition from The Data Warehouse Institute (TDWI) with addition is 'BI programs usually combine an enterprise data warehouse, and a BI platform or toolset to transform data into usable, actionable business information' (TDWI, 2012). From the above definitions, BI can be understood as an analytical process that transforms enterprise and markets' fragmented data into a piece of performance-oriented information or knowledge about objectives, positions, and opportunities for an organization to achieve its goals. In order to support this analysis process, BI software, software products such as data warehousing software, digital dashboards software, data mining software, is designed. BI tools are the Business Intelligence software products deployed in an organization and a collection of applications, processes, technologies related to BI tools is called a BI system that is used to support the BI.

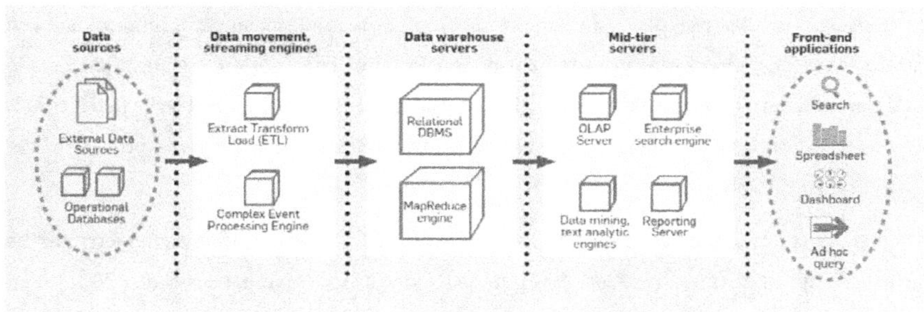

Figure 2.1: Typical Business Intelligence Architecture (Source: Adopted from Surajit Chaudhuri, Umeshwar Dayal and Vivek Narasayy (2011)

However, the information tools present in the *Business Intelligence systems* ease the users to obtain the information required in an efficient and simple manner. On-Line Analytical Processing (OLAP) is such an analytical tool for real-time data processing. Encompassed with the software, it allows the users to convert any amount of large data which is opaque into useful information as well as one can create their self-reports, inquiries and viewing modes, making Business Intelligence systems is more an improved one than the existing transactional ('OLTP') information systems.

A Business Intelligence system is not based on a single application but a group of different components yet have a close relationship with each other, which enable the selection, analysis, aggregation of data by the users and obtain easy and understandable results. The architectural viewpoint of such a system is as follows,

- Operational and external databases as data sources.

- Data sources, from the existing operational and external databases.

- *The Extract, Transform, Load* process, the process of data collection from various sources, Quality checking for errors, transformation to a unique form and storing in a data warehouse.

- Separate from operational systems, a *data warehouse* (in its various forms) meant to be the entire company's central database storage to access data.

- *Tools for data access and analysis* (analytical tools): Data transformation to information is their prime use. Reporting tools, control panels, OLAP tools, Query tools, data mining, advanced analytical solutions (What-if scenarios, optimization, statistical analyses, etc.) are the commonly used analytical tool types (Hočevar & Jaklič, 2010)

2.2.2. *Business Intelligence Advantages*

Business Intelligence plays an important role in decision-making for operations and strategic business by creating present information. In spite of decisions in business being made at different hierarchy in an organization, the daily operations take BI as the base when it comes to business politics and rules respectively. In contrast, BIS support decisions process at the analytical level to be specific.

A study conducted by IT strategies, Inc. (2008) stated that information asymmetry can be achieved by BIS which possess the potential to do so (Marchand et al., 2002) and differentiating from the competitors respectively and thus reach the competitive advantage with IT.

Williams and Williams (2007) stated that it is important to recognize and properly manage the business and technological factors which impact on investment returns, to ensure the BI investment returns.

For instance, the study by Thompson (2006, p 1) points out the following advantages for the company which adopts Business Intelligence

Business Intelligence benefits are also listed by other authors such as Carver and Ritacco (2006, p.6) who's views which are grouped into four are as follows

Adding to the above mentioned four groups, the most commonly mentioned Business Intelligence benefit is that its support for better decision-making and Carver and Ritaco (2006, p. 11) incorporated this aspect in the third group itself. The categorization of Business Intelligence by Atre & Moss (2003, p. 39) is as follows.

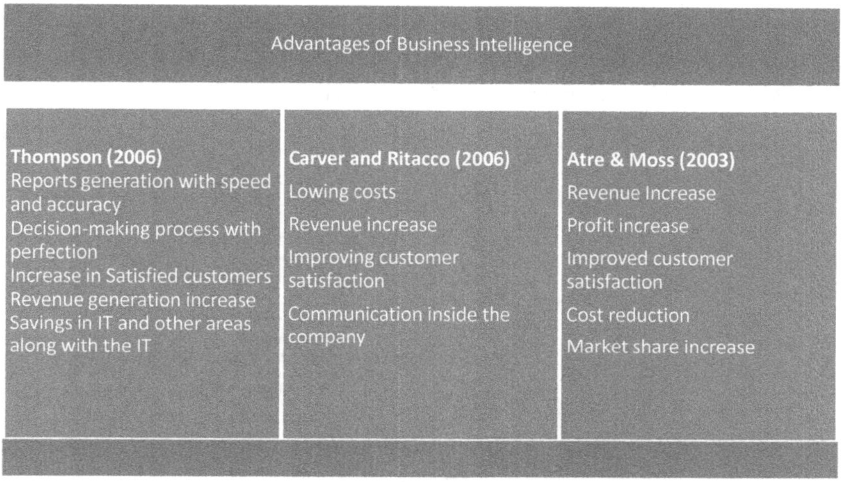

Figure 2.2: Advantages of Business Intelligence

2.2.2.1. *Implementation based on Requirement*

Before implementing a project, assessing the business need and futuristic thinking on business benefit through implementation is another critical thing to be done due to the close relationship with the senior management. Sometimes, the implementation needs and benefits are determined by competition and to achieve the market advantage. Acquiring other organizations, which actually increase the original organization's size is another reason to implement the BI in a business-driven approach. This merging can be beneficial for the implementation of DW or BI to create much better oversight.

The Available Data's Amount and Quality

Good data is considered as the most important factor since it has an impact on successful BI implementation, in spite of good management sponsorship and business-driven motivation. Without data or without quality data, it is sure that the BI implementation meets failure. Data profiling is considered as a good idea before implementation as this describes the "content, consistency and structure [..]"(Kimball et al ., 2008) of the data. Data profiling should be preferably done as early as possible in the process and if the results show about the lacking data, it is a safe and good idea to shelf the process temporarily meanwhile the department of IT finds the best way to collect the data with expected quality and quantity.

In addition to the above mentioned three factors, Naveen Vodapalli mentioned in his theses about various factors, which affect final BI product titled "Critical Success Factors of BI Implementation" (Kimball et al., 2008). The list which he mentioned about the seven important factors for a successful BI project implementation is as follows,

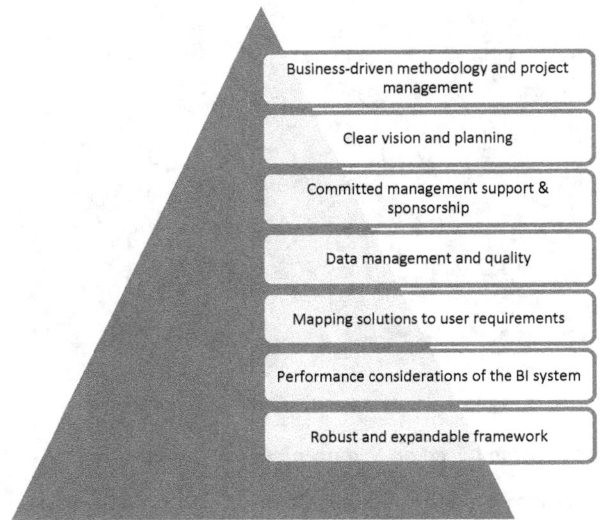

Figure 2.3: Factors for a Successful BI Project Implementation

User Aspect

It is important to consider certain things in a company to integrate the usage of Business Intelligence systems in a successful manner. Kimball et al., (2008) mentioned that the users must utilize the BI system which is acceptable, for value addition to the organization and if there is a poor usability, users may find it difficult and consume more time in just learning about 'how to use the system' or it may also lead to non-usage of the system. The users do not prefer to use the system if it doesn't add value to their mission.So it is advised to consult the business users during the early stages of the DW/BI lifecycle (such as the phase of gathering initial requirements) to make sure the BI system has increased user acceptance. This leads the clear understanding of the business processes and requirement of users from the BI system. This kind of information can be collected through interviews or survey questionnaires.

Whenever the requirements are gathered from the business users, the perspectives of the local IT department members should also be considered in order to decide on how far the business needs can be fulfilled with the data available (Kimball et al., 2008).

Further, he also added that the BI system can be easily adopted rapidly by the users if the approaches during the design and development stages are focused on the users. Alongside focusing on the experience of BI applications users, the possibility of adding a competitive element in the system is high which in turn motivate the users to utilize the system. Kimball et al. (2008) suggested that a function is found, which is implemented in the Business Intelligence portal website in order to generate reports on system usage.

The result would be an effective comparison between departments by their managers in their performance, which would also encourage other employees increased utilization of the BI system. H.J. Watson (2007) described how the competitive element can play the role of the incentive.

He described the implementation of performance dashboards for all the agents in a big call center and tying up the monthly incentive bonuses to that of the performance metrics. This enabled the agents to compare their own performance with their colleagues. Thus, the performance measurement implementation and resultant competition showed a significant improvement in their performance.

Watson (2007) suggested involving the senior management also in the BI system to increase its success rate as well as making BI as an organizational culture through effective training and providing with necessary tools and support.

Training enables the users to utilize the BI application in an effective manner as per Kimball et al. (2008). User support at all levels is critically important to ensure the BI system is maintained in a proper way and assist the human resources (Kimball et al ., 2008) which can be achieved in many ways, the one method being a website creation with rich content that is easily accessible with relevant tools to find necessary information.

The other ways can be helpdesk support, which consists of highly skilled manpower i.e., Power users or the DW/BI projects team (Kimball et al., 2008).

Market Place

Business Intelligence vendors are many in number whom can be categorized into consolidated "Megavendors", which entered the market through BI industry current acquisitions trend, and the remaining "pure-play" independent vendors (Kimball et al., 2008). Some companies prefer BI software from different product offerings rather than from a single integrated and comprehensive solution, i.e., best-of-breed is picked up than full-service.

Industry-Specific

The Business Intelligence systems for some sectors need some specific considerations; for example, in governmental banking regulations, the information collected by banking institutions and the analyses done using BI software must be available to some groups or individuals while the others must be restricted to access the data. So sensitivity for specific needs must be a part of BI solutions, which must be flexible enough to customized requirements and ready to adopt new regulations as per the changes in existing laws.

2.2.2.2. Semi-Structured or Unstructured Data

Merrill Lynch mentions that 85 percent of the total business information exists in the form of information called as *semi-structured or unstructured* data, which comprises of news, web-pages, e-mails, memos, presentations, notes from call-centers, user groups, marketing material and news, video-files, chats, and image files. Watson et al., (2007) highlighted that these documents are mostly used only once by the organization. In the Information technology industry, semi-structured data management is found out as the unsolved problem in a majority. Gartner (2003) projected that around 30-40 percent of the time is being spent by the white-collar workers to search or find or assess the unstructured data. Business Intelligence uses Structured as well as the unstructured data but the structured data is easy to explore but the unstructured possess a huge amount of required information for decision making and analysis (Mundy et al., 2006). According to Kimball (2008), a particular decision or a project or simply a task could influence the poorly-informed decision-making when the unstructured or semi-structured data is not drawn by the organizations because of practical difficulties in searching, retrieving and assessing these data from the huge information database. So Mundy et al (2006) suggested accommodating the exact problems that are correlated with semi-structured, Unstructured as well the structured data whenever the Business Intelligence/DW-solution is designed.

With regards to the relational database systems, the data which is unable to be stored in rows and columns is referred. It must be in the Storable format of the BLOB (Binary Large Object), a catch-all data type, which is available in most relational database management systems. But PowerPoint Presentations, Word processing text files, video-files, image-files and emails, i.e., many data types conform to a standard that offers the metadata possibility. A relational database can store this metadata in which the author name and creation time can be included. So these documents can be mentioned as semi-structured documents or data (Kimball, 2008) to be accurate though the exact consensus is yet to be reached.

Problems Pertaining to Semi-Structured or Unstructured Data

Several challenges associated with the development of BI with semi-structured data as per Inmon and Nesavich (2008) is as follows.

1. Unstructured textual data access through physical mode – unstructured data is stored in a huge variety of formats.
2. Terminology – Standard terminology to be developed for usageresearchers and analysts
3. Semi-structured data exists around 85% which is quite a big volume and this is coupled withthe need for word-to-word and semantic analysis.
4. Searchability of unstructured textual data – If a precise search team is used, for example, Apple, this result in links where there is a reference. An example provided by Inmon and Nesavich (2008) "a search is made on the term felony. In a simple search, the term felony is used, and everywhere there is a reference to the felony, a hit to an unstructured document is made. But a simple search is crude. It does not find references to crime, arson, murder, embezzlement, vehicular homicide, and such, even though these crimes are types of felonies."

2.2.2.3. The Use of metadata

It is mandatory to know the content which is being searched in order to solve the problems of search ability and assessment, and this can be achieved by adding context through the metadata use.

Some metadata such as filename, size, author, etc., is already captured by a lot of systems but the metadata relevant to the actual content, i.e., topics, summaries, people or companies mentioned is the most useful one.

In order to generate metadata about the content, two technologies, information extraction and automatic categorization are designed.

2.2.3. Business Intelligence Environment

A usual environment in an organization allows the business information access to its business users through transactional applications and other enterprise applications in which most information presented will be about the current status of the business. This is organized to provide support for structured decisions instead of supporting the complex requirements which BI addresses. BI serves the complete decision-making range from strategic decisions and tactical decisions to operations decisions as per Taylor & Raden (2007).

Therefore, English (2005) defines the BI environment (English, 2005) as *"quality information in well-designed data stores, coupled with business-friendly software tools that provide knowledge workers timely access, effective analysis and intuitive presentation of the right information, enabling them to take the right actions or make the right decisions."*

The BI environment comprises of all the developmental activities with information processing and support, which is requisite for the delivery of reliable business information with accuracy possessing the business analytics capabilities organizations to ensure to design and implement the BIS successfully within their own BI environments. The scenario is defined as achieving the organizational goals by proper guidance to business through analytical decision-making supported by the quality information from information systems. The Business users utilize the information help rendered by the BIS analyses (of business operations) to understand, improvise and focus on business operations (White, 2005)

BIS represents a broader concept by covering the areas of knowledge management, data mining though it is used as the decision support system. Query and reporting, Statistical analysis, OLAP, Forecasting and Data mining tools comprise the BI solution which is divided into two parts architecturally such as 1) Data warehousing and 2) Access to data, Analysis of data, Reporting, and delivery. A more application orientation makes the traditional information system (e.g., executive information system, decision support systems, etc.,) different from that of the current BIS. Executive information systems have previously used BIS technologies such as dashboards, filtering, KPI, graphical interfaces and drilldown. But the organizational data was scattered in different sources of data, which is mostly connected to one decision support solution.

Providing Uniform and Integral data viewing forms a prominent problem. This problem was handled with a data-oriented approach (Frolick & Ariyachandra, 2006) by the Data warehousing and later broader concept of BIS in which the architectural center represented the integral data sources for analytical decision-making.

Thus, the analytical tools and infrastructure i.e., the data warehouse is included in the state-of-the-art BIS. Based on the focus of the content and various terminologies referring to BI (that include strategic intelligence, competitive intelligence and competitor intelligence), the BI understanding also varies.

Figure 2.4 shows the relevant areas of BI. The term Competitive Intelligence (CI) is used frequently in the literature of North American authors and it highlighted the external environment and external information sources.

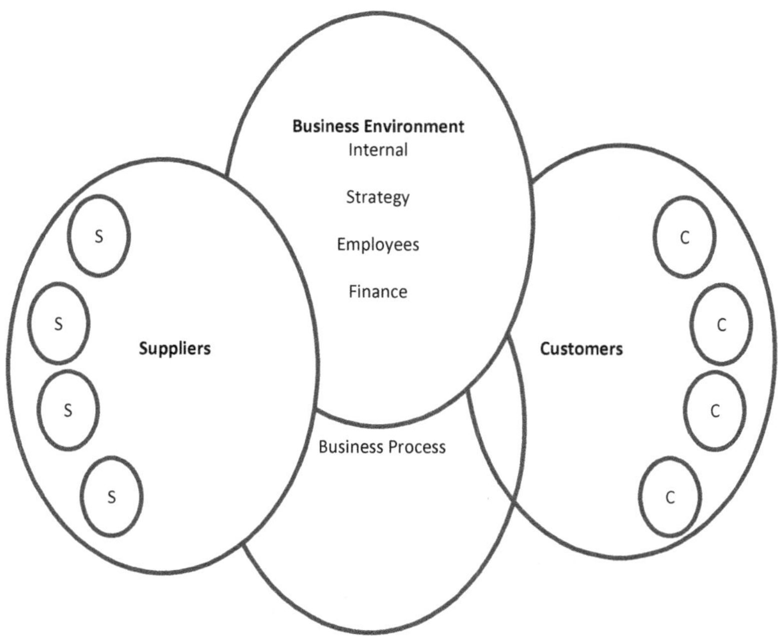

Figure 2.4: Broad Concept of the Term BI Source (Adopted from Popovič et al., 2006)

The BI is viewed as a broad concept for CI and additional terms related to intelligence in the European literature which focuses on the internal environment (e.g. strategy, technology, culture, employees) (Lonnqvist & Pirttimaki, 2006) and external environment (e.g. markets, competition, suppliers, customers). In spite of BIS offering the necessary tools for improving the decision-making inside the organizations, it did not provide proper systematic means of planning, monitoring, controlling and managing the strategic business objectives implementation (Frolick & Ariyachandra, 2006). This can be achieved by embracing the Business Performance Management (BPM) concept by the means of merging the business strategy and technological structure to make sure the entire organization accomplishes the common organizational objectives.

BI and BPM have grown in parallel in the last few years which have been considered as same, but not as per Schiff (2006). But much intertwined, they share a synergistic relationship. The tools important for the BPM applications delivery is provided by BI. In turn, by tying to a strategic business initiative, BPM helps drive the BI adoption. BPM is thus designated at the BIS service specialized in the specific domain (i.e., prepared information for business decision-making).

2.2.4. Tools of BI

The applications of BI include the query and reporting, decision supports activities, statistical analysis, Online Analysis Processing (OLAP), forecasting and data mining (Saunder School of Business, 2000). The business intelligence solution brings the required information to the experts or the users who actually need it: those include the consumers (dynamic queries and simple analysis) analysis and experts (multidimensional analysis, statistics) and information users (reports). (Microsoft, 2004)

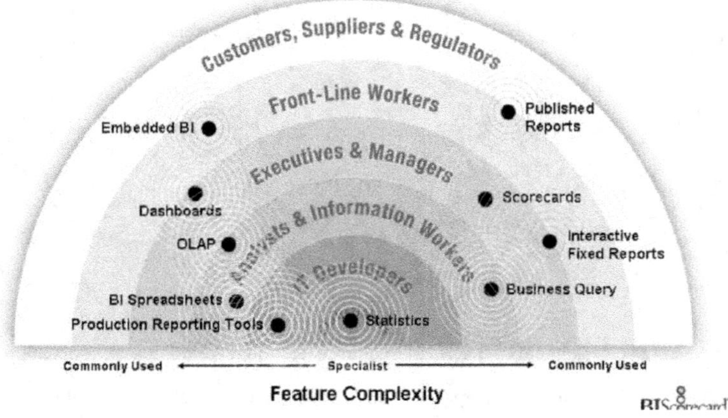

Figure 2.5: BI tools and User Types (Source: Adopted from Venkatraman & Brooks, 2012)

The analysis was done for the prominent Business Intelligence platforms by Gartner: Micro Strategy 9.3, SAS 9 Enterprise Intelligence Platform, QlikView, Oracle BI Foundation Suite 11g, WebFOCUS 8, IBM Cognos 8, Microsoft SQL Server and SAP Business Object BI Platform. The above-mentioned platforms were assessed using a total of 16 technical capabilities, which were inturn divided into five categories that are Scorecards, Mobile integration, Infrastructure and Development Analysis, and Data Visualization. Mobile Integration became an important requirement and important share in this analysis when it comes to the business environment since managers are equipped with the opportunity to acquaint with the progress of the company and quick, efficient decision-making wherever they are. A short description of the 16 capabilities is listed below.

I. Infrastructure & Development

    a.   BI integrated infrastructure: common security, administration, query engine:

    b.   Development: Development tools and SDK for developing applications or tools;

c. Metadata: The storage and reusing capability of metadata objects across the variety of users and applications.

II. Analysis

a. OLAP: The capability to raise fast queries, sophisticated sorting, inter-row calculations, hierarchies, ROLAP calculations

b. Data mining services: The prediction modeling creation with the help of complex algorithms such as clustering, optimization and statistical models like Beta distribution, Average Deviation and Fisher transformation.

III. Scorecards

a. Six Sigma: Support to enhance this process management methodology;

b. Balanced Scorecards: support for strategic management methodology;

c. KPIs: supporting KPIs (Key Performance Indicators) in order the measure the company's performance, classification or forecasting

d. Statistical modeling: Analysis of data using software

IV. Data Visualization

a. Reports: From multiple operational and analytical sources, the ability to create reports that is interactive with complex settings.

b. Dashboards: To publish key indicators, interactive reports creation using a web-based interface which uses gauges, dials or traffic lights to emphasize the information and making it easier to understand.

c. Microsoft Office integration: In order to achieve data export and import, dashboards, render reports and scorecards, gaining the ability to integrate to MS Excel.

V. Mobile Integration

a. Data Visualization & Exploration: Interaction, exploration, and modification of the data with touch-optimized graphs, grids

b. Analysis: Interaction with the scorecards, OLAP analysis, and dashboards

c. Alerts: Receive alerts during the instances such as a change in key indicators or requiring manager approval;

d. Offline Analysis & Data Exploration: Interaction, exploration, and modification of the reports, dashboards, graphs, and grid when the BI server is not connected also.

Table 2.1: Scores for Business Intelligence Platforms

Platforms / Characteristics	IBM Cognos	Oracle BI Foundation Suite	SAS Enterprise Intelligence Platform	SAP Business Objects BI platform	MicroStrategy	QlikView	WebFocus	Microsft SQL Server+ MS SharePoint Server
BI Infrastructure	100	75	75	100	100	75	75	50
Development	100	75	75	75	100	75	100	75
Metadata	75	100	100	75	100	25	50	50
OLAP	75	100	100	75	75	50	50	100
Data Mining	25	100	100	75	75	0	75	75
Statistics	50	25	100	75	75	0	75	50
Predictive Modelling	25	25	100	75	75	0	75	75
Six Sigma	0	75	75	25	100	50	75	25
Balanced Scorecard	100	75	75	25	100	50	75	50
KPIs	100	75	50	25	100	50	75	75
Reports	100	100	75	75	100	75	75	75
Dashboards	100	75	75	75	100	100	75	75
MS Office Integration	75	75	75	75	75	50	75	100
Mobile Data Visualization	75	75	75	100	75	75	100	75
Mobile Analysis	75	100	75	75	75	75	100	50
Alerts	0	50	0	75	75	75	75	0
Offline mode	75	75	0	75	75	50	0	0

Source: Adapted from Rusaneanu (2013)

Table 2.2: Global Scores

BI Platforms	Overall Score
MicroStrategy 9.3.1.	88.33
SAS Enterprise Intelligence Platform	81.93
Oracle BI Foundation Suite	74.72
WebFocus (Information Builders)	72.50
SAP Business Objects BI Platform	70.97
IBM Cognos	70.00
Microsoft SQL Server + MS SharePoint server	65.97
QlikView	45.97

Source: Adapted from Rusaneanu (2013)

MicroStrategy 9.3.1 scores the maximum in this platform table with a score of 88.33 which means that this platform has functionalities with various range and customization options. In addition to that Oracle BI Foundation Suite as well as SAS Enterprise Intelligence also possess similar characteristics and placed at the first position.

Scored in the range of 50 to 75, the other platforms possess characteristics with an average range of features, which need to be customized with the help of programming tools. From the above, it is understood that the companies have to invest its human and financial resources for implementing these platforms or the vendor must be paid for the implementation (Alexandra RUSANEANU, 2013)

2.2.5. Business value of Business Intelligence

Determining the added value by investing the new technology remains the major agenda for both practitioners as well as researchers in the area of IT management. Grover et al (1998, p.157) stated that due to various methodological approaches, non-establishment of this critical link is there along with the existence of intervening variables, lump-sum treatment of IT investment and inconsistent measurement of productivity.

As per Williams (2004b) and Williams & Williams (2007), the previous decades' most IT investment was done for the better systems to maintain the day-to-day operations. These investments are little debated on its necessity to operate new enterprises (Williams & Williams, 2007; Davenport & Short, 2003; Dewett & Jones, 2001; Li & Ye, 1999), but an interpretation from the research both through scientific and professionals state that these organizations lack or have less information with more data (Williams & Williams, 2007, Forslun, 2007; Gibson et al., 2004). From the above statement, it is understood that these organizations do not possess the information required for action or tools required for analysis for improving the performance and profits.

Lonnqvist & Pirttimaki (2006, p. 32) inferred that BI application consumes resources, but benefits obtained are not with clarity.

So an organization faces two important questions such as how to measure BI and Why to do so. The reviews of the literature have two answers for these questions such as following.

- The first and foremost reason often cited for BI measurement is to prove whether the investment is worthy (e.g., Sawka, 2000). Williams & Williams (2007) suggested that a greater value is delivered by the IT investments when the business value capture responsibility resides on the business side.

- The Second reason to measure BI activities is to help manage the BI process by which ensuring that the BI products meet the user's requirements and an efficient process if followed (Herring, 1996).

Lonnqvist & Pirttimaki (2006, pp, 34-36) summarized the approaches for measuring the BIS values and BI process management process that is used currently.

At present, practically BI is not being measured as there is no suitable measurement method or unavailability of resources for such activities. BI activities can be proved as viable, cost-cutting and valuable to the board of management (not yet started operations) by utilizing the apt measurement methods.

It is quite simple to evaluate the costs in BIS, but tough to predict the benefits (Turk et al., 2006, Lonnqvist & Pirttimaki, 2006; Williams & Williams, 2007) since this cannot be measured on the market directly. It is hard to define the benefits driven from BIS through the terms of greater productivity, which is actually an assumption in IT investments. With a strictly utilitarian view, executives, knowledge workers, and managers view the IT in general. Due to this orientation and magnitude and considering the importance of investment in BI, the business leaders and managers are expected to expand their nature of understanding about BI initiatives (Williams & Williams, 2007, pp. 122-123).

An important technological element of BIS is represented by the frameworks and several types of research, which were conducted to justify investments in data warehouses. Sentry Market research and IDC study (Power, 1997), Watson and Haley (1998) and Watson et al. (2002) provided such investments' possible sources of benefits. Wu (2000) emphasizes the importance of or assessing the tangible and intangible benefits before commissioning a BI project.

A comparative study conducted by Morris (2003) taking two elements, the one being developed one's own data warehouse and analysis application, the other being bought one. The research conducted by Taub (1999) is important to support our findings in this study. In his paper, Taub established that the data warehouse does not act as a source of data warehousing investment returns, but only the new or improved business processes which this data warehouse enable act so.

In contrast to the business value, the BIS' development path can be discussed within the organizations through a variety of BIS maturity stages. Presented with models commonly, where in the maturity model, stage-wise progress leading to goal achievement, in the end, can be viewed. BIS maturity model figures out the evolution of BIS from a cost-center and less-value operations to High-end, strategic utilities which drive the market share (TDWI, 2005). These maturity models are no scarce in the current business trend (Williams & Williams, 2007;TDWI, 2005)and these models provide the organizations about the status' 'instant perspective' and the BIS initiative's perspectives. A six-stage BI maturity model in Table 2.1 is proposed by the TDWI institute (2005).

Table 2.3: Six-stage BI Maturity Model

Stage	Architecture	Analytics	
Parental	Reporting	Paper Report	**INSIGHT**
Infant	Spreadmarts	Briefing Book	
Child	Data Marts	Interactive Report	
Teenager	Data Warehousing	Dashboard	**ACTION**
Adult	Enterprise DW	Cascading Scorecards	
Sage	Analytical Services	Embedded BI	

Source: Adapted from TDWI (2005)

The currently proposed model defines maturity as the architecture of the system, attainment of the system, its users and through the focus of the system (to the questions that BIS can provide answers).

2.2.6. *Information Quality Enhancement Goals of BIS*

The BIS information quality improvement goals' benefits can be easily assessed in general. The primary objective is to reduce the gap that exists between the collection of data by the organizations to the amount of quality information accessible to the users to utilize it for business decisions during tactical and strategic levels. It should be noted that there is a slow increase found in the amount of information when compared to the number of decisions, which was supported by appropriate information. It is generally important in business to consider the intuition but has been moved to the place of the supplementary element where there is a structured decision process is involved based on the available information, i.e., fact-based decision-making,

Though the information gap arise in different forms in business practice, the following are the commonest ones,

- Inconsistent data sources and those data present in various places, which are hard to integrate for analysis.
- Rarely used reports with extensive information or inappropriate reports to management.
- Organizations are unaware of some data about their organizations themselves.
- The improper arrangement of data inside the operational databases to supportthe decision of the management.
- It is a quite hard and time-consuming process to prepare reports and query execution for non-technical analysts, and it is hard to use the traditional tools for raising queries and report generation inspite of Graphical User Interface.

- IS staff play a role of data steward (integration of data from various sources, reports generation, aggregating data) due to the increased requirement of information in analytical decisions processes.
- Instead of analyzing the information, analysts take more time just to gather the same.
- Lack of external and/or competitive information for a better decision-making process, restricted access to information by the data owners and incompatible software/hardware systems act as a limitation.

From the above information, it can be inferred that the Information Quality (IQ) is poor in all cases thus the important issue related to BI and BIS is IQ in such an environment (English, 2005).

In connection with the BIS maturity stage, IQ remains an important issue to achieve the business value which a system provides for decision-making. In order to gain competitive advantage, quality information is required which is recognized by the organizations (Salaun & Flores, 2001; Redman, 1995; Ruževičius & Gedminaitė, 2007; & English 2007). Researchers have defined which information can be considered as good information in the IQ field. In spite of differences in the research contexts, methods or goals, researchers have developed an exemplary consensus regarding the criteria to validate the good information. (Eppler 2003, p.41).

The literatures in the IT, communication and management have plenty of information about IQ criteria's (i.e., adjectives which describe about the information characteristics to make the useful information for its users) conceptual frameworks and simple lists (Morris et al., 1996; Eppler, 1997; Davenport, 1997; Kahn et al., 2002; Lesca & Lesca, 1995). Eppler (2003) stated that an IQ framework could provide an organized and precise set of criteria based on which the information can be evaluated, IQ problem-solving schema and the IQ measurement and benchmarking basis. Huanget al. (1999, p. 43) define IQ as "information that is fit for use by information consumers"; IQ is defined by Huang et al (1999, p.43) as "information that is fit for use by information consumers".

As per Kahn et al. (2002), IQ is considered as the information characteristics to meet or exceed the expectations of a customer. And IQ was defined by Lesca and Lesca (1995) IQ as "characteristic of information to be of high value to its users".

In the 1970s and 1980s, early important studies are conducted on IQ in which Grotz-Martin (1976)'s study is about IQ and decision processes. Deming (1986) mentioned 14 quality points for managing the transforming business effectiveness.

There are recent studies conducted by Crump, 2002; English, 1999; Ferguson & Lim, 2001; Lillrank, 2003 which handle the issue of IQ from the perspective of various disciplines, which range from pedagogy, medicine, legal, rhetoric, and accounting. Either explicitly stated or not, these disciplines' IQ definitions are purely dependant on the use of information. From an IS perspective, Huang et al. (1999, p.17) stressed the IQ in their study as *"Clearly, the notion of IQ depends on the actual use of information"*

BIS has provided, some frameworks which are suitable to evaluate the IQ. The broadest study conducted by Eppler in the year 2003 have done a complete analysis of IQ literature and scrutinized 70 criteria for quality with partial or complete overlapping. Further, the review of 20 selected IQ frameworks marked that the frameworks are mostly domain-specific and the interdependency between the IQ criteria have been rarely analyzed. Adding to the above, the information specificity in knowledge-intensive processes is not considered along with the cost dimension of IQ, which is really important when it comes to evaluation of IQ in the BIS. With 16 criteria, Eppler's framework was designed covering all the aspects of IQ, which further was divided into two categories, the one being the criteria which affect information content quality and the other one being the criteria which affect information access quality. IQ is not only considered as an IT topic but also conceived as a management issue which must be correlated with the investments in order to achieve the expected quality. So the Eppler's IQ framework (Eppler, 2003, p. 68) is being adopted, with 16 criteria, which covered all the aspects in IQ (See Table 6), in order to analyze the attainability of BIS information quality improvement goals.

Table 2.4: Information Quality Criteria

	Criterion name	**Description**
QUALITY OF INFORMATION CONTENT	Comprehensiveness	Is the scope of information adequate? (not too much nor too little)
	Conciseness	Is the information to the point, void of unnecessary elements?
	Clarity	Is the information understandable or comprehensible to the target group?
	Correctness	Is the information free of distortion, bias, or error?
	Accuracy	Is the information precise enough and close enough to reality?
	Consistency	Is the information free of contradictions or convention breaks?
	Applicability	Can the information be directly applied? Is it useful?

QUALITY OF INFORMATION ACCESS	Timeliness	Is the information processed and delivered rapidly without delays?
	Traceability	Is the background of the information visible (author, date etc.)?
	Maintainability	Can all of the information be organized and updated on an on-going basis?
	Interactivity	Can the information process be adopted by the information consumer?
	Speed	Can the infrastructure match the user's working pace?
	Security	Is the information protected against loss or unauthorized access?
	Currency	Is the information up-to-date and not obsolete?
	Accessibility	Is there a continuous and unobstructed way to get to the information?
	Convenience	Does the information provision correspond to the user's needs and habits?

Source: Adapted from Eppler (2003)

The fulfillment of information quality improvement goals can be defined and later checked with the analysis conducted between the BI solutions and IQ criteria connections. Thus, the information versatility can be contributed by the data warehouse (comprehensiveness criterion) since, through the integration of data sources, the business operations' whole view can be acquired, which acts as the subject of interest when a business problem is specifically solved. The important perceivable benefit from the view of information quality improvement goals is that this includes the IQ increase by fast and convenient gathering of information, interactivity, etc., Due to this, the time available for business decisions-taking is short, specifically due to information gathering and analysis which acts as a base for acceptance of the decisions. However, the extension of decision times can also happen. It is noteworthy to know that BIS enables the beginning of earlier decision processing as it identified the events that are worth reacting to.

2.2.7. Building BI System

Academic researchers and practitioners researched building BI systems in which Olszak and Ziemba (2007) and Moss and Atre (2003) provided the academic models which are normative. Ryzebol (2004), in his research, detailed about IBM's approach in facilitating the development of a BI system, which is primarily focused on its own DB2 database product. A BI life cycle for system development is provided by Gangadhara and Swami in the year 2004. But the methodology illustrations about the BI system implementation are only limited in the literature and fewer insights about the choice and preferred analytics in the BI systems is observed (O Leary, 2011).

2.2.8. Summary

Deploying business information and business analysis tools is the business strategy for leveraging BI so as to make sure the detailed, precise and timely information is provided to the front-line managers about the productivity. This will enable for closer monitoring, clear overview of performance trends and prompt corrective actions the most important. Deploy business information and business analysis tools, which will be in-turn provide a widerange of the entire disability claims process. This will end up in a meeting or exceeding the customer expectations by correcting the service issues from the top managers, front-line supervisor, and middle managers' perspectives. Change remains the only constant in today's world. Being proactive and agile acts as a unique competitive advantage by itself, this is enabled by business intelligence. This denotes the survival of the quickest along with the survival of the fittest.

2.3.   Decision-Making Support System

2.3.1. Introduction

A historical, current and futuristic predictions are provided by BI technologies to business operations. The business intelligence technologies' general functions include data mining, reporting, online analytical processing, process mining, analytics, business performance management, and text mining, benchmarking and predictive analytics. BI aims for providing the best support in decision-making in business which made it call as Decision Support System (DSS) (Kobielus, 2010). BI uses processes, technologies and applications to assess the internal (mostly), structured data and business processes, while the competitive intelligence collects, assess and disseminate the topic focused information from the company's competitors. From the above statement, it is clear that BI is different from CI though they both support the decision-making process. Competitive Intelligence (Miller Devens, 1865) can be included as a subset in Business Intelligence.

Power & Sharda (2007) stated that about the necessity to develop strategies to enhance and improvise the decision making of both an individual as well as an organization through the usage of an automated tool in decision systems with the available huge amount of unstructured information. Lack of the ability to capture the ill-defined data and dynamics is the flaw in Traditional decision support system. Quantitative data is being processed by current existing decision support tools where the systems analyze the factual value specifically. Froelich & Ananyan (2008: 609) stated that both the structured and unstructured data should be analyzed even in large volumes for decision-making challenges.

Unstructured problems can be solved by help decision makers using data and models through the computer-based interactive system as suggested by Druzdzel & Flynn (2002). As per Stewart (2003), the decision support system is a "computer system which assists decision makers in exploring the consequences of decisions in a structured manner and in developing an understanding of the extent to which each decision alternative or option contributes toward goals". After considering the system's capabilities, Laudon & Laudon (2007) proposed a definition for a decision support system as "DSS Provided simulation, analytical, and data modeling tools to optimize decision making. This system addresses problems where the procedure for producing the information aids is not fully predefined in advance. Therefore, the decision support system has more analytical power than other information systems".

Based on the different definitions drawn, the researcher listed out the major capabilities for Decision Support System as suggested by Morana, et al (2010)

1. By human judgment and objective information, providing support to all the managers who are the decision makers during the unstructured situations.
2. Support for various decisions that are interconnected.
3. Enabling support during the complete phases of decision making process intelligence, choice, design, and successful implementation.
4. Based on the changing conditions, adaptability to the user to deal with.
5. Easy to construct and Multi-cases usage.
6. Often uses quantitative models (that are custom made or standard or both).
7. Very complex problems are handled with efficient and effective solutions provided by the advanced Decision Support System Equipped with a Knowledge Management component.
8. Easy to access via Web-portal.
9. Eases the simple execution of sensitivity analyses.

The list mentioned above consists of the capabilities which a Decision Support System should possess. In the year 2005, Holsapple & Sena suggested the potential benefits of this above list, which include the system's capability to improve the ability of a decision maker to process knowledge, reduce the time taken to decide, handle complex problem, improve the decisions' reliability, a decision maker to be encouraged to discover, stimulate novel approaches in problem thinking, support decision with a proof and create competitive advantage over the competitor organizations.

Decision alternatives such as 'what-if' and 'goal-seeking' analysis are generated and evaluated in nowadays Decision Support Systems during the stages of choice and design.

There are various models in Decision Support System, for example, an accounting model that facilitates the future planning by estimating the outcomes of planned actions on the estimate of balance sheets, Income statement and other financial statements. Another one, the representational model evaluates the outcomes of future actions that include all simulation models. The optimal solutions are generated by the optimization models and specific suggested decision provided by Suggestion models for a clearly structured task (Eom, 2001).

2.3.2. *Rationality and Problem Solving*

With reasonable rationality, a decision is made from the multiple alternatives provided. In both personal and professional life, every individual continuously takes decisions, which is more or less important. This section discusses the knowledge workers' decisions both in private as well as public enterprises and organizations. These decisions which are interlinked and impact on the strategic plan development, making substantial investment choices, predicting the sales with defining marketing initiatives and production plan design to effectively and efficiently utilize the available human and technological resources.

Usually referred as problem-solving, the decision-making process is an integral part of a broker subject, in which an individual bridge the gap in a process between the existing system operation conditions (as *it*) and future better operations conditions (*to be*). It is not so easy to attain for a transformation to happen from one system to the desired state after overcoming certain obstacles. These obstacles enable the decisions makers to think for an alternate solution always to achieve the desired goal, and make a decision after comparing each option's advantages and disadvantages. So it is necessary for the decision to be put in practice and verify whether it achieved the planned objectives. If not, again the problem is reconsidered based on the recursive logic.

2.3.3. *Characteristics of DSS*

Although the term decision support system has many connotations, based on Steven Alter's (1980) pioneering research the following characteristics: Steven Alter's (1980) excellent research of the Decision Support System has the following characteristics though the connotations are many.

1. DSS is designed to facilitate the decision process specifically
2. DSS should support instead of going for automatic decision making
3. DSS should have the ability for a quick response as per the decision makers' changing needs.

In their book 'Decision Support Systems: A Knowledge-Based Approach' during the year 1996, Clyde Holsapple and Andrew Whinston, identified five characteristics, which is expected in a DSS (see pages 144-145). Though it is very general and abstract, this study provides an even broader perspective on the DSS concept. The characteristics of a DSS system as per Holsapple and Whinston are:

1. A DSS should include the knowledge body describing the various aspects of the decision-makers world which specifies on accomplishing various tasks that denote that conclusions are valid in different circumstances.

2. A DSS has the potential to obtain and retain all the kinds of knowledge (i.e., procedure keeping and rule keeping) as well as descriptive knowledge (i.e., record keeping)

3. DSS which has the capability to exhibit the knowledge in an ad-hoc basis in different customized as well as standardized reports.

4. During the problem recognition and/or problem-solving course, a DSS must possess the ability to select any wished subset of stored knowledge for both presentations as well as deriving new knowledge.

5. A direct interaction between DSS and decision maker or a participant is possible in order to make sure the decision maker has got flexibility in choosing and sequencing of knowledge management activities.

Decision Support Systems are broadly defined by Sprague and Carlson (1982) as interactive computer-based systems which help decision-makers to employ the data and models in order to solve the semi-structured, unstructured as well as ill-structured problems. Bonczek, Holsapple, and Whinston (1981) argued the "system must possess an interactive query facility, with a query language that ... is ... easy to learn and use (p.19)".. Decision-makers are helped by different kinds of DSS to utilize and manipulate huge volumes of databases; some of them which help by applying checklists and rules, and some make use of extensive mathematical models.

In the past 25 years, it is understood from various case studies that management activities can be supported in many ways. Managers are helped by some DSS by fast access to information, which is actually unavailable or have some difficulty to obtain. Some other systems contain explicit models, which provide structure for particular decisions while some other acts as primary tools for individuals who work alone in decision-making. Some other systems just coordinate people through proper communication. Specific types of DSS are named with different terminology, which also includes business intelligence.

2.3.4. *The Decision Support System Components*

An accurately formatted 'Decision Support System' is an interactive software-based system to assist people who make decisions to gather helpful data from unprocessed information, records, own understanding, as well as corporate prototypes to recognize and resolve setbacks and take decisions (Ahmadi & Salami, 2010). Advancement of the needs, features, working, and contents of the decision support structure rely on the purpose of the structure, like plan, function or creation. These fields might require diverse data; however, the kind of decision backing might be similar. As per (Druzdzel & Flynn,2002) Basic DSS (Decision Support System) outline comprises of DBMS (Database management system) prototype based management structure as well as DGMS (Dialog generation management system).

1. DBMS: Database management system is a structure that functions as a data bank for DSS. Here an extensive amount of information can be stored, which are linked to the set of issues which the DSS is formatted for, it further offers rational data arrangements that the customer can interact with. It must be able to provide information to the customer regarding the kind of information that can be accessed.

2. MBMS: The basic purpose of a Model base management system is to offer freedom between definite prototypes, which are utilized in a Decision Support System from the applications which utilize them. Its function is to change information from DBMS to data, which is helpful to make decisions and be able to help the user in formatting a method.

3. DGMS: Generally speaking 'Dialog generation and management system' is a user interface. It assists to interrelate with a Decision Support System so that the Decision Support System is provided with user-friendly interfaces. These interfaces assist in creating methods as well as interaction with them, like acquiring suggestions from them. Mardjono (2002: 20) reveals that DSS contains the elements mentioned forth with: databases, database and knowledge management, reasoning engine, rule base, in addition to a user interface. The database is a compilation of information stockpiled in a methodical manner. With the help of database management, information can be accessed, included as well as removed. Decision Support System is further provided with a rule-based element, which is a compilation of policies that can be utilized while making a decision, knowledge management is utilized to manage information transactions; a reasoning engine might be required in a Decision Support System design that is formatted as a computer program, an interface is required to link the databases and main program to assist the user interact with DSS.

Him et al.,(2002) stated that the internet setting is a vital platform for the enhancement of DSS, by means of utilizing a web infrastructure for creates a DSS to enhance decision-making agendas and supports more reliable decision making on recurring chores. Thus, the Decision Support System groups comprise data warehousing, Online Analytical Process (OLAP), web-based Decision Support System, data mining, collaborative support systems, in addition to optimization based Decision Support System. A web-based Decision Support System is a programme structure which offers data via a web browser to the user, by transferring the requirements to a database server that produces the requested findings and delivers it back for utilization, wherein it functions constantly with data warehouses and Online Analytical Process.

Druzdzel and Flynn (2002) authenticated that the excellence as well as dependability of modeling implements, and the internal structural designs of DSS are important, their user interface is extremely vital, a superior user interface to DSS must back model building and assessment, however difficult or vague user interfaces or, which need exceptional abilities are hardly helpful or received in reality. Additionally, if the structure is founded on normative codes, it could function in an oversight role; that customers would understand the field prototype and the way to handle it in time, and enhance their opinion that DSS utilizes numerous methods, which incorporate artificial intelligence. Particularly, expert systems comparable to artificial intelligence could be incorporated with additional customary methods for functions like statistics, mapping and data restore to shape structures, which offer additional effectual decision support in a research field. Moreover, it is employing rules to programme domain Knowledge, with inference engines, to construe assumptions from data which customers give (Booty et al., 2009).

2.3.5. *Quality of Decision Making*

The ambiguity of the corporate environment, as well as the transforming needs of establishments, necessitates that managers are bold, have the determination and capacity to take hard decisions. Taking decisions is a manager's responsibility. An excellent manager can be distinguished from an incompetent manager by the decisions he takes. The range of decisions renders it hard, at times impossible; to scrutinize and assess the capability of a manager in decision-making will achieve the firm's goals at the same time guarantee the interests of the workforce (Nonaka & Takeuchi, 1995). Making decisions is a cognitive procedure leading to a specific path of action from numerous choices available. All procedures in decision making result in an ultimate choice. The outcome could be an act or a view of selection (Abou Aish, 2001). Making decisions is a vital facet of leadership.

Decision making is what executives and leaders are salaried to do. However, every day one wonders who really makes decisions in a firm when news articles appear in papers regarding certain firms. This might have been the case always, yet in the first ten years of the second millennium it seemsadditional so everything is, "too big, too fast, too much, and too soon." (Goll & Rasheed, 1997).

The actuality is that the majority of establishments do not have good decision makers, leave alone excellent ones. When questioned, people do not find it easy to accept any decision as an excellent one. Accounts of not so good decisions madecome to one's mind easily (Harung, 1993). This could be due to our inclination to remember exceptions against times when things fare better (Papadakis, 1998). There are numerous vital features that impact making decisions. They comprise previous experiences, a range of cognitive prejudices, a rise of obligations and dashed results, personal disparities, like age in addition to socioeconomic standing, and a conviction in the individual bearing. These influence the process of decision making and also the choices taken (Sabherwal & King, 1995).

Previous occurrences could influence prospective decision making. Juliusson, Karlsson, and Garling (2005) revealed that earlier decisions impact the choices individuals take in days to come. It is understandable that when a decision results in constructive outcomes, future decisions will be similar, supposing the circumstances are the same. Contrarily, individuals refrain from making the same mistakes (Sagi, & Friedland, 2007). This is important to the degree that prospective decisions taken founded on previous experiences are not essentially the most excellent decisions. In economic decision making, extremely successful individuals refrain from making investment choices founded on previous ruined results, relatively by probing decisions disregarding previous occurrences; this method differs from what one might anticipate (Juliusson, et al., 2005).

Added to previous occurrences, there are numerous cognitive prejudices, which impact making decisions. Cognitive prejudices are thought processes founded on scrutiny as well as overviews, which might result in memory inaccuracies, mistaken decisions, and defective reason (Evans, Barston, & Pollard, 1983; West, Toplak, & Stanovich, 2008). Cognitive prejudices comprise, but are not restricted to belief prejudice, the excess reliance on previous understanding in making choices; retrospective prejudice, people are easily inclined to describe an experience as unavoidable, after it has occurred; omission bias, normally, individuals have a tendency to leave out facts seen as hazardous; and confirmation prejudice, where individuals notice only what they anticipate to notice (Marsh, & Hanlon, 2007; Nestler. & von Collani, 2008; Stanovich & West, 2008).

When making decisions, cognitive prejudices impact individuals by making them depend extensively or give additional credibility to anticipated observations as well as past experience, when rejecting facts or observations, which are seen as doubtful, not viewing the wider perspective. Though this impact might result in taking not very good decisions at times, cognitive prejudices allow people to take resourceful choices with the support of heuristics (Shah & Oppenheimer, 2008). Besides earlier occurrences as well as cognitive biases, making decisions might be impacted by an increase in obligations as well as dashed outcomes that are expenses that cannot be retrieved. Juliusson, Karlsson, and Garling (2005) deduced that individuals made choices founded on an illogical increase of obligation, to be precise, people spend more time and funds, as well as an effort into a choice that makes them feel obligated; moreover individuals will go on taking hazardous choices if they think that they are accountable for the losses on a venture. Consequently, making decisions sometimes are impacted by 'how far in the hole' the people think they are in (Juliusson, et.al., 2005).

An excellent decision is accompanied by a warrant: a guarantee. Not an assurance of a definite result— bear in mind that this is actual circumstances we are dealing with, and some instances cannot be perceived till they take place —but an assurance that the procedure you employed to get at the decision was an excellent one. The quality theory is old, actually as ancient as the Medieval Ages. It is a constant apprehension of the colleges from the time of their initiation in olden days, constantly a fraction of the educational culture. Van Vught (1995) disputes that it was previously feasible to differentiate two methods of quality evaluation in the century, the French method of giving a command in an outside authority (Cobban, 1988) being the model of quality evaluation pertaining to answerability, and the English prototype of an autonomous society of fellows being a paradigm of quality evaluation through a peer review.

As per Massy (2003), this can be done more effectively, with the help of constant and unrelenting work on the development of "decision quality without spending additionally, dismembering their research project, or coming down from their basic standards" (Massy, 2003). Nevertheless, this might be hard work as Trow (1994) stresses: "Trust cannot be ordered but should be given freely". As per Vroeijenstijn (1995), the current thought given to excellence might make one assume that this is an innovation from recent times and that people were unaware of it before 1985. Yet this is not so. The quality decision will at all times related to the leaders made decisions. It is interrelated to their decision approaches. Consequently, conclude their management method.

The change of decision-making accountability to the makers has had "considerable inferences for organizational authority and administration" (Dill, 1995). Beginning in the '80s, and particularly at the political level, numerous people were vocal in opposition to the conventional method of control and administration, believed to be incompetent and obsolete to tackle the recent problems faced by these establishments (Rosa, Saraiva & Diz, 2005). Actually, nearly all over establishments are being pressurized to be "more answerable and receptive, competent and effectual and, simultaneously, more entrepreneurial as well as self-managing" (Meek, 2003). Therefore, in the past twenty years, we can see the incursion of the oratory and management practices of the private segment that has resulted in vital alterations in the functioning of establishments.

As per Elsass and Graves (1997) who argue that the core of leadership is making decisions as well as imagining that the main choices are progressively becoming decentralized to people and clusters within establishments, it is vital to comprehend how the growing variety in the segment concerns Malaysia Colleges' decision-making ability. Making decisions could be categorized at three major levels. At the personal level, the person experiences common problem resolving cycle to take decisions regarding personal matters, to which one looks for answers. On the basis of its involvedness, time and other resources on hand, personal choices pertain to a range, from extremely planned and sensible to unplanned and illogical (Foskett & Hemsley-Brown, 2001). At a collective or diminutive faction level, the propensity is to include more planned methods that usually, at least in hope, entail logical problem resolving plans and connect to functional matters. The third level includes choices taken for an establishment, and they are additionally tactical and usually entail the senior management panel, which carries the tactical accountability for the establishment.

2.3.6. *The Decision-Making Process: The Process*

Decision support a model-based concept could be used in a RE procedure management to enhance the class of the choice, its outlay, and agenda of the RE procedural outcome. Several experimental types of research back this statement by representing that DSS have enhanced the administration of different public as well as private organizations (Mallach, 1994; Sprague and Watson, 1996; Turban, 1995 and Young, 1989). One can find a distinct connection between decision-making procedure and decision results. This concept-based method utilizing SD could reveal the way the procedure impacts results to the decision maker (stakeholder) as well as the Software Development Organization. Decision Support Systems are formatted to back RE process stakeholders in the decisions they make (Williams, Hall and Kennedy, 1999). This backing is given at the different stages of the decision-making procedure.

As revealed in diagrams three and four, there are likely associations among process stages; results; and between the procedure and results of decision-making. Numerous structures were formatted to define the decision making procedure in human beings. Simon's (1961) three-stage model of acumen, design, and option is extensively utilized in decision support efficiency researches. As portrayed in diagram 3, this model was developed by including an execution stage and by integrating stages documented in the paper pertaining to the four stages (Mallach, 1994; Turban, 1995 and Young, 1989). A convincing depiction of the decision-making procedure was suggested in the 1960s, and even now is a key procedural citation. The method incorporates three stages, namely *intelligence, design, and choice.*

Diagram 5 illustrates that the established edition of the initial system that is the outcome from the insertion of two extra stages that is *implementation and control.*

Intelligence: Intheintelligence stage, the vital information that is filtered, condensed, and traced by other data systems could be captured in a Decision Support System database. The Decision Support System could be utilized to manage this acquired data, produce well-timed focused accounts, as well as scheme styles. This kind of dealing out assists the individual who makes the decision to speedily supervise the decision setting, set goals, and assesses the developed data for openings or challenges (Sprangue and Watson, 1996; Turban, 1995)

The Design Phase: Necessitates engineering procedures, resources, as well as goods data structures, and numerical methods could be detained in a Decision Support Systems model base.

The Decision Support Systems, improved by the needs of managers' (or perhaps analysts) insights as well as decisions, could be utilized to develop these detained concepts and prototypes into norms, occurrences and options required to develop a prototype of the decision issue (Mallach, 1994; Sprage and Watson, 1996; Williams, Hall and Kennedy, 1999). Extra development with the numerical procedure management techniques could approximate the structures necessary to functionalize the developed decision issue prototype decision (Young, 1989).

Choice: The formulated model, augmented by the managers' insights and judgments, are used to evaluate alternatives in a systematic and analytic fashion and to recommend alternatives (Fripp, 1985). In the decision-making process, these evaluations typically involve: (a) simulating performance outcomes from stipulated actions and policies under specified internal and external conditions and (b) solving specified models for the most preferable actions and policies for implementation (Turban, 1995; Young, 1989).

Implementation: A System Dynamics model-based DSS can provide the analyses in rich and varied detail with tables, graphs, and iconic animation of variables of interest. Systems thinking can facilitate the synthesis of soft and hard data identified in the problem. Such iconic animation supported by many SD simulation packages increase the decision maker's confidence in the recommendations, improves the decision maker's perception of support system effectiveness and enables the decision maker to better explain, justify, and communicate the decisions during implementation (Dean and Sharfman, 1993 and Tan and Benbasat, 1993).

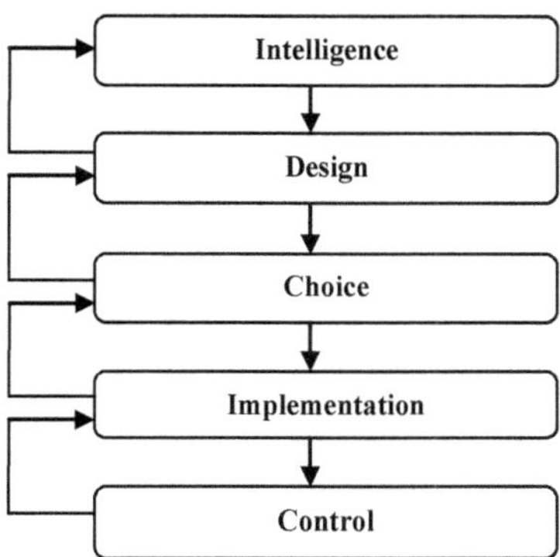

Figure 2.6: Phases of Decision Making

The most pertinent features typifying a decision-making procedure could be summed upon short as given below:

- Decisions are frequently formulated by a panel of people rather than by an individual decision maker.

- The figure for optional activities might be extreme and at times limitless.

- The impacts of the decision taken are normally felt afterward, not instantly.

- The decision taken in a public or private organization is mostly interrelated and decides broad outcomes. Every choice has outcomes for several persons and numerous divisions of the establishment.

- At the time of the decision-making procedure, knowledge workers are requested to retrieve information and operate on them on the basis of a theoretical as well as investigative structure.

- The response has a vital part in presenting data and awareness for prospective decision-making procedures in a particular establishment.

- In a majority of cases, making decisions has numerous objectives, having various pointers of the functionality, which may further be in divergence with each other.
- Several choices are taken in vague circumstances and involve danger. The degree of tendency or distaste to danger differs considerably amid various people.
- Trials undertaken in realistic circumstances, pertaining to a *trial-and-error* method are very dear as well as unsafe to be of real use for making decisions.
- The dynamics, wherein organizations function, fiercely impacted by the stress of a rival atmosphere, entails that knowledge workers require tackling circumstances and take decisions speedily and in time.

2.3.7. Types of Decisions

Describing taxonomy of decisions might be helpful at the time of designing a Decision Support System, as it is possible that making decisions with comparable features might be theoretical by a similar collection of methods. Choices could be categorized into two major facets, pertaining to their *nature and scope.* Each facet would be further classified into three divisions, thereby arriving at nine feasible groupings, as revealed in Table.

Pertaining to their nature, choices could be categorized as *structured, unstructured or semi-structured.*

2.3.7.1. Taxonomy of Decisions

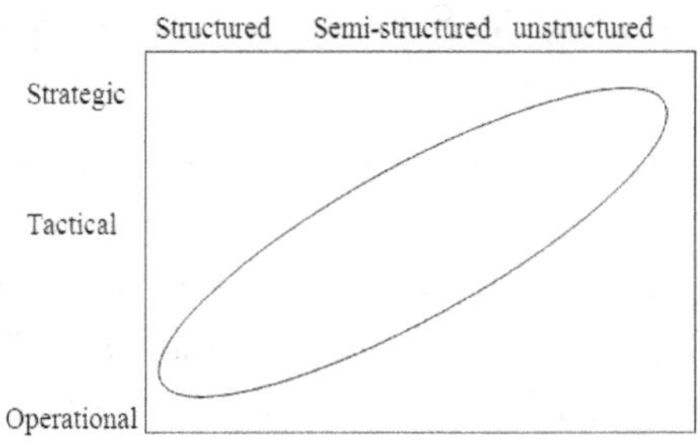

Figure 2.7: Decision Making Model

Structured decisions: A choice is planned or structured if it is founded on a distinct as well as the habitual process. In the majority of instances, planned choices could be tracked to an algorithm that might be relatively unambiguous for people who make decisions, and are thus more suitable for computerization. More particularly, we have a planned choice if input and output flows and the alterations carried out by the system could be lucidly defined in the three stages of intelligence, design, and decision.

In this instance, it could be stated that every stage is planned in its time. In fact, even choices that seem to be completely planned to mostly need the direct involvement of decision makers to handle with unanticipated occurrences, due to atypical values of certain input flows.

Unstructured decisions: A choice is stated to be unplanned if the three stages of intelligence, design, and decision are also unplanned. That is, in each one of the stages there happens to be some component in the system; either the input or output flows, or the alteration procedures; that is not possible to be defined fully and diminished to a predefined series of stages. This could happen if a decision-making procedure is encountered for the initial time or occurs rarely. Here the part played by knowledge workers is basic, and business intelligence systems might offer to back to people who make decisions with the help of appropriate as well as adaptable access to data.

Semi-structured decisions: A choice is semi-planned if certain terms are planned and others are unplanned. Most choices confronted by knowledge workers in administering public or private establishments are semi-structured.

Therefore, they could take advantage of Decision Support Systems and corporate intelligence surroundings largely in two methods.

For the unplanned stages of making decisions, corporate intelligence instruments might proffer an inactive kind of backing that transforms into suitable as well as adaptable access to data.

For the planned stages, it is feasible to offer a dynamic style of backing via numerical prototypes and algorithms that permit important stages of decision-making to be computerized.

At times, circumstances might come up wherein the character of a choice is impossible to be effortlessly recognized, unmistakably. When confronting similar issues, like ascertaining the selling cost of goods, diverse decision makers functioning in diverse enterprises might make different decisions.

For instance, an initial decision maker might think about the decision stage of decision-making as planned.

Contrarily, the person who makes a decision for the second time might think that the flexibility curve fails to mirror every element impacting the reaction of the market price variations as certain of the components are not possible to be measured. For such a person, the decision stage is unplanned or structured or at best semi-planned.

Table 2.5: Characteristics of the Information in Terms of the Scope of Decisions

	Operational	Tactical	Strategic
Accuracy	High	←——→	Low
Level of detail	Detailed	←——→	Aggregate
Time of Horizon	Present	←——→	Failure
Frequency of use	High	←——→	Low
Source	Internal	←——→	External
Scope of information	Quantitative	←——→	Qualitative
Nature of information	Narrow	←——→	Wide
Age of information	Present	←——→	past

From the fore stated samples it can be deciphered that the character of decision making procedure relies on several features, namely:

- The features of the organization wherein the system functions
- The biased approaches of the people who make the decisions.
- The accessibility of suitable issue -resolving methods
- The accessibility of effectual support instruments

Based on their range, choices could be categorized as *strategic, tactical and operational.*

Strategic decisions: Choicesare considered asstrategic if they impact the whole enterprise or at the slightest, a considerable division of the enterprise for an extended time. Strategic choices convincingly impact the common goals as well as strategies of an organization. As a result, strategic choices are made at the top level of the organization, mostly by the firm's top management.

Tactical decisions: Tactical choices influence merely divisions of an organization and are generally limited to a particular division. The period is restricted to a medium-term perspective, characteristically to twelve months. Tactical choices are within the framework established by strategic choices. In a business leadership order, tactical choices are taken by managers in the middle order, like managers of particular divisions in the firm.

Operational decisions: Operational choices are precise actions executed within an enterprise and have a moderate effect on times to come. Operational choices are formatted within the components as well as situations decided by strategic as well as tactical choices. Thus, they are typically taken in the organization's lower rung. They are made by knowledge workers accountable for a particular action or job, like sub-divisional heads, workshop foremen, back-office heads.

The features of the data needed in the procedure of making decisions alter pertaining to the range of the choices to be backed, subsequently also the direction of a Decision Support System will altercorrespondingly. Figure12 illustrates variations in the features of the data as the range of the choice alters. The system could be employed as an evaluation instrument when formatting a Decision Support System when the range of the choices wherein the scheme is meant to be established; the system could be employed to decide if the procedure of making the decision is sufficiently backed by correct data. Even though the character and range are not faultlessly related, the majority of real-world choices are within the curve illustrated in figure 2.7: the majority of strategic choices are unplanned, whereas the majority of operational choices are planned and most tactical choices are semi-structured. The experimental statement is helpful when describing earlier the features of a Decision Support System to assist a procedure of decision-making of precise character as well as the range.

In multifaceted enterprises, both public, as well as private, choices, are taken based on continuation. This kind of choices might be relatively significant, containing short or long- term impacts in addition to involving individuals at different levels in the hierarchy. The capacity of these people to make decisions, as individuals and as a panel, is the major feature that impacts the functioning as well as the viable soundness of the said enterprise. A majority of people, who make decisions, take them, mostly by utilizing effortless as well as intuitive methods that consider precise components like experience, awareness of the application field and accessible data. This method results in dormant decision-making due to the unsteady circumstances decided by recurrent as well as quick alterations in the physical setting. Comparatively, the procedure of making decisions within today's enterprises are frequently very complicated and forceful to be successfully handled via an intuitive method and need to be founded on investigative methods as well as numerical prototypes.

2.3.8.   *Decision-Making Methods*

- Stagnant decision Making:
    - The majority of people, who make decisions, take them largely by utilizing effortless and intuitive methods that consider precise components like experience, understanding of the application field as well as access data.
- Dynamic Decision Making:
    - The procedures of making decisions in an enterprise today are usually very complicated and forceful to be successfully handled via an intuitive method and need to be founded on investigative methods as well as numerical prototypes.

Phases in the Development of Mathematical Models for Decision Making

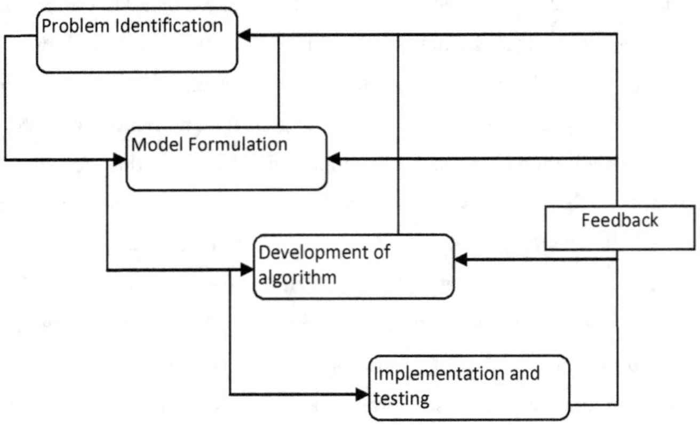

Figure 2.8: Phases of Decision Making

2.3.9. Decision-Making and Models

Modeling makes real-world situations simple and assists in abstracting decision options (Mallach, 1994). The advantages of modeling are presented in Appendix 2. Mallach (1994) categorized prototypes as *graphical, narrative, physical or symbolic.* An information flow chart is a sample of a graphical prototype. A narrative prototype explains a scheme in a common language like English. A physical prototype is a smaller or idealized version of the actual scheme. These three prototypes usually do not belong to the DSS. The fourth prototype: symbolic or numerical is generally employed by DSSs. It is further referred to as a data-based prototype. Certain prepared management science setbacks and modelinginstruments are accessible to resolve the setbacks (Turban et al2001). Standard prototypes will not be able to resolve administrative issues, which are unstructured. These setbacks are generally categorized as tactical or strategic and need to the utilization of a Decision Support System.

Table 2.6: Problem and Tools

Problem	Tool
Allocation of resources	Linear and non-linear programming
Project management	PERT, CPM
Inventory control	Inventory management models, simulation
Forecasting results	Forecasting models, regression analysis
Managing waiting lines	Queuing theory, simulation
transposing and distributing goods	Transportation models
Matching items to each other	Assignment models
Predicting market share and other dynamically orientated situations	Markov chain analysis, dynamic programming, simulation

Source: Adapted from Turban et al. (2001)

2.3.9.1. The Seven Groups of DSS Models

Several Decision Support Systems include prototypes of different types. Prototypes of a specific variety have a tendency to contain several features in general. Mallach (1994) contrasts DSS prototypes as stated forthwith:

- System versus Process
- Static versus dynamic
- Continuous versus discreet-event
- Deterministic versus stochastic

Turban (1995) further allocates the aforesaid features to Decision Support System prototypes, however, classified the prototypes additionally into seven clusters:

- Complete enumeration – a few options
- Optimization through algorithm
- Optimization through an analytical formula

Simulation

- Heuristics
- Other descriptive models
- Prescriptive prototypes

Prototypes contain processes and principles to operate their information components or to obtain other information components. An exterior database or other exterior information sources might be employed to obtain these values. A helpful feature of these prototypes happens to be that the prototype is still applicable when information varies (Mallach 1994). The subsequent parts offer brief descriptions of the seven clusters as specified by Turban (1995).

Complete Enumeration

A limited, as well as small numbers of options, are represented by decision examination. Two kinds are differentiated: solitary goal and multiple goals. Decision tables or decision trees are two methods employed in solitary goal decision examination. There are numerous methods of multiple goals. The goal in the two kinds is to choose the most appropriate option subsequent to making a list of them and evaluating every goal predicted input towards their goals. The decision table is a numerical prototype. Two features which could impact the prototype are ambiguity as well as risk. In ambiguity, the likelihood of every state of nature is unidentified. In the risk factor, the likelihoods are identified.

Adequate data is collected regarding the case to assess the risk. An option to the decision table is the decision tree. A decision tree illustrates the associations of the setback and will be capable of handling circumstances, which are additionally complicated.

Optimization Via a Mathematical Algorithm

Numerical encoding offers a comparatively impartial slant in resolving the setback. Linear encoding is the best acknowledged numerical method employed in optimization. Another encoding, as well as network prototype that are available, is non-linear encoding, goal encoding as well as distribution problems. The aim is to seek the most appropriate choice from innumerable options. Appropriate setbacks generally exhibit the subsequent features and require some suppositions:

- An inadequate number of fiscal resources on hand for distribution (labor, capital, machines, water).
- The resources are employed in the generation of goods or services.
- Two or more ways exist to user resources, everyone called a solution program.
- Each product or service generates a return pertaining to a said objective.
- Numerous restraints limit or confine the distribution.
- The returns from different resources are calculated with an equivalent general unit.
- The return of a particular allocation is free from other allocations.
- The entire return is the total of the return of various services or goods.
- All information is acknowledged with conviction.
- The resources are to be utilized in the best financial manner Optimisation utilizing investigative methods.

Numerous inventory prototypes are there in this group. The aim here is to seek the most favorable result utilizing a single-line method. The method is, "Optimisation utilizing a numerical procedure", might be utilized also. Many other inventory prototypes are there incorporating statistics, fiscal examination, as well as accounting and management science prototypes. Statistical and financial operations are incorporated into numerous Decision Support System generators. There are innumerable management science models varying from inventory to project management. Numerous Decision Support System generators incorporate optimization as well as simulation abilities. A Decision Support System generator could invoke these prototypes by passing a solitary command. A Decision Support System generator could further interface with strong quantitative methodologies in stand-alone packages. Pre-programmed quantitative prototypes could be retrieved through templates.

A few of these prototypes could be the basis for other prototypes, for example, the regression method could be a fraction of the predicting prototype which backs the economic planning prototype. SQRT estimates the square root and could be a fraction of the inventory prototype.

Simulation

Simulation is a method for carrying out trials. Simulation generally emulates actuality contrasting to prototypes that represent actuality (Turban 1995). That is there are fewergeneralizations of actuality in simulation prototypes as compared to other prototypes. Yield values of the choice provided with particular input variables are monitored. Simulation is a descriptive rather than a normative instrument. It lacks automatic search for a most favorable result. Simulation foresees or defines a system in a particular situation. The most excellent one among the options could be chosen.

The procedure frequently subsists on several recurrences of a trial. Simulation is generally utilized if the issue to be resolved is very complicated to be carried out by mathematical optimization methods. A precise simulation prototype needs a thorough awareness of the setback. The prototype is formatted considering the viewpoint of the person making the decisions and in his decision structure. The simulation prototype is formatted for a specific issue and thereby will not be capable of resolving all issues. The person making the decision could try out various input variables to decide the ones that are vital. The decision maker could try out various options to decide the best variable set. It permits the person who makes the decision to put forward "what-if" kind of queries. Decision-makers, who utilize the trial-and-error method for solving issues, will be able to do it quicker, with fewerexpenses and risk. A vast amount of time compression could be achieved, providing the decision-maker with a proposal of the long-term impacts on different strategies in just a few minutes.

Some drawbacks of the simulation are stated forthwith:

- An optimal result is not assured.
- Building a simulation prototype is often a time-consuming and expensive procedure.
- Solutions, as well as inferences from simulation research, are frequently not assignable to other issues.
- Simulation is at times selected in place of investigative solutions, which could generate optimal solutions. It is better to use a heuristic method.
- The input information is inaccurate or restricted.
- The actuality is so complicated that the optimization prototype is oversimplified.

- A dependable precise prototype is unavailable.
- The calculation period foroptimization is very extreme.
- It is feasible to enhance the competence of the optimization procedure by utilizing heuristics.
- Issues are resolved often and utilize maximum computer time.
- Multifaceted issues which are uneconomical for optimization.
- When representative rather than mathematical processing is concerned.

Certain benefits of heuristic prototypes are that they are simpler to comprehend and thus simpler to execute. They could generate numerous answers, which could be useful to orient individuals to be resourceful and format regulations for complicated issues, save formatting and computer implementation time.

2.3.9.2. Other Descriptive Models

Other descriptive methods incorporate non-quantitative prototypes conveyed as rules or methods. These prototypes might be formatted individually or in amalgamation with quantitative methods like fiscal prototypes and waiting for lines to seek answers to "what-if" situations by the employment of a procedure.

Prescriptive Models

The chief aim of this kind of prototype is to foresee the future for a particular situation. Representative methods comprise Markov-analysis as well as forecasting prototypes. Forecasting foresees the worth of prototype variables at times to come. Two kinds of estimates are differentiated by Turban (1995): short run that is to 12 months, where predictions are utilized in deterministic prototypes and long run where predictions are employed in both deterministic as well as probabilistic prototypes. Frequently, numerous features, many of which are unmanageable, are entailed in the complex job of predicting. Recognized predicting techniques could be classified as for groups:

- Judgment prototypes founded subjective estimations as well as an expert view rather than hard information employed where historical information is inadequate or unavailable.
- Counting techniques, comprising a type of trialing or reviews of the marketplace founded on hard past information usually segregated between time-series and causal techniques.
- Time-series examination where past information is employed to foresee future occurrences.

- Association or causal techniques that comprise more variables than time-series techniques and utilize superior numerical techniques in producing the options.

Dialogue Subsystem or User Interface

This subsystem is the means to triumphant utilization of the Decision Support System. Different interface methods are there that decide the way data is presented as well as utilized. Dialogue modes, as well as conversation arrangements all, donate to the effortlessness of utilization of the Decision Support System. Modes like menu interface, command language, query and solution, form interface, natural language,and object management aremethods employed to help the dialogue subsystem of a Decision Support System. Graphics are particularly vital for resolving issues, as they assist people who make decisions envisage information, associations as well as reviews.

Graphical User Interfaces (GUIs) are direct management schemes where the user has straight control of the noticeable objects like icons or buttons to substitute complicated command syntax. An extensive range of graphics like: text - in the form of titles as well as depictions, time-series graphs, bar and pie charts, scatter diagrams - illustrating the correlation between two variables, 2D or 3D maps, room plans, hierarchy tables, series graphs, animated graphics, and desktop publishing are feasible choices when creating user interfaces. A division of the aforesaid alternatives could be employed to improve the particular Decision Support System, irrespective of if Decision Support System generates reports or just envisage issues and probable answers.

User interfaces could be enhanced by the utilization of interactive multimedia. One new category of multimedia is known as hypermedia and comprises numerous kinds of media like text, graphics, audio as well as video components as instruments to direct knowledge and information and attain outcomes.

Associated awareness could be correlated with hypertext permitting the user to manage to maneuver to different elements. Virtual actuality, offering a 3-D user interface, presents rich chances for dominant interactions. The execution of 3-D is complex as well as costly. In virtual reality, an individual "thinks that what they are doing is real", all though it is falsely generated (Turban et al., 2001).

Numerous issues can be played down or at times removed if the user can convey to the computer utilizing the user's personal native language. The computer has to be competent to construe this input despite its layout. NLP (Natural Language Processing) is a fraction of AI (Artificial Intelligence).

Two methods are employed in Natural Language Processing: key work search (pattern matching) as well as complex language processing (syntactical and semantic examination). Keyword analysis hunts for chosen words or phrases. Once detected, the program reacts with the connected group of answers. Language processing is even now developing know-how. As communication incorporates language in context, it is hard for the computer to comprehend what is precisely intended when free-format orders are given.

Heterogeneity is present among customers and handling styles of Decision Support System (Turban et al2001). Diverse customers have dissimilar cognitive penchants and capabilities, diverse means of getting at a choice and thus require dissimilar kinds of backing in taking the ultimate choice. Certain customers are expert in utilizing Decision Support System and require a dissimilar user interface than other customers who are not very skilled.

2.3.10. Previous Work

Liao and Hsu (2004) in "An Intelligent Decision Support System for Supply Chain Integration", try to attain a viable lead by utilizing an intelligent DSS for supply chain incorporation, chiefly there are three main concerns in addition to associated Information Technologies (IT), counting a multi-agent structural design, data cube method, and an ANN-founded method, are examined to investigate the incorporation of supply chain actions. A multi-agent founded structural design is suggested to back the choice as well as negotiation of acquiring bids and help in making decisions.

The notion of the data cube is employed to examine the multidimensional information of ordering data and assessing the decision norms of buying and ordering procedures. A system merges supplier choice assessment as well as ANN (Artificial Neural Network) method is fashioned to assess and envisage the supplier's functioning. The findings reveal that the suggested arrangement and connected IT (Information Technologies) could help the person making decisions for supply chain administration as well as assimilation.

Negash (2004) in "Business Intelligence" illustrated that BI systems merge functional information along with investigative instruments to represent multifaceted and viable data to planners and people who make decisions.

The aim is to develop the appropriateness and excellence of inputs to the decision procedure. BI is employed to comprehend the abilities obtainable in the company; the technology, tendencies, and potential trends in marketplaces, know-how, and the regulatory surroundings wherein the firm functions, and the activities of rivals and the insinuations of these activities.

Fries (2006) in "The Contribution of Business Intelligence to Strategic Management" endeavors to examine the input of Business Intelligence to strategic management. It showed that BI not merely provided inputs to the tactical level of an establishment, but even to the strategic and functional level. In addition, it deduced that generating or offering intelligence for the initial group of tactical choices and concerns was comparatively effortless as internally linked information are developed. Information on the firm and its chief competitors and clients is comparatively effortless to access and to process.

Lee and Cheng (2007) in "Development Multi-Enterprise Collaborative Enterprise Intelligent Decision Support System" illustrate intelligent decision support that incorporates BI, user intelligence, supply chain intelligence in addition to business analysis. The multi-organization joint theoretical ERP-IDSS structure includes supply-chain management as well as customer relationship management. This structure is an integrated answer for venture resource scheduling, customer relationship, and supply-chain management. This incorporates a DSS with knowledge management, to offer direction to making choices while in the scheduling stage. This research noted that the IDSS (Intelligent Decision Support System) contained the capability to acquire the knowledge and offerable direction at the time of the scheduling stage. Whereas the information and model management is carried out via the Decision Support System, individuals who make the decisions can concentrate on planning concerns.

Olszak and Ziemba (2007) in "Approach to Building and Implementing Business Intelligence Systems" endeavor to define procedures of creating BI structures. The deliberations are centered on goals and operational fields of Business Intelligence in enterprises. Therefore, the method to be utilized when creating and executing Business Intelligence comprises two main phases, which are of interactive character; that is Business Intelligence formation and Business Intelligence utilization. A great segment of this paper is centered on portraying goals as well as missions, which are attained when creating as well as executing Business Intelligence.

Lupu et al., (2007) in "The Impact Of Organization Changes On Business Intelligence Projects" endeavors to portray subject attitudes of BI pertaining to ERP ventures, and the familiarity of a real business venture, its advancement and the issues it confronted. It allows a perception into the three major stages of the venture and it assesses the influence of technological issues and business alterations on Business Intelligence ventures, portraying the positive and negative aspects of the suggested results.

The deduction of the paper could be helpful for everyone concerned with creating BI solutions to disclose certain success aspects, to avoid or resolve certain inbuilt issues connected to this kind of ventures.

Pirttimaki (2007) in "Business Intelligence as a managerial tool in large Finnish companies" endeavored to study Business Intelligence as an instrument for administering company data in huge firms in Finland. The outcomes illustrated the part played by Business Intelligence in Finland has enlarged ever since the 1990s. The utilization of Business Intelligence augmented in the foremost fifty firms in Finland, during the timeframe of the investigation, and Business Intelligence is expected to be a vital element of these firms' operations.

Sahay and Ranjan (2008) in "Real Time Business Intelligence in Supply Chain Analytics", examined the concerns for utilizing BI structures in supply chains and attempted to recognize the requirement for real-time Business Intelligence in supply chain analytics. Additionally, they centered on the need to evaluate the conventional Business Intelligence notion that incorporates as well as merges data in an enterprise to assist the companies that are service intended and looking for client allegiance and retention. The author deduced from this research that supply chain analytics utilizing real-time Business Intelligence in establishments will have enhanced functional competence. A perfect Business Intelligence scheme offers an enterprise's workforce, associates, and dealers to effortless accessibility to data they require to successfully do their tasks, and the capability to examine as well as effortlessly share this data with others. So that company functions get new proceeds and save expenditure by offering decision support data.

Rus and Toader (2008) in "Business Intelligence for Hotels Management Performance" endeavored to portray the benefits of utilizing BI Schemes hotel's decision- making procedures. Following a brief examination of the research papers, the authors assess the major elements of a BI System and will classify the Business Intelligence answers for hotel business accessible on the worldwide market and in the Romanian marketplace. It proffers vital instruments for assessing and representing information to executives to help them make knowledgeable choices. Hotels have huge amounts of functional information, produced from everyday deals, in operational databases. These databases hold exhaustive data; while the executive requires comprehensive, brief data for the procedure of making choices. Utilizing BI, the information from different source systems is uploaded into a data warehouse channel, a procedure of withdrawal, alteration, and loading, and the information is changed to helpful data and understanding.

Alnoukari (2009) in "Using Business Intelligence Solutions for Achieving Organization's Strategy: Arab International University Case Study" endeavored to describe the part played by Business Intelligence that offered enterprises a means to structure and attain their business stratagem. We will research this function utilizing an example in the area of higher education, particularly serving a recent private college in Syria (Arab International University) in structuring and attaining their business stratagem. Tabatabaei (2009) in"Evaluation of Business Intelligence maturity level in the Iranian banking industry" endeavored to study the development standard of BI actions and the view pertaining to BI in banks in Iran. The research revealed that Business Intelligence is an administrative notion that assists executives in the establishments to organize data as well as take accurate decisions. The researchers deduced that the development standards of BI as a complete procedure in banks in Iran were at level three of ability.

Stefan (2009) in "Improving the Quality of the Decision Making By Using Business Intelligence Solutions" endeavored to stress the vital part played by BI to augment the excellence of decisions, pertaining to utilizing data warehouses, and the major regions where BI solutions proffered by Microsoft SQL Server 2008 could be used productively. Kursan and Mirela (2010) in "Business Intelligence: the Role of the Internet in Marketing Research and Business Decision – Making" puts forward the determinants of the BI order, as functional in promotional practice. The study scrutinizes the part played by the Internet in the promotional study and its insinuations on the corporate decision–making procedures. The study attempted to emphasize the significance of web chances in carrying out Web segregation as well as gathering user information. Owing to the presence of various views pertaining to the part played by the Internet, this study attempts to stress its endeavor of an interactive channel which supplies the purpose of not merely of informational character, but as an influential study instrument also. Numerous information gatherings, as well as study methodologies, are dealt with, which will assist firms to benefit from the Internet as an important business resource.

Ahmad and Shiratuddin (2010) in "Business Intelligence for Sustainable Competitive Advantage: Field Study of the Telecommunications Industry" try to emphasize these topics pertaining to the Telecommunication sector. Qualitative field research in Malaysia was carried out in this study, where every one of the four telecommunication service providers, at different standards of Business Intelligence operations, was examined. The research is carried out through interviews with top executives, who are concerned with making decisions in their firms.

Contents examination is later carried out to obtain the aspects as well as variables and all-inclusive prototype of Business Intelligence for Sustainable Competitive Advantage is formatted.

The findings of the interviews recognize nine main variables impacting winning Business Intelligence use like; Quality Data, Quality Users, Quality Systems, Business Intelligence Governance, Business Strategy, Utilization of Business Intelligence Tools, and Organization Culture. Business Intelligence is thought to be the chief source for attaining knowledge in maintaining the viable lead. Popovic & Jaklic (2010) in "Benefits of business intelligence system implementation: an empirical analysis of the impact of business intelligence system maturity on information quality" endeavors to experimentally substantiate the input of BI systems in offering excellent data, and to examine thoroughly the extent to which the execution of these systems really supply to resolving the key problems concerning data quality. The outcomes of the examination illustrated that BI systems really have a constructive effect on the excellence of the data. The findings revealed that the excellence of information content is vital for taking improved business choices and offering better worth of BI systems. The findings, therefore recommend that there is yet a void between accessible data quality and knowledge workers' requirements.

Ozceylan (2010) in "A Decision Support System to Compare the Transportation Modes in Logistics" utilized an AHP-based prototype (analytical hierarchy process) to choose a most favorable Transportation means that was assessed for logistic actions. To resolve this issue, the most excellent transportation means is established as well as debated by developed DSS. The AHP prototypes are utilizing a hierarchical association amongst decision levels. It is competent of dealing with manifold norms and facilitates to integrate seven diverse norms features while evaluating the transportation means. The researcher deduced that Seaway is the most excellent transportation means on the whole.

Beheshti (2010) in "A Decision Support System for Improving Performance of Inventory Management in a Supply Chain Network" endeavors to put forward a decision support prototype for enhancing supply-chain management. The prototype hopes to offer a holistic outlook of the supply chain as an incorporated scheme by examining inventory alternatives to assist in making decisions by business associates. The findings for the research reveal that the prototype could be utilized as a forceful Spreadsheet foundation that could be developed to find a solution to diverse supply chain Structures cost-effectiveinstruments and negotiation queries.

Garza et al. (2010) in "Managerial Cultural Intelligence and Small Business in Canada" examines (122) managers in small enterprises in Canada, to find out the level to which executive cultural intelligence was a causative aspect to the institutional efficiency of small enterprises. It was noted that the cultural intelligence of executives in small enterprises handling global businesses was more than that of executives in regional companies. Following calculating for company entrepreneurial direction, the author noted that executive cultural intelligence was constructively linked to business standing as well as worker loyalty, however, not to the fiscal feat of small enterprises. Moreover, these associations were comparable for small enterprises that carried out global trade and enterprises that merely regionally based. For global small enterprises, executive cultural intelligence was not affected by the global extent of company actions. One inference is cultural intelligence is an executive skill which is not limited to global business frameworks. Courses for a prospective study on cultural intelligence are recognized.

Karim (2011) in "The value of Competitive Business Intelligence System (CBIS) to Stimulate Competitiveness in Global Market" endeavors to define as well as calculate that viable leads could be attained via BI. It assesses the effect of major features of characteristic Business Intelligence Systems on enhancing business operations to carry on in a viable marketplace. Additionally, the research revealed that BI is the combination of the collecting, assessing and incorporating information from different sources, and initiating solutions in a manner, which could improve corporate choices. Business Intelligence Systems offer an adequatebasis for the evaluation procedure.

Riabacke et al. (2011) in "Business Intelligence as Decision Support in Business Processes: An Empirical Investigation" endeavors to examine part of BIS and the apparent business worth of executed schemes and their role to assist the accomplishment of institutional aims. The research develops on a survey carried out with 43 participants from various big enterprises in Scandinavia.

The survey had queries on the way ideas, goals and policies are backed by Business Intelligence Systems, on the way corporate standards are gained from these schemes, and on the way plan and execution matters impact the solutions. The general deduction of the research is that there are noticeably various extents of difficulties in the fields. The majority concerns noticed was in the incorporation of Business Intelligence data and decision procedures, and development is needed to a great extent and additional effort within all fields from execution to requirements engineering for BIDSSs.

Isik et al. (2011) in "Business Intelligence Success and the role of Business Intelligence Capabilities" endeavors to recommend that the cause for failure is the absence of awareness of vital features that describe the achievement of Business Intelligence functions, and that Business Intelligence abilities are amongst those vital aspects. We put forward results from a survey of 116 Business Intelligence experts that offers a view of customer contentment with different Business Intelligence abilities and the association between these abilities and customer contentment with Business Intelligence. Results propose that customers are usually content with Business Intelligence in general and with Business Intelligence abilities. Nevertheless, the Business Intelligence abilities with which they are mainly content is not essentially the abilities, which are convincingly linked to Business Intelligence success. Taking into consideration five abilities which were extremely linked with general contentment with Business Intelligence, merely one was particularly linked to information. Another remarkable result entails that, even though customers are not very content with the intensity of an interface of Business Intelligence with other schemes, this ability is greatly connected with Business Intelligence success.

Ramakrishnan, et al. (2012) in "Factors influencing business intelligence (BI) data collection strategies: An empirical investigation" investigates outside stress, which impacts the association between a firm's BI information gathering method and the intent for which Business Intelligence is executed.

A prototype is suggested as well as experimented that is viewed in organizational concept, a study on competitive stress, and study on the intent of Business Intelligence. Two information gathering methods, namely, comprehensive and problem-driven methods, and three Business Intelligence intents namely, insight, constancy, and transformation, were studied. Results reveal a hypothetical view to comprehend better the motivators as well as success features connected to gathering large quantities of information needed for Business Intelligence.

This research offers executives an intellectual prototype wherein to base decisions regarding the information needed to achieve their aims for Business Intelligence.

Woodside (2012) in "Business intelligence and learning, drivers of quality and competitive performance" endeavors to represent the associations between Business Intelligence Systems, knowledge, quality organization and competitive functioning, and calculate the impact that Business Intelligence Systems have customer insights of excellence and viable functioning from a learning standpoint.

Qualitative as well as quantitative techniques counting survey, interview, and case study tools to calculate the connection between Business Intelligence systems, learning prototypes of intellectual-model development and maintenance, quality administration, and viable functioning. Personal, institutional, scheme, data, and service features are investigated to calculate the association among variables. A projected prototype is initiated to enhance the illustrative influence of the previous prototype and broaden hypothetical, realistic, and strategy roles within a healthcare background. Outcomes reveal an important association among knowledge, quality,and viable functioning while using Business Intelligence Systems. Data, as well as system quality, features to impact the degree of knowledge. The prototype augments the illustrative strength compared to earlier data support systems and knowledge prototypes and attaches vital inputs to healthcare study and practice.

2.3.11. Associated Work: ANN in Consumer Segmentation

2.3.11.1. Decision Support System Employing Algorithms

Managers require a decision making draw near that's strong, capable, effective, competent, & integrative to deal with multidimensional organizational bodies. The decision maker copes with numerous players in an association like products, competitors, customers, site, geographic structure, reach, inner organization, & cultural dimension (Porter, 1980). Sound decisions contain two vital conceptions: efficiency (return on the invested resources) & effectiveness (reaching fixed goals). Swarm cleverness, based on combined artificial intelligence, happens to be an emerging region in the sector of optimization. A lot of researchers have built up algorithms, which model the behavior of a diverse swarm of animals & insects like ants, bees, termites, fishes, birds, & elephants.

In the 1990s, researchers brought in two vital algorithms – ant settlement optimization (Dorgio et al., 1991) & particle horde optimization (Kennedy & Eberhart, 1995) founded on fish schooling & bird flocking. PSO does mimic the movement of the birds inside a flock sharing info with one another & the way they cooperate with one another (Acan & Gunay, 2005) described by topology. Birds inside the swarm symbolize parameter samples known as particles. Birds fly about arbitrarily, but monitor others to go after the bird nearest to food. Likewise, every particle inside the swarm does keep track of its individual finest solution found, until now, & does share the info with the topological neighbors for flying in the direction of optimal solutions (Brits et al., 2007).

Such algorithms have encouraged a lot of researchers to make fresh versions to crack problems/difficulties in diverse areas.

The researchers have utilized such models to crack hard real-world problems/difficulties like networking, traffic routing, games, robotics, industry, economics, & design of non-natural self-organized spread problem-solving tools. Among challenges in PSO is to find global optima while not getting ensnared in the local optima (Hendtlass, 2003). Researchers propose diverse topologies to develop the triumph rate of locating global optima (Brits et. al., 2007). Eberhart et al. (1996) identify gbest & lbest topologies for original PSO.

Then again, Kennedy & Mendes (2002) exemplify von Neumann topology, & Suganthan (1999) recommends spatial topology. Likewise, Brits et. al. (2002a) NichePSO, a multi-modal optimization algorithm which utilizes the Guaranteed Convergence PSO (or GCPSO) (van der Bergh and Engelbercht, 2002) for improving local convergence even as preserving the multiplicity of particles by making the formation of subswarms. Li (2004) did introduce the Species-based algorithm (or SPSO) to ease the failings of the k-means algorithm. Similarly, over the most recent decades, the clever behavior of bee horde has encouraged researchers to build up fresh algorithms. Abbas (2001) did propose a fresh horde intelligence method, Honey Bee Mating Optimization (or HBMO) founded on matrimony in honey bees. This model does simulate the fruition of honey-bees beginning with a lone settlement (solitary queen with no family) to the materialization of a Eusocial settlement (one / additional queens having a family).

Abbas did apply the model to a 50 propositional Satisfiability problem (or SAT) with 50 variables & 215 constraints & 3-SAT problem/difficulty (Abbas 2001a, b). From that time, researchers have put forward numerous variations of bee horde intelligence. By way of 50 variables & 215 constraints & 3-SAT problem/difficulty (Abbas 2001a, b). Lu & Zhou (2008b) built up the Bee Collective Pollen Algorithm by faking the honeybees' combined pollen as a worldwide convergence probing algorithm.

Researchers have employed such algorithms to crack the travelling sales individual problem/difficulty utilizing heuristically approach like the ant settlement optimization (Dorgio & Gambardella, 1997), honey bee mating optimization (Marinakis &marnakis, 2009), & particle horde optimization (Pang et. al., 2004; Lope & Coelho, 2005). The fundamental PSO & its variation have moreover, been utilized to crack problems like bin-packing problem/difficulty (Liu et. al., 2008) & flow shop stringing (Tasgetiren et. al., 2007; Tseng & Liao, 2008).

Similarly, researchers have moreover utilized ant optimization algorithm for developing a hybrid routing modus operandi like works by Rajgopalan& Shen, 2006, Baras & Mehta, 2003, & Camara and Loureiro (2000) amongst others.

Likewise, HBMO has been productively applied to answer problems/difficulties like partitioning & design of the embedded systems (Koudil et al., 2007) & cluster examination (Fathian, et. al., 2007), only to name some. Such algorithms have found countless industrial applications. For instance, US maker of American Air Liquids has accomplished significant monetary savings by employing a computer model founded on algorithms encouraged by the foraging actions of ants to analyze each combination of plant scheduling, gas costs, and weather& truck movements. Additional applications consist of telecoms data routing & delivery vehicle armada scheduling (Bogue, 2008).

It's just late; researchers have begun using horde intelligence to the monetary service industry. Nenortaite & Simutis (2006) employ a clever decision-making model to work out a day forward judgment for buying of stocks. The decision model's founded on the application of non-natural neural networks & horde intelligence technology, PSO. The enormous financial-services company Capital One has substituted its inflexible command-and-control administration style with an additionally supple approach better matched to a fast-developing business. Similar to a medium-size ant settlement whose terrain is marched into by a larger rival, Capital One continually looks for & targets fresh market openings.

The application of the neural networks in the marketing region is fairly novel but is turning out to be popular due to their capability of detaining nonlinear relationship among the variables. Plentiful applications of the NNs models in the marketing discipline are obtainable, to bring up some are Market Response Prediction, Market Segmentation, fresh Product Launch, customer Choice Prediction, Sales Forecasting, and that. Market segmentation does have some advantages over mass marketing because it makes available the chance to develop a marketplace after fulfilling the specific requirements of definite consumers (MacQueen et al., 1967).The info of the segments assists the decision makers to get to all customers efficiently with one fundamental marketing mix up. Thus, it assists them to set up resources more efficiently & establish the particular competitive plans (i.e. low cost, differentiation, / focus strategy) (Aaker, 2001).

Segmentation assists to construct closer relationships among the customers & the company. Where the company can produce an additionally fine-tuned manufactured good / service offering & price it properly for target section (Kotler, 2000) for which company can additionally easily choose the most excellent distribution & communications channels, & moreover have a more obvious picture of its rival. Market modeling is a very important matter in marketing. At the collective level, marketplace share models are usually employed in marketing for numerous diverse purposes.

These contain the assessment of cost & advertising elasticity & more normally, forecasting the effects of alterations in marketing variables. Cluster analysis's an ordinary tool for marketplace segmentation. The conventional study usually uses multivariate analysis processes. Kuo et al., (2002a,0020b, 2006) did compare 3 clustering techniques & proposed that SOM does perform better clustering compared to the other usual methods. Lewis et al., (2001) productively implemented SOM founded a neural network to make out the housing property sub marketplaces. A data mining association rule founded on SOM has been grown & applied to a section of sales records from the database for marketplace fragmentation (Changchien and Lu, 2001).

Intelligent systems vary in ways in which they get, stock up & apply the information, cope with uncertainty & incomplete info & knowledge, become accustomed to fresh knowledge, keep up the knowledge & so on (Khebbal et al., 1995). Mazanec (2001) did apply a topology susceptible vector quantization process for marketplace structure analysis. Hope field neural network was found to be more helpful to retailers for segmenting marketplaces (Boone & Roehm, 2002).

Bayesian neural networks present a feasible alternative for the purchase incidence modeling to make out if a consumer makes use of the credit provisions of the direct mailing corporation (Baesens et al., 2002). Adaptive resonance hypothesis, mainly ART2, the neural network has been applied in the form of a toolkit to build up a plan for acquiring consumer necessity patterns (Chen et al., 2002). Kauko et al. (2002) studied on neural network modelling making use of SOM & Learning Vector Quantization (or LVQ) with application to housing marketplace of Helsinki, Finland that shows how it's possible to recognize diverse dimensions of housing submarket place formation by revealing patterns inside the dataset, & also demonstrates the classification capabilities of 2 neural network methods.

A non-natural neural network includes neurons that have been connected with special preparation. Neurons are inside layers & each network includes a few neurons inside the input layer, one / more neurons inside the output layer & neurons inside one / more concealed layers. Algorithms & architectures of non-natural neural networks are diverse through discrepancy in neuron model & relationship among neurons, & their weights. The education point in non-natural neural networks is mass updating, such that with the presenting set of inputs, required outputs are got. The most ordinary kinds of non-natural neural networks consist of feedback, feedforward, & competitive (Menhaj, 1998). Training is a method that ultimately causes learning. Every network is skilled with presented patterns.

Throughout this procedure, the connection masses amid layers are altered until the dissimilarities among forecasted values & target (experimental) are lessened to the allowable limit. Weights infer the memory & information of the network. The pros of making use of ANN are: high calculation rate, learning capability via pattern presentation, the forecast of unknown pattern & suppleness affront the boisterous patterns (Heristev, 1998)

A genetic/hereditary algorithm approach's been taken on to ensure that consumers in the identical cluster have the closest buying patterns (Tsai &Chiu, 2004). A 2 stage system, including SOM & GA (or genetic algorithm) set up for wireless telecommunications business marketplace segmentation & the end results, did show that the proposed system has improved productivity in segmentation (Kuo et al., 2004). A GA founded intelligent method approach was found to be resourcefully used in consumer targeting (Kim & Street, 2004). The rear circulation neural network based application set up in Cape Metropolitan Tourism information has been demonstrated to track the shifting behavior of travelers within & among segments (Bloom, 2005). It happened to be found that the NN models do better than the multinomial logit model in finding out the most money-making time in a buying history to categorize & target potential customers new to their groups (Kaefer et al., 2005). Kim et al. (2005) set up an ANN directed by genetic algorithms (or GAs) productively to target the households. Targeting of the consumer segments with custom-made promotional activities happens to be a key aspect of consumer relationship management.

Kianget al. (2006) did apply the SOM networks to one consumer data set from American Telephone & Telegraph Company (or AT&T) & the study found that SOM network outperforms the 2-step process that unites factor analysis & K-means cluster scrutiny in finding out market segments. Reutterer et al. (2006) empirically found proof of major positive impacts on profitability as well as sales for segment-specific custom-made direct marketing operations. Huang et al., (2007) put into practice support vector clustering (or SVC), SOM & k-means in the case study of a drink corporation and on account of the numerical outcomes; they did find that SVC does better than the additional techniques. SOM has been demonstrated to produce major segments with definite traits are found in themature marketplace (Bigné et al., 2008). A lesser sized market is also able to be targeted utilizing the Marketing segmentation that's of use for decision makers to get to all customers efficiently with one fundamental marketing mix. A back-propagation neural network model's been demonstrated to be of use in making out present patterns of consumers of hospitals (Lee et al., 2008). Chan (2008) did demonstrate that segmentation employing GA based system can more efficiently target precious customers compared to haphazard selection.

ANN & particle horde optimization techniques have been put into practice to produce accurate marketplace segmentation for marketing plan decision making & extensive application (Chiu et al., 2009). Wang (2009) did adopt a hybrid kernel-founded clustering methods for outlier classification & strong segmentation in a real application. Hung & Tsai in the year 2008, implemented with success an approach of segmentation of the novel market, by the use of the model of Hierarchical Self-Organizing Segmentation (HSOS), in order to deal with the practical data set for the segmentation of market of multimedia that is in demand in Taiwan. In order to cluster the customers according to the variables of their characteristics and to visualize the segments by the produced market maps the method of Fuzzy Delphi, maps that are self-organizing (SOM) & some visualization techniques are developed & implemented successfully as per Mirzazadeh and Hanafizadeh in the year 2011.

A firm, operating in various regions, a method of market segmentation, which can collect data from various regions in order to obtain a set of segmentation rules, could greatly influence the company's competitiveness. Mo et al in the year 2010 did apply the network technique of a self-organizing map (SOM) as a reduction of dimension as well as the clustering tool in order to market segmentation by using data of the largest bank in terms of issuing credit cards in China, which include surveys of the attributes of customer satisfaction & the history of transaction of credit card & did show that the SOM for segmentation in multiple regions would be an effective & efficient method as compared to the other approaches. The researchers developed a system by using the method of Fuzzy Delphi & a model of the neural network and have applied it to the data of the customers for the selection of perfume with more rate of correct classification as per the Hanafizadeh et al.in the year 2010.

The Chen et al in the year 2010 did apply a CBR system based on 3NN+1 by various means of the algorithms of the genetics to the case of the market of the notebooks in order to demonstrate the usefulness of it for the market segmentation. From the real case results, it is shown that this system will be of great value to the enterprises, in order to develop the marketing strategies. The systems have been explained well by Wickramasinghe, Amarasisi & Alahakoon (2004), Kohonen (1982), Hamilton & Selen (2008), Shirazi & Soroor (2007) and Hamilton (2009). Here, a request of the user is matched in terms of the environment of the three-dimensional packages, where none of the exact matches has been deliverable, the best option has been selected or another solution has been found. The option is remembered, then added to the database, & the next request is more adjusted & improved, therefore, the result is improved to be the customer request's exact representation. Alternatively, more data that are relevant is sought & obtained, and then it is added to the map that is self-organized.

As slightly various data has been added to this system, growth is created in the self-organizing map & therefore it would be possible to gather greater intelligence & synthesis.

A distribution of 64 articles is categorized by the scheme of proposed classification has been based on the publication year, name of journal, title, tools of ANN that have been used and the authors.

The fourteen types of the ANN algorithms have been found to apply on the research of the market segmentation between the span of the years 2000 to 2010 in some reviewed journals that are selected: a) NN algorithm, b) Meta-Heuristic tools, c) ARNN, d) adaptive resonance theory e) Bayesian NN, f) Back Propagation NN, g) Data Mining, h) hybrid fuzzy tools, i) Genetic Algorithm (GA), j) hope field NN, k) hybrid NN, l) Self Organizing Map (SOM), m) Support Vector Machine (SVM), n) Vector Quantization

Applications of the techniques of neural network that are artificialare the emerging inclination in terms of industry and academics for the segmentation of the market. It has been paying attention of the researchers, of the industry practitioners & academics. This work did identify 64 articles that are related to the application of the techniques of the neural network in the segmentation of the market, & is published between the years 2000 & 2010. The article does aim to give a review of research in the applications of the neural network in the domain& technique of the market segmentation that is used often.

The work of review can't claim to be an exhaustive one, but presents some reasonable insights & show the research's prevalence in the area of discussion. **More detailed work on Application of ANN can be found in Appendix 2.**

2.3.12. Summary

This chapter comprehensively deals with Decision Making Support System, which is provided by BI and its necessity to develop the strategies that manage the decision making for both organization and individual by using the automated tool that contains the enormous amount of unstructured data.

This chapter discusses the Rationality and problem solving, Characteristics of DSS, components of DSS, Quality of Decision Making, Types of the decision, Decision Making Methods, previous work.

The research revealed that Business Intelligence was an administrative notion that helps executives in establishments to organize data and also to attain accurate decisions.

2.4. Data Mining

2.4.1. Introduction

Many companies do collect the vast amounts of the data; however, they just fail in terms of extracting the necessary information in order to support managerial decision-making. The discoveries of Knowledge in the databases came to the attention during the nineties with growth in the need for analyzing the data & turning it to be useful information. For instance, for evaluating the applications of the loans, by improving the ability to predict bad loans, the company could reduce the loan losses. In the area of medics, we can predict the probability of the presence of heart diseases in new patients by studying the historical data. In the industrial field, reducing the fabrication flaws of a certain product, processing large quantities of the data that have been collected while the fabrication process in order to name some.

2.4.2. Definition

The mining of data is a search for the relationships and the global patterns that are "hidden" in large quantities of the data in the databases. **More detailed definition and explanation could be found in Appendix 1.**

The Tasks of Data Mining

Some main tasks of the data mining have been the classification, the dependencies modeling, the associations (sequential patterns) and the clustering.

2.4.2.1. Classification

This task is the most researched in data mining. Its aim has been to deal in finding mutual properties of the set of various elements in the dataset and classifying them onto the various classes, as per the classification rule.

The desirable properties of the discovered rule are its power of predicting &assigning of the classes of the new elements, for example evaluating the applicant of the new loan by considering the characteristics of him. When the dataset has been already divided into the training and the test set.

Another case is when there would only be one dataset & specialized methods for the evaluation of the algorithm are been used like the cross-validation of the N-fold. The method does divide the dataset onto N that is an exclusive sub-dataset of a similar size. In each of the steps of the total number of steps of the algorithm, the different sub-datasetis used in order to test, while the rest of the sub-datasets for learning the algorithm.

2.4.2.2. *Dependencies Modeling*

The task is the generalization of the classification task. The difference is the goal attribute, which isn't selected advance & more attributes could be in the part of the rule. The lone limitation has been the goal attributes couldn't be appearing in IF (predicting) of the similar rule. The training and the testing are done as it was in the problems of problem.

2.4.2.3. *Associations*

Its rules have the following set of

$$X_1 \wedge " \wedge X_m \Rightarrow Y_1 \wedge " \wedge Y_n,$$

Asdata mining gets the discovery of the list of customers who are associated with the concerned buying patterns.

2.4.2.4. *Clustering*

In the problem of classification the class has been given as the input of the algorithm, the algorithm of clustering must be detecting the class by itself, therefore creating clusters of an elemental dataset. The clusters have been derived from data & have been formed of the elements, which are the same as the other, here similarity measured with a respect to the all-available attributing values. The goal is to identify the clusters, which is considered to be classes.

2.4.3. *Data Mining Techniques*

Data mining techniques differ widely in a way of the representation of the data. All the methods supposed to have individual elements in the dataset, which could be explained by the characteristics, in such a way that the elements belong to a concept or class having similar characteristics. If elements are explained with the attributing values, they might be represented to be the points in the n-dimensional space of the attributes, where n would be the number of the attributes.

The model's aim is to find adequate representations of the cluster. Data could be represented in a lot of ways like by etalons, functions that have been assigned to each cluster and the division of space of the attributes in the forms that are easy to explain etc.

2.4.3.1. *Decision Trees*

The Decision trees have been the structures of tree-shape, which represents the decisions & rules for classifying the dataset. The advantage of the method is that it is easier to understand the representation as well as has the ability to select the significant variables.

For such a reason, the technique has been suitable for the datasets, where quite a number of predicting attributes are irrelevant. "Divide and conquer" method is kept in mind while making decision trees.

The training data is gradually divided into small & smaller subsets for having subsets, which contains elements of a similar class as much as possible. Every step of the algorithm selects one attribute for nodding the tree. The aim is to choose the attribute, which will distinguish the elements of the different classes into subsets.

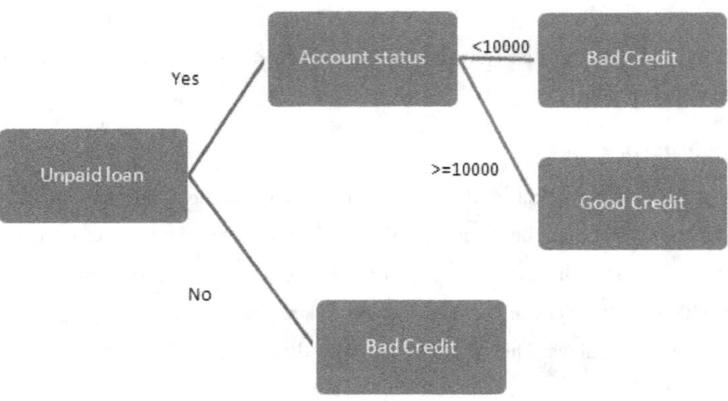

Figure 2.9: Quality Attributes

2.4.3.2. *Rule Induction*

Since the rule representation has been widely used for data mining, a number of greedy algorithms are also used for the creation of the same. One of such methods for the creation of the decision rules has been the algorithm of sets covering the utilization of the concept of "divide & conquer". The examples have been removed from the dataset & the search continues in order to find the other rule with similar characteristics unless the dataset has been emptied. The results of such a method are equivalent to the decision tree, i.e. the rules could be rewritten for the decision tree & vice versa.

IF (UnpaidLoan="yes") THEN (Credit="bad")

IF (UnpaidLoan="no") and (AccountStatus<10000) THEN (Credit="bad")

IF (UnpaidLoan="no") and (AccountStatus>=10000) THEN (Credit="good")

Another method for rule discovery ina search of the attribute space, either depth-first or breadth-first search. Rules are being generated by adding one attribute value at a time and evaluated for "interestingness". Rules are usually evaluated by computing the support and confidence of the rule. Support represents the number of elements in the dataset that satisfy both the IF and THEN part of the rule, whereas confidence is the conditional probability of THEN part of the rule if IF part is satisfied.

2.4.3.3. Neural Networks

Artificial neural networks have been mimicking the human brain's neurophysiology. They do have an ability to learn from the examples for finding the patterns of data and classifying them. Once get trained in training data they would have the ability to predict new data. They usually perform the global searches on the data however the shortcoming of them is that it represents a black box, which the user could hardly understand the principles underlying that have been used in order to classify data. It could also perform well in recognizing images and such similar tasks, while it isn't necessary for understanding the process. The most common method that is used in order to learn the neural network has been an error.

2.4.3.4. Genetic Algorithms

Principles of the technique have been explained in the two chapters of the past; here it would be discussed about the applications of the data mining. Each of the individuals in the population of the genetic algorithm does encode a solution of the task of data mining as possible, usually classifying, dependence modeling or various associations. Suppose every individual does represent a single rule for classifying. The individuals are generated randomly for the generation first. Each individual could be the potential solution for the algorithm. Each of the individuals has been evaluated in terms of the dataset of training; the function of evaluation could be the number of classified elements (correctly) within the database. While the algorithm has been finished, the result would be that an individual has best values of evaluation (or fitness – in chapter one) – in such an example the result would be the rule of classification with the highest prevailing accuracy. The advantage of such a method would be that it can perform global searches on the dataset. Such methods have proved to be of great help in making the theories understandable to a greater possible extent.

2.4.3.5. K-Nearest Neighbour

The concerned method as used for classification and clustering task. The classes or cluster are represented with their concerned examples. Suppose isthe "n" attributes gets considered & each element along the dataset gets placed along this space.

The elements which have a similar attribute of values form the clusters along the concerned attribute space. Hence, analyzing those clusters, either along the representative of each of the cluster gets chosen or the functions get noted as divided along the attribute of spaces along the subspaces which contain only the elements from 1 cluster (Takač, 2003)

2.4.3.6. Limitations in Existing Algorithms

Restrictions in GA

The drawback of GAs happens to be in the working out time. But as we're able to stop the calculation at any time, the more extended run is tolerable (particularly with faster & faster computers) (Gupta, 2006). For, getting an idea on some problems/difficulties solved by GAs, here's a short listing of a few applications:

1. Nonlinear dynamical systems – forecasting, information examination
2. Designing neural networks, architecture as well as weights
3. Robot trajectory
4. developing LISP programs (or genetic programming)
5. Approach planning
6. Finding the shape of the protein molecules
7. TSP & sequence setting up
8. Functions for making images

Restrictions in ABC

- The most excellent solution established by onlooker/bystander bee, which did adopt the local search plan is not able to arrive at the perfect intensity of accuracy.
- ABC algorithm has been stated to suffer from a small number of demerits such as poor utilization ability (Gao et al., 2007), more sluggish convergence (Akay & Baraboga, 2012) & local optima trapping (Gao et al., 2012).
- ABC's good at discovery but poor inutilization; its convergence swiftness is moreover an issue in a few cases.
- In the ABC algorithm, the procedures of the discovery & utilization contradict with one another, so the 2 abilities have to be steady for achieving first-rate optimization performance.

2.5. Summary

This chapter discusses the importance of gathering related data in order to assist managerial decision making.

This section enables to provide the importance of data mining in the research area in order to extract high knowledge. Further, this chapter deals with the major task of data mining such as dependencies modeling, classification, the clustering and the associations (sequential patterns). Data mining techniques have been explained in this chapter in order to find the adequate representation of the cluster.

CHAPTER 3

Overview of Problem Definition

3.1. Introduction

In this chapter elaborately discuss about the optimal state problem in Business intelligence and provides the limitations of BI and define the proposed solution using the existing studies which is briefly discussed in previous chapter (Refer chapter II) in context to Indian banking Industry, thus identified research gap will lead to the proposal of new meta-heuristic algorithms. Today's knowledge economy, it is no longer sufficient for only key individuals in any organization to have all the information. Competition is shortening business-cycles, forcing businesses to be more agile and thus pushing more decision-making responsibility to not just strategists and analysts, but all tactical and operational decision-makers. Indeed, these are some of the main reasons why Business Intelligence (BI) initiatives continue to be front and center for most enterprises, and BI-related activities keep on rising. BI is becoming popular and used by more and more organizations for better decision-making in business (Gartner Research, 2009).

3.2. Business Intelligence in Banking Industry

BI in banking has evolved by the Manual System so as to manage the information systems along with computerization, though these sectors have an efficient transaction in the recording system. The manual systems also provide effective reports for the management and regulatory requirement and these were consolidated manually and the final reports were represented to the higher level. As a result of the expansion of the banking network, transactions were also increased, which resulted in the error-prone manual operations. Thus banking system switched over to the computerization and become fully automated. This previous initiative leads to the foundations of BI in the banking industry. It remarks that even though the organizations are rich in data, but they seem to be poor in information that is completely inappropriate. The challenge is how to transform data into useful information (Carver & Ritacco, 2006, p. 3).

The BI environment comprises of all the developmental activities with information processing and support, which is requisite for the delivery of reliable business information with accuracy possessing the business analytics capabilities organizations to ensure to design and implement the BIS successfully within their own BI environments.

The scenario is defined as achieving the organizational goals by proper guidance to business through analytical decision-making supported by the quality information from information systems. The Business users utilize the information help rendered by the BIS analyses (of business operations) to understand, improvise and focus on business operations (White, 2005).

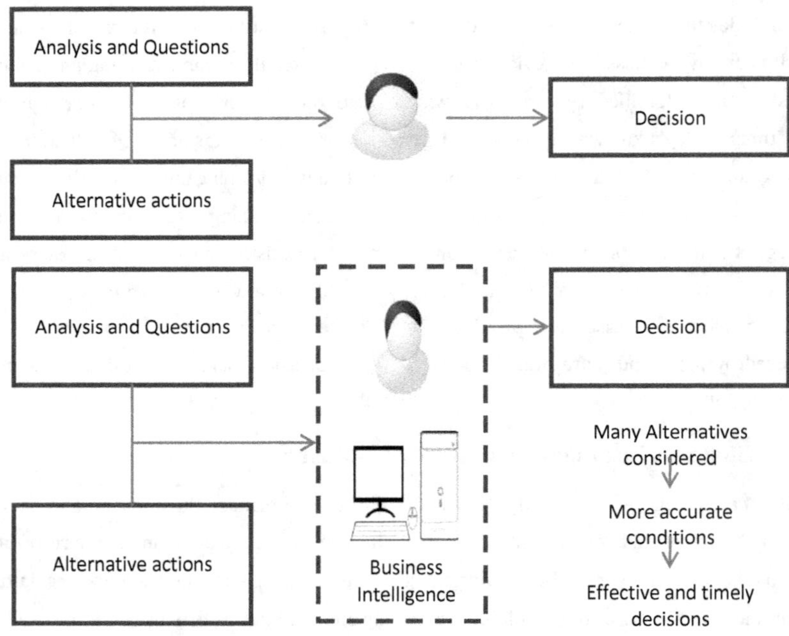

Figure 3.1: Benefits of a Business Intelligent System

BI programs usually combine an enterprise data warehouse, and a BI platform or toolset to transform data into usable, actionable business information (TDWI, 2012). BI is an analytical process that transforms enterprise and markets' fragmented data into performance-oriented information or knowledge about objectives, positions, and opportunities for an organization to achieve its goals. Due to the competitive pressures in businesses, the intelligent decisions are made based on their incoming business data, and these decisions must be made quickly (Business Intelligence and Data Warehousing, 2005, p. 5). Thus the business intelligence is the tool that enables the manager to make the decision. In the organization, this system had become the most indispensable part of the success. Customer segmentation is one of the most significant methods used in studies of traditional marketing.

Mostly, they define and create new variable for clustering procedure or use different variables in sequential clustering steps (Such as Hwang et al., 2004; Kim et al., 2006; Chang et al., 2007; Chan 2008; McCarty & Hastak, 2007; Cheng & Chen, 2009 and Seog et al ., 2005). Lifetime Value (LTV) has an important role in the current literature on customer segmentation. Using artificial neural network practices in market segmentation methodology was proposed are relatively fewer articles with the Meta-Heuristic, ART2, data mining, Genetic Algorithm, and fuzzy algorithms. Even though it does not mean the application of artificial neural network in this aspect, the fewer number of articles related to the above category of artificial neural network application to market segmentation is less mature than in the others.

3.3. Problem in the Existing Work

Deploy business information and business analysis tools, which will be in-turn, provide a widerange of the entire disability claims process. This will end up in a meeting or exceeding the customer expectations by correcting the service issues from the top managers, front-line supervisor, and middle managers' perspectives.

In order to maximize an organization's profits through segmentation, strategists have to segment the market and thus increase the profitability of the organization. In addition to the real-life problem based by the marketers, previous studies to our knowledge only attempted to explain the purpose of Business Intelligence and proposed to explain the theoretical methodology of BI such as Predictive analysis, Forecasting analysis, Supply chain management, Scorecards,andDashboards.

The homogeneous enterprise – extensive BI methodology isn't established as of now. There's a requirement for High intensity of interactive and Adhoc reporting necessities. Present business intelligence tools put up with a shortage of analysis & visualization abilities and usual result listing displayed by the search engines frequently engulf business analysts by means of irrelevant info and every day raising of the information volumes. The standard execution time for some greater BI solutions isbetween approximately 3 to 6 months. A lot of Business Intelligence applications happen to still be hard to use.

The main problem is that the huge amount of data must be converted into useful information in a timely manner in order to provide the manager with solid information for their decision. By converting the non-transparent data into useful information in real time, could contribute a significant competitive advantage for the company. However, none of the research had focused on a standard methodology that would be applicable for enterprise-wide BI methodologies.

Even the existing methodologies, failed to provide a high level of interactive and Adhoc reporting requirements as still, enterprises tend to use only excel and spreadsheet functions. Although the people are employing the BI apparatus & techniques for exploring the database, actually people happened to be doing is making a theory concerning the BI matters. Generally, they've talked regarding the building for their individual real-time difficulty. They don't make available adequate support in managing future challenges in the BI industry, like real-time decision making

3.4. Research Gap

The BI methodologies and its limitations and expectations were briefly explained in the previous chapter (Chapter II). Hence there will be a good response to the new methodology to overcome the limitations of the existing methodology and fulfill the expectations. In the existing papers, there is no consistent enterprise-wide BI Methodologies. Still, now the business analysts are using Excel and spreadsheet functions. Existing BI tools suffer from a lack of analysis and visualization capabilities. Daily rising the data volumes is the biggest hectic to manage the big data set.

Only 10% of BI users are sophisticated enough to utilize a BI Tool. The inconsistency of the respond produced by more than one advanced user is also known as multiple versions of the truth. The decision-making process is an integral part of a broker subject, in which an individual bridge the gap in a process between the existing system operation conditions (as it) and future better operations conditions (to be). It is not so easy to attain for a transformation to happen from one system to the desired state after overcoming certain obstacles. These obstacles enable the decisions makers to think for an alternate solution always to achieve the desired goal, and make a decision after comparing each option's advantages and disadvantages.

3.5. Objectives

In order to accomplish the optimal customer the following five stages were adopted: Database preparation and Normalize the data in the first stage, Applying the existing Meta-heuristics algorithms individually is the second stage, Applying the proposed new algorithms in the third stage, Compare and analysis with the existing Meta-heuristics algorithms with the new algorithms is in the fourth stage and Intelligence concept is implemented with Backpropagation algorithm in the fifth stage. The following are the specific objectives developed for the present book.

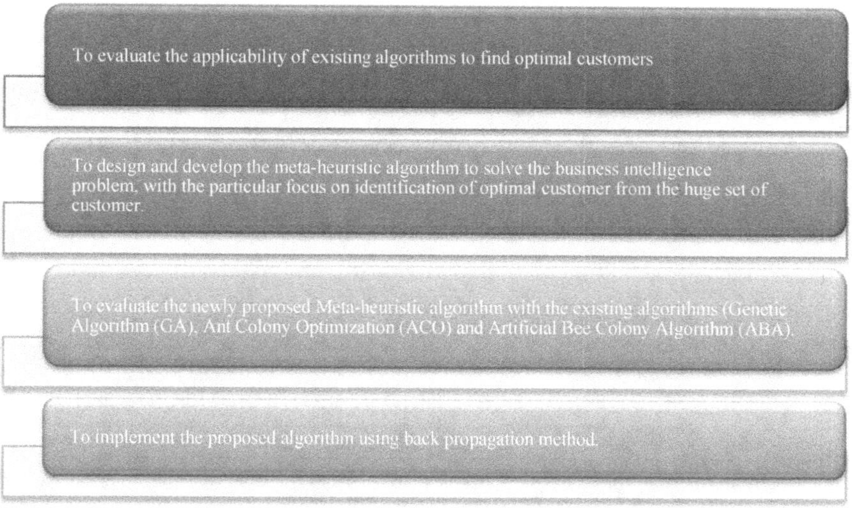

Figure 3.2: Objective of the Proposed Algorithm

3.6. Overview of Proposed Model

The research will propose a new algorithm considering the limitations of existing ANN and genetic models. In addition, the study also evaluates existing algorithms in terms of its benefits and drawbacks of each and how best to find the most suitable algorithm. This will not be a comprehensive review of commercial tools but instead provides a method for evaluating tools and as a point of reference for selecting the best BI tool for the particular problem. A BI life cycle for system development is provided by Gangadhara and Swami in the year 2004. But the methodology illustrations about the BI system implementation are only limited in the literature and fewer insights about the choice and preferred analytics in the BI systems is observed (O Leary, 2011). The present study will restrict and implement the new optimization techniques to overcome the limitations of existing optimization techniques and lacking the understanding behind in the meta-heuristic algorithms.

3.7. Summary

This chapter comprehensively described the overview of the problem in Business intelligence, existing in the present situation and the need to develop the strategies using the automated tool that contains the enormous amount of unstructured data. Further, this chapter discusses the BI in the banking industry, problems in the existing work, research objective and overview of the proposed model.

CHAPTER 4

Normalization and Optimization

4.1.　Normalization of Data in Business Intelligence

In today's information society, the concept of information is seen as an essential component that actors of the business environment (e.g. organizations, enterprises, etc.) need to leverage in order to acquire a deeper understanding of the occurring processes, improve the decision making, and increase the reaction to change. The abundance of existing internal and external data and information may be effectively exploited in the benefits of organizations and enterprises by means of intelligent systems, such as Decision Support and Business Intelligence Systems. Business Intelligence systems comprise a broader category of applications and tools, from data acquisition, transformation, and storage, to on-line analytical processing and interactive presentation to the end users. Their main goal is to offer a framework for improved decision -making process by supplying business people with the right information at the right time. While BI represents a comprehensive technology, DSS is smaller in scope and mostly reduced to a computer program or application; moreover, Decision Support Systems may be integrated into the Business Intelligence environment, as part of the overall BI framework.

From the mathematical algorithm perspective, BI establishes the data as a component of the repository element and the foundation upon which is built. The development of BI systems follows a generic cycle specific to most information systems, which includes planning and direction activities, data collection, information processing and storage, analysis and production operations, and dissemination of the produced information among intended addressees.

The presented technologies are meant to facilitate the processing of data from multiple enterprise-wise sources into understandable and valuable information which business user may use to improve their decision-making process. Regardless of their complexity, the employment of either one, according to users' needs, significantly increases responsiveness to changes occurring in the business environment. Initially, BI was coined as a collective term for data analysis tools. Meanwhile, the understanding broadened towards BI as an encompassment of all components of an integrated decision support infrastructure.

In the normalizationprocess, all many-to-many relationships are removed and modeling the data entities in the precise data attribute level.

The next more granular level of information entities might be added as well to a model to handle the business information requirements (Corr &stagnation, 2012). Normalization is accomplished by designing the database according to the normal Forms.The most important concept of relational databases is normalization. Normalization is done by adding constraints to how data can be stored in the database, which implies restrictions to the way data can be inserted, updated and deleted. The main reasons for normalizing database design are to minimize information redundancy and to reduce disk space required to store the database. Redundancy is a problem because it opens up the possibility to make the database inconsistent. Codd talked about update anomalies, which is classier into three categories; insertion anomalies, deletion anomalies and modification anomalies (Elmasri & Navathe, 2004).

A normalized database makes sure that every piece of information is stored in only one place, thus medication of the data only has to be done once. Storing the same data in one place instead of once per entry will also save a lot of storage space. One crucial step in the analysis of microarray data is normalization. Since the overall brightness of the scanned images can differ substantially between arrays, normalization is usually required to allow direct array-to-array comparisons. A very simple way to normalize a set of arrays is to compute a multiplication factor forcing equal overall intensity, for example, measured by the mean or median intensity. However, quite often there exist non-linear relationships between the intensities of arrays, and thus more flexible solutions are required. However, a direct application of the loess normalization results in a non-continuous normalization in that intensity being equal on one array prior to normalization may not be equal after normalization.

Cyclic-loess is a generalization of the intensity-dependent normalization procedure proposed by Yang et al. (2002). With only two arrays Cyclic-loess is a direct application of the loess normalization. With more than two arrays Cyclic-loess iteratively performs loess normalization on all pairs of arrays, until all pairs of arrays are sufficiently normalized. Contrast normalization is another generalization of the loess normalization. Normalization is the process of removing unwanted non-biological variation that might exist between chips in a microarray experiment. It has long been recognized that variability can exist between arrays, some of the biological interest and other of non-biological interest. These two types of variation are classier as either interesting or obscuring by Hartemink et al. (2001). Comparisons of normalization methods for high-density oligonucleotide arrays are considered in both Bolstad et al.(2003) and Schadt et al. (2001).

In (Hochbaum, 2010), Normalized Cut and Normalized Cut' were compared upon the objective standard of having the closest value to the "optimal" when the results were used to calculate the normalized cut criterion. Even though Normalized Cut approximates the entire normalized cut criterion and Normalized Cut' solves for a variant of the criterion, it was found that Normalized Cut' actually arrived at a better result of the normalized cut objective. The Normalized Cut algorithm has been evaluated as part of a study in creating an image segmentation benchmark. Data should only be stored once and avoid storing data that can be calculated from other data already held in the database. During the process of normalization redundancy must be removed, but not at the expense of breaking data integrity rules.

The goal of quantile normalization, as discussed in Bolstad et al. (2003), is to give the same empirical distribution of intensities to each array. There are three levels at which normalization can occur: probe-level, probe set-level and after computing expression. The topic of probe-level normalization is considered extensively in Bolstad et al. (2003). At this level, it is raw probe intensities, possibly after a background correction, which are Normalized. The goal of the Quantile normalization is to produce identical empirical distributions of intensities on all arrays analyzed. The concept, as well as the algorithm of the Quantile normalization method, is very simple, and in terms of speed, Quantile normalization is superior over the other methods based on curve fitting. In summary, with favorably performance in terms of speed, variance, and bias, it is recommended that quantile normalization should be used in preference to the other methods.

Optimization has a key part of today's plan and decision-making procedures. The term, 'optimize' just denotes 'to render as perfect, effectual or purposeful as feasible' (Schwartz & Connor, 1996). The word 'optimized' was employed earlier to denote that produce has been enhanced to attain the goals of a development scientist (Singh & Ahuja, 2004). Nevertheless, currently, the word denotes that computers and statistics were used to attain the goals. Regarding BI, optimization is an occurrence of discovering "the best" feasible means to augment proceeds (Lewis, 2002). Therefore, optimization is described as the execution of methodical methods to attain the most excellent amalgamation of product and procedural features under a particular group of situations (Tye, 2004). Earlier, the majority of researches were centered on seeking the most favorable equivalent to a solitary objective like least expenditure or highest functioning (Kaveh & Talatahari 2010; 2011). For this intent, the optimization algorithm explores through feasible, viable answers, and finally arrives at the best possible solution. This kind of result mostly does not impact other similarly vital aims.

4.2.   The Basic Components of an Optimization Problem

Objective function: An **objective function** states the major objective of the prototype that is either to be minimized or optimized. For instance, in a production procedure, the goal might be to optimize the proceeds or reduce expenses. When assessing the information recommended by a user-defined prototype with the experimental information, the endeavor is minimizing the overall divergence of the forecasts founded on the prototype from the experimental information. In planning a bridge pillar, the aim is to optimize the strength and lessen the size. A group of variables manages the value of the objective purpose. In the production concerns, the variables might comprise the quantities of diverse resources employed or the period spent on every action. In fitting-the-data concern, the variables are the strictures of the prototype. In the pillar plan issue, the unknowns are the outline and measurements of the pillar.

Constraints: A group of constraints is that which let the variables to acquire on definite values but prohibit others. In the production concern, it is impossible to use unconstructive time on whichever action, thus one limitation is that "time" unknowns should be positive. In the pillar plan issue, one might possibly seek to restrict the width of the base and to confine its dimension. The maximization concerns to seek values of the unknowns which minimize or maximize the objective performance whilst fulfilling the limitation.

Currently, applied optimization has been improvised, principally with the accessibility of proficient multi-goal maximization concepts that allows a planner or a person who makes decisions to take into consideration several contradictory objectives concurrently. Practically, a superior plan needs a good balance between diverse goals. This endeavor contains two major sub-tasks: (a)A maximization process to determine high-performing answers, trading-off diverse contradictory objectives of the plan and (b) a decision-making mission to select a solitary favored answer. The word "mathematical programming", was formatted in 1945, and is equal to optimization. Respectively, linear maximization, wherein the limitations as well as goals are linear feats of the unknowns, is commonly called "linear programming," whilst optimization issues, which comprise limitations and contain nonlinearity found in the goal or in any case certain limitations, are called "nonlinear programming" concerns (Kumar, n. d).

4.3.   Optimization Prototypes

The three major categories of controlled optimization prototypes are called linear, integer, and nonlinear programming prototypes. These are very widespread. They have similar arrangements of optimization with constraints.

Linear programming is the easiest of the three categories. As the term reveals, a linear programming prototype merely contains linear expressions (AIMMS, 2012).

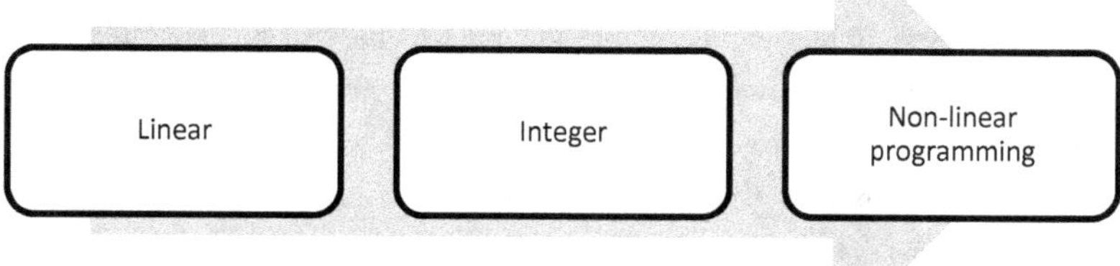

Figure 4.1: Optimization Models

4.3.1. *Formulating Linear Programming Models*

Linear programming was formatted at the start of the numerical programming period and is still today is largely utilized constrained optimization prototype. This is because of large amounts of the theory that is available, the accessibility of resourceful solution techniques, and being able to apply the linear programming to numerous realistic issues.

4.3.2. *Optimization-Modelling Process*

Optimization concerns are omnipresent in the numerical modeling of real-world schemes and encompass a wide variety of applications. Optimization modeling needs a suitable time. The common process which could be utilized in the procedure series of modeling is to: (i) define the issue (ii) suggest an answer and (iii) manage the issue by evaluating and modernizing the optimal solution incessantly, even as altering the structures and arrangement of the issue. Obviously, one can find feedback circles amongst these common stages.

Mathematical Formulation of the Problem: Develop a numerical prototype or structure to symbolize actuality to invent and utilize an optimization solution algorithm. The issue has to be authenticated prior to being proffered an answer. A superior numerical format for maximization should be inclusive as well as exclusive, that is, incorporate what belongs to the issue ward-off that which does not belong to the issue. Seek an Optimal Solution: This is the recognition of a solution algorithm and its execution phase. The only superior plan is an executed plan that remains executed. Managerial Interpretations of the Optimal Solution: When one identifies the algorithm and decides the suitable unit of software to operate, use the program to gain the most favorable plan.

Subsequently, the result would be offered to the person who makes the choice, in a similar fashion and language employed by the said person. This refers to offer administrative construal of the tactical answer in common terms, not merely giving the person who makes the choice a computer printout. Post-Solution Analysis: These actions comprise modernizing the most favorable answer to manage the setback. In these transforming circumstances, it is vital to regularly fill in the most favorable solution to any specified maximization setback. A prototype which was suitable might not be suitable owing to altering circumstances, therefore, turning out to be an erroneous depiction of actuality and unfavorably impacting the capability of the person who makes the decisions to make excellent choices. The maximization prototype developed must be able to deal with transformations in circumstances.

The Importance of Feedback and Control: It is essential to consign great importance on the significance of reviews and manage features of a maximization issue. It will not be appropriate to talk about the background of the optimization-modeling procedure and overlook the detail that one could not anticipate to discovering an unfaltering, irreversible answer to a decision concern.

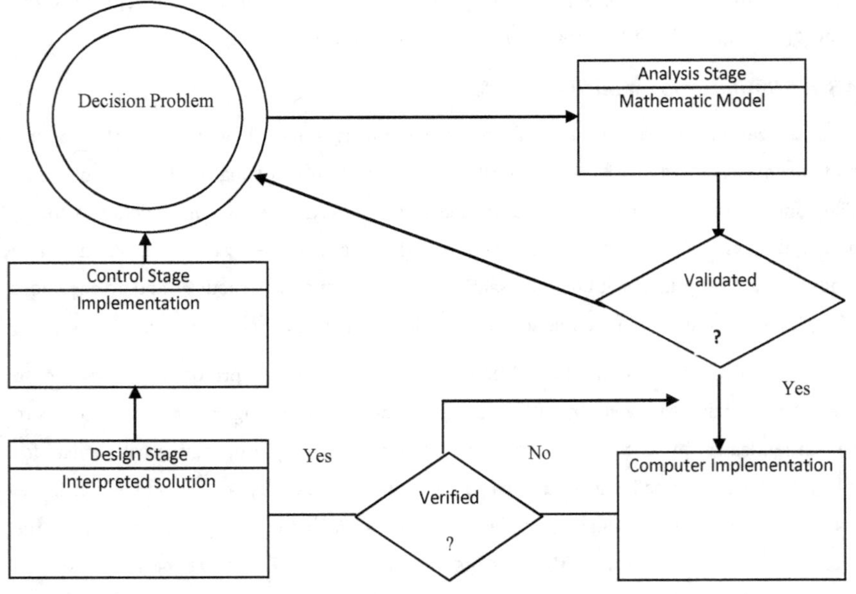

Figure 4.2: Feedback Loop

The key character of the optimal policy's setting is altering, and thus response and management are a vital fraction of the maximization-modeling procedure. The fore said the procedure is portrayed as the Systems Analysis, Design, and Control phases in the subsequent flow chart, as well as the substantiation and confirmation actions:

Thus, the concluding answer must gratify two stipulations: it must be a Pareto-optimal point, and it must moreover, be the best appropriate answer in accordance with the predilections of the person who makes the decisions.

To integrate decision making procedure in a maximization process, three feasible techniques are there in the research paper; that is, the *prior*, the *progressive* (interactive) and the *posterior* (Deb, 2001).

Owing to the benefits of the last, in this study the posterior technique is utilized. In this technique first, a multi-objective optimization procedure meets a separate illustration of the Pareto front, and then the decision making procedure selects the ultimate solution. Several real-world engineering plan issues could be developed as multi-goal maximization concerns. A vital example is to reduce the sum weight of a truss whilst minimizing.

With the initiation of competent methods for Multi-goal Evolutionary Optimization (EMO), real-world hunt and optimization concerns are resolved more and more for numerous contradictory goals. In the last ten years of study and implementation, maximum importance was laid on seeking the absolute Pareto-optimal set, even though EMO investigators were constantly conscious of the significance of methods that will assist to select the one specific answer from the Pareto-optimal group for execution.

This is further a vital matter wherein the traditional and EMO beliefs are alienated on. In this study, we deal with this continuing concern and propose an interactive EMO method that would encompass a decision-maker in the evolutionary optimization procedure and assist to select a solitary answer finally.

This research utilizes several decades of study on EMO and will expectantly support both users and authors to give additional thought in scrutinizing the multi-objective optimization as a collective mission of maximization and decision-making (Chaudhuri & Deb, 2010).The design examination could be divided into several stages, wherein every "sub-structure" could be handled and maximized in a comparable manner.

By utilizing design computerized methods, the complete design procedure or the particular sub-issues could be examined methodically, by ways of:

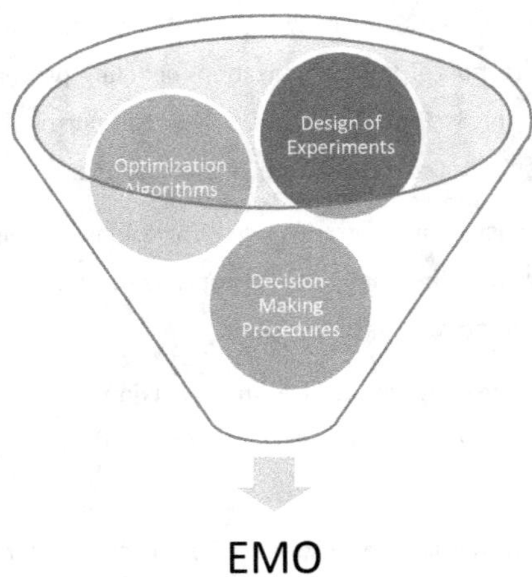

Figure 4.3: EMO Optimization

4.4.   Optimization Models

Several decision-making procedures confronted by firms or multifaceted businesses could be classified as per the structure stated forthwith:

1. The problem at hand
2. The person who makes the decision describes a set of *possible* choices and ascertains a norm for the assessment and comparison of optional choices, like financial expenses or payoffs.
3. Here, the person who makes the decision should recognize the *best* decision as per the assessment norm described, that is, the option equivalent to the lowest amount or to the maximum payoff.

The theoretical model delineated decides an extensive as well as the accepted rank of numerical prototypes for decision-making procedures, symbolized by *optimization* prototypes. Generally, optimization prototypes emerge spontaneously in decision-making procedures wherein a group of restricted resources should be assigned in the best effectual manner to diverse units.

These resources might be employees, manufacturing procedures, raw materials, components or monetary aspects. Amongst the key application fields needingthe most advantageous allocation of the resources, we notice:

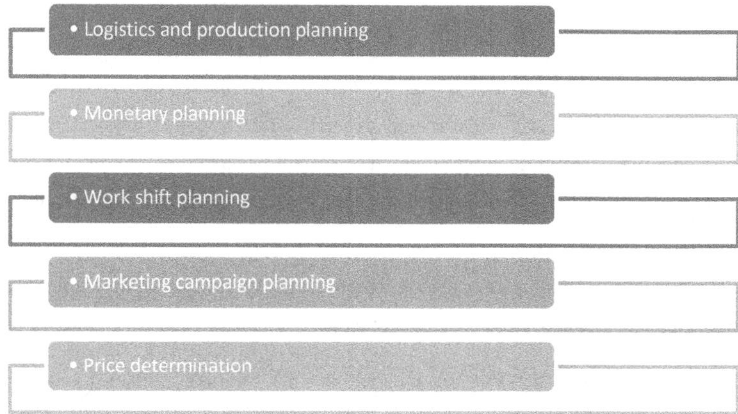

Figure 4.4: Dimensionless optimization (or DO)

Mathematical optimization prototypessymbolize a moderately sizeable group of optimization concerns, which are obtained while the goal of the decision making procedure is a role of the decision variables, and the norms defining possible choices could be articulated by a group of numerical equalities as well as inequalities in the decision variables. Pertaining to the arrangement of the objective purpose and its limitations, optimization prototypes might presume various outlines:

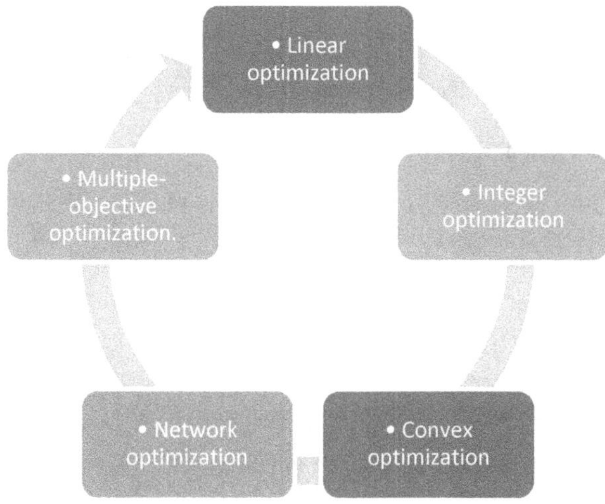

Figure 4.5: Mathematical Optimization Prototypes

4.4.1. *Stochastic Models, or Project Evaluation and Review Techniques (PERT)*

A *project's* a compound set of interconnected activities performed to get to a specific objective, which might correspond to a building, an industrial plant, an information system, a fresh product/ a fresh organizational make-up, depending on the diverse application domains. The carrying out of such a project does require a setting up & control a procedure for the inter-reliant activities & the human, technological & monetary resources essential to accomplish the final objective.

Project management techniques happen to be based on the roles of a variety of disciplines, like business association, behavioral psychology & operations study.

Mathematical models for result making do play a vital part in project management techniques. Particularly, network models are made use of to stand for the component doings of a project & the priority relationships amongst them.

Such models let the by and large project implementation time to be established, presuming deterministic information of the length of every activity.

Stochastic models, conversely, usually talked about as *Project Evaluation &Review Techniques* (or *PERT*), are made use of to derive the implementation times when stochastic suppositions are made about the length of the activities, symbolized by random variables.

In the end, diverse groups of optimization models let the study to be widened to the compound problem of most favorably assigning a set of restricted resources amongst the project doing in consideration of execution costs & times.

Disadvantages of Steepest Decent

As per examples, the drawbacks of this technique are as follows (Miettinen, 1999); for additional detail see the Comments below:

- It's comparatively slow near to the least amount
- the linear search might cause difficulties
- It may 'zigzag' down the valleys.

Other key mathematicians in the field of optimization consist of:

Multi-objective optimization (programming) (Miettinen, 1999) moreover acknowledged as **multi-criteria / multi-attribute** optimization happens to be the procedure of concurrently optimizing 2/more contradictory objectives subject to definite constraints.

Multi-objective optimization difficulties are able to be found in a variety of fields: product & process design, aircraft design, finance, the oil & gas industry, vehicle design, or anywhere optimal decisions require to be taken in presence of transactions between 2/more contradictory objectives.

Maximizing profit & minimizing the price of a manufactured good; maximizing performance & minimizing fuel using up of a motor vehicle; & minimizing weight even as maximizing the strength of a definite component are instances of multi-objective optimization difficulties. In the event of a multi-objective difficulty being well-formed, there ought to not be one solution that concurrently minimizes every objective to its fullest.

In every case, we're seeking a way out for which every objective's been optimized to the point that in the event of us trying to optimize it any more the additional objective(s) are going to suffer consequences.

To find such a way out, & to quantify how much improved this solution is in comparison to beingadded such as solutions (there is generally going to be many) happens to be the objective while setting-up & working out a multi-objective optimization difficulty.

4.4.2. *Multi-objective Optimization*

Putting in over a single objective to an optimization difficulty does add complexity. For instance, in the event of us optimizing a structural design, we would wish for a design that's light as well as rigid.

For the reason that these two objectives do conflict, a trade-off does exist. There is going to be a single lightest design, a single stiffest design, & a countless number of designs, which are some conciliation of weight & stiffness. This set of trade-off designs happens to be referred to as a Pareto set.

The curve generated by plotting weight against the stiffness of the most excellent designs is identified as Pareto frontier.

A design's adjudicated to be Pareto optimal in the event of it not being dominated by additional designs: a Pareto optimal design has to be better compared to a different design in no less than one aspect. In the event of it being worse than a different design in every respect, it's dominated & isn't Pareto optimal.

4.4.3. *Multi-modal Optimization*

Optimization difficulties are frequently multi-modal, that's they have multiple first-class solutions.

They are able to be globally excellent (identical cost function worth) or there is able to be a blend of globally excellent and locally excellent solutions. Obtaining every one ofthe (or no less than some of) multiple solutions is the objective of a multi-modal optimizer. Orthodox optimization methods because of their iterative approach don't perform suitably when they're made use of to find multiple solutions, because it isn't guaranteed that diverse solutions are going to be getting even with diverse starting points in numerous runs of the algorithm. Evolutionary Algorithms happen to however be an awfully trendy approach to acquire manifold solutions in a multi-modal optimization assignment. Dimensionless optimization (or DO) is made use of in design difficulties, and does consist of the following subsequent steps:

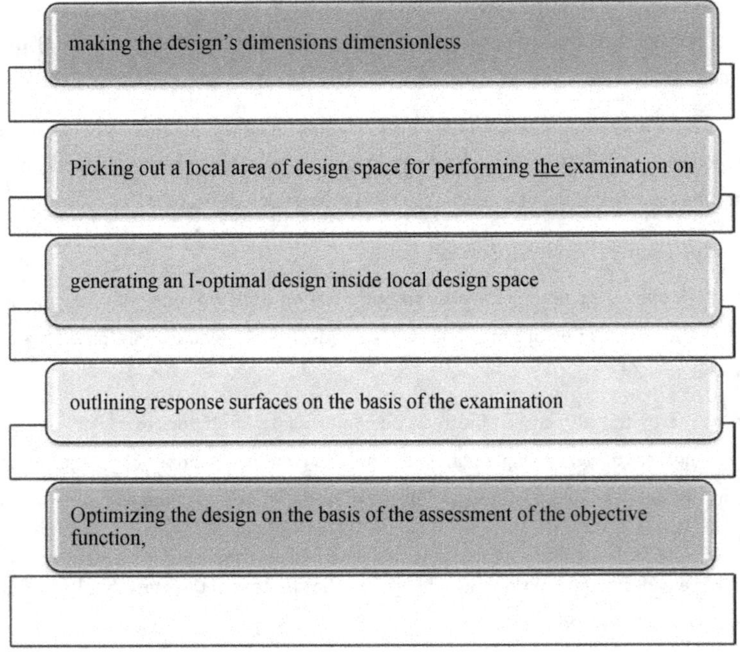

Figure 4.6: Dimensionless optimization (or DO)

Optimization talks about selecting the most excellent element from some set of accessible alternatives. Optimization implies solving difficulties in which one does seek to minimize/maximize a real function by methodically selecting the values of real / integer variables from inside a permitted set. The oversimplification of optimization hypothesis & techniques to additional formulations includes a great part of applied mathematics.

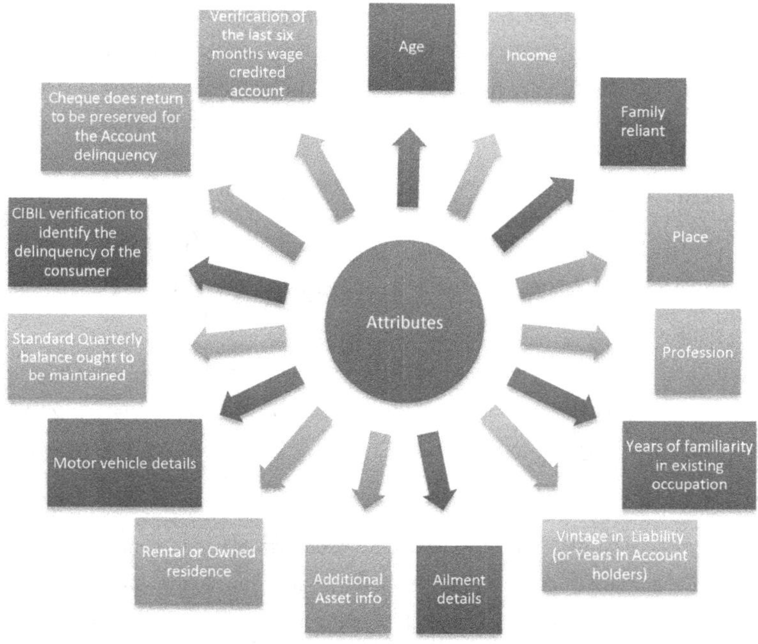

Figure 4.7: Sample Attributes (Decision Variables) for the Identified Problem

4.5.　Related Works

The notion of Business Intelligence (or BI) is an administration philosophy and a tool that's made use of to assist companies to deal with and process business info and to make additionally efficient business decisions (Ghoshal & Kim, 1986, Gilad & Gilad, 1986). Jayanthi Ranjan (2005) does explore the notion ofBI, its components, coming out of BI, advantages of BI, factors influencing the BI, know-how requirements, designing & carrying out of business intelligence, & a variety of BI methods (EIS, MIS, Trend analysis). A dedicated field of business intelligence acknowledged as competitive intelligence does focus exclusively on the competitive setting.

Stackowiak et al. (2007) classify business intelligence to be the procedure of taking a large quantity of information, studying that data and presenting the first-rate report that abbreviates the actual meaning of the information into essential of business acts, enabling the administration to make basic everyday business decision. BI happens to be the procedure of compilation, treatment & dispersal of info that has a purpose, the lessening of ambiguity in the making of every planned decision (Zeng et al., 2006).

In keeping with earlier researchers, BI happens to be a term which does enclose a wide variety of analytic software & solutions for getting-together, securing, analyzing & providing access to info in a manner that's supposed to let a project's user make trade decision (Adelman et al., 2002). There isn't any common notion of the substance of BIon the country, every one upholds their ideas.

Access to info is imperative in being able to manage the organization, this happens to be to keep an eye on activities & gauge performance. Gangadharanet al. (2004) explain the life cycle, including a variety of stages in the expansion of a BI structure. The paper does elaborate on the execution matters of BI in an association spotlighting a case study.

Business Intelligence (or BI) solutions have been put into practice for quite a few years in companies & institutions for fulfilling such role. Tvrdikova (n. d) talked briefly about the matters of business intelligence applications.

Major Elements of Business Intelligence Tools

A novel approach to BI, referred to as Business Performance Management (or BPM), is materializing from his outline: it consists of DW but it, in addition, requires a reflex component competent of supervising the time-critical functioning processes to permit tactical & functioning decision-makers to adjust their actions in line with the company plan. Golfarelli et al. (n.d) did aim to persuade the research society to recognize the coming of the 2nd period in BI, to put forward an all-purpose architecture for BPM (or Business Performance Management), the needs rising from contemporary companies & discussed the way in which they meet into a novel architecture, referred to as BPM, that does promise to lead business aptitude further than information warehousing.

DW systems did lead to put a figure on business info, to make it quickly available & certified. Conversely, the responsibility of BPM happens to be to put a figure on the enterprise strategy & targets, to be able to distribute decision making. The BI society has only slightly faced the difficulties connected to their modeling& handling (Buglione 2000).

A human-source intelligence set of connections comprising an organization's lead employees is an important intelligence benefit because the employees hold early on and interpreted info concerning the business surroundings. (Viitanen & Pirttimaki, 2006) did work on how this info can effectively be made use of in the BI procedure and more, to scrutinize how BI canbe smoothly incorporated in the procedure of strategic administration. To achieve such objectives, literature study & case study approaches happen to be applied.

Seufert (2005) did work on the building for improved business intelligence, which does aim to add to the worth of business intelligence by decreasing action time & linking business procedures into decision making. (Zeng et al., 2006) did review the notion of Business Intelligence, makes available a survey, from an all-inclusive standpoint on, the BI technological framework, procedure, & enterprise solutions. For the triumphant application of BI, an enterprise ought to consider convincing, incorporated, in-time information, & conversion of the information into decision info. Enterprise solutions & platforms for company intelligence have been urbanized. Such vendors & platforms consist of commercial solutions like IBM DB2 with company Intelligence Tools (Gonzales, 2003).

Jayanthi Ranjan (2008) did present customary and real-time trade intelligence & their responsibility in business firms. It explains the insights on the part and prerequisite of real-time BI by studying the business requirements. Oleskow et al., (n. d) did focus on the business intelligence & includes the way to effectively implement BI systems on account of practical cases, what prospects and benefits arising out of their application and how to successfully triumph over challenges facing ERP systems credit to incorporation with BI systems.

Beye Network did work on the challenges of putting into practice self-service BI tools & scrutinizes the different kinds of users & tools that are going to meet their requirements. Self-service has been an indefinable objective for BI professionals for over a decade. There're a couple of main classes of self-service BI apparatuses and they're top-down reporting apparatuses, which usually make available a semantic cover that allows super users to make custom queries & reports & bottom-up analysis apparatuses that allow power users to issue interactive dashboards to the casual users. To achieve something with the self-service BI, organizations require taking a nuanced approach which can map users to tasks & apparatuses.

Prashant Pant, Deloitte Consulting LLP does take into account the truth that too frequently what's missing from BI happens to be the conversion of insight into the act and therefore, failure to make the most of the full possibility of BI. It does require amindful approach, an amalgamation of enterprise reserves to deliver an absolute, steady, & dependable basis of information to accomplish the pledge of BI. Reach of BI should consist of making the finest use of info for planned, tactical, and operational requirements. BI plan ought to support parallel expansion tracks where manifold steps are able to be performed concurrently & manifold activities inside the steps can happen simultaneously. BI trends and the avant-garde approaches are building thriving BI strategies. Usage of the BI tool is chaotic therefore the requirement of the straightforwardness of usage is ignored and when weighed against BI tool, BI applications happen to be most excellent for reporting services (Quinn, n. d).

4.6.   Limitations of Existing Work

The present study on Business intelligence does revolve in the region of the clarification, reach, purpose & current strategies. The hypothetical explanation of method which is made use of in BI consists of Predictive & forecast study, Supply chain supervision, Scorecards & Dashboard. The homogeneous enterprise – extensive BI methodology isn't established as of now. There's a requirement for High intensity of interactive and ad-hocreporting necessities. Still, at present, the business analysts are making use of Excel & spreadsheet functions. Present business intelligence tools put up with a shortage of analysis & visualization abilities and usual result listing displayed by the search engines frequently engulf business analysts by means of irrelevant info and every day raising of the information volumes.The standard execution time for some greater BI solutions between approximately 3 to 6 months. A lot of Business Intelligence applications happen to still be hard to use. Generally, they've talked regarding the building for their individual real-time difficulty. They don't make available adequate support in managing future challenges in the BI industry, like real-time decision making. Although the people are employing the BI apparatus & techniques for exploring the database, actually what people happened to be doing is making a theory concerning the BI matters. Only 10 percent of the BI users are sufficiently advanced to make use of a BI apparatus. The irregularity of the answers produced by in excess of one advanced client is also recognized as numerous versions of the fact.

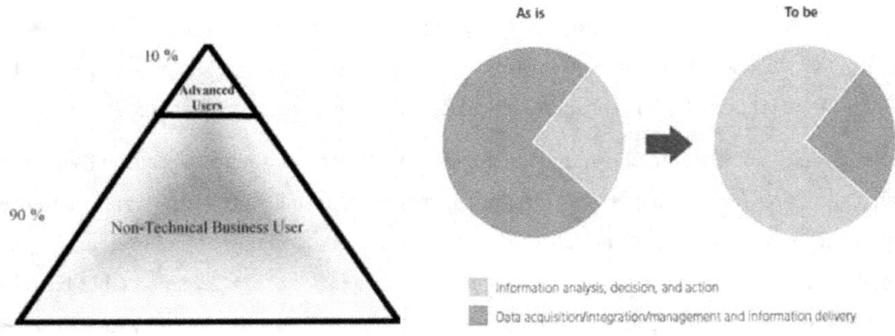

Figure 4.8: Change of BI Focus from Current State to Future State

1. Piling of Historical Data

The user might not be having an interest in historical information as many marketplaces that the corporation controls are in recurrent alteration.

1. **Cost**: The employment of such a system is able to be costly for fundamental business transactions. When weighed against profit, expense's extremely high.

2. **Complexity**: intricacy in carrying out of data.

3. **limited use**:similar to all enhanced technologies, business aptitude was primarily established considering the buying capability of well-off firms. Even at the moment, the BI system is unable to be afforded by the majority of companies. Even though, traders in the last small number of years have begun altering their services towards medium & small sized industries the fact remains that a lot of such firms doesn't deem them to be highly indispensable, for its intricacy.

4. **Time-consuming carrying out:** A lot of firms in the fast-paced industrial situation of today aren't tolerant enough to await the implementation of Business intelligence in their association. It does take approximately 18 months for information warehousing system to totally put the system into practice.

2. *Handling the Business Process Way is Different When We Compared with the Tools*

The entire idea of gathering Sales Intelligence happens to be to gain insights into manufactured goods/services you're selling, who you're selling to &who are interested in purchasing, the sales performance of the sales force of yours & others. The notion of monetary Intelligence is to achieve insights into where you're acquiring your revenues from, the way in which you're managing your hard cash, collections & disbursements, where you're using up your money, and others. As far as Process /Operational Intelligence are concerned, the difficulty becomes somewhat different. Post mortem, back view mirror type of info isn't very helpful. Understanding that you did screw up surgery experience / Automobile Insurance Claim of a patient, after the truth isn't as helpful as acquiring real-time info as & when it's occurring &you have a possibility of setting things right.

3. *Lacking in the Procedure Flow*

Business Intelligence solutions require capturing and reporting on Key Performance Indicators (or KPIs) which are vital for the implementation of business procedures in slice & dice report formats such as Sales &monetary Intelligence solutions make available.Soit requires capturing Business Process Flow & having the usual information Warehousing & study capabilities that survive currently. Therefore, we see that usual Business Intelligence solutions do have ways to go prior to effectively addressing, BI applications in the region of Process development!

4. Open source BI system

a. Features are not as Robust

Traditional BI software traders put in a great deal of wealth & resources into R&D, & the end result is that the manufactured goods have a well-off feature set. Open source BI apparatuses, conversely, depend on social support and thus don't have as sturdy a feature set.

b. Consulting Help not as Readily Available

The majority of the usual BI software is Business Objects, MicroStrategy, Cognos, Oracle & all that have been around for a lengthy time. Consequently, there're many people having experience with such tools, and to find consulting assistance to put these solutions into practice is typically not extremely difficult. Open source BI apparatuses, conversely, are rather recent progress, and there area a relatively small number of people having implementation experience. Thus, it is additionally difficult to come across consulting assistance in the event of you going with open source BI.

c. Open Source BI Apparatus Vendors

- Eclipse BIRT Project
- JasperSoft
- SpagoBI
- Pentaho
- OpenI

4.7. Summary

This chapter discusses the optimization and its algorithm that explores via viable answers, feasible, and finally obtained from the best possible solution. This section enables to provide a clear insight about the importance of optimization in order to attain the goals. Three major models of optimization were also discussed. Further, this section describes the components of optimization, optimization models, related work, and limitation of existing work.

CHAPTER 5

Meta-Heuristics Algorithms and Proposed Algorithms with Forecasting Analysis

5.1. Efficiency of Genetic Algorithm [GA] with Manual Decision Making [MDM]

5.1.1. Introduction

The population-based optimization algorithms hit upon near-optimal ways out of the difficult optimization difficulties by enthusiasm from nature. An ordinary feature of every population-based algorithm is that the populace consisting of likely ways out of the difficulty is adapted by applying a few operators on the ways out based on the info of their fitness. Therefore, the populace is moved towards improved solution regions of search space. The vital groups of populace-based optimization algorithms happen to be.

Optimization applications and their processes are countless and have much potential. There is not a single firm that is involved in solving the issues of optimization. This occurs with a minimum amount of time, risk, profit maximization and costs that are involved. A huge number of optimization issues in the field of businesses, science, economics, and engineering are very difficult and tough to solve. It is not possible to solve it within less time period in the right way. With the help of approx. algorithms, the problems of different classes can be solved to some extent. The algorithms can be divided into two such as specific heuristics and meta-heuristics. Specific heuristics are dependent on problems and are designed according to the nature of each problem. Meta-heuristics represent general approximate algorithms that are related to a huge class of organizational issues.

Meta-heuristics can solve tough problems that are usually hard to decipher exploring the huge search spaces that are related to instances. This is achieved by the algorithm by lowering the huge size of the space and exploring it effectively. Meta-heuristics is useful for three different purposes like solve the problems quickly, solve big problems and achieving the right algorithms. However, they are easy to design and practice as it is highly flexible.

Computing the optimal solution is essential for maximizing the issues that are related to industrial and scientific areas. Traditionally we were content with the good results we obtained using Meta-heuristics or heuristics algorithms.

Meta-heuristics is related to a family of presumed techniques of optimization which has received immense popularity during the last 2 decades. Meta-heuristics can offer acceptable outcomes within a reasonable period of time by tackling tough and complex issues related to science and engineering. This is the reason why Meta-heuristics domain experience a high level of growth. When compared to other algorithms, there is no guarantee from Meta-heuristics regarding the solution it offers. It does not define how near are the solutions it arrived at are optimal with natural motivation. The common feature of algorithms that are based on population comprises of solutions to those issues which were derived by some few operators based on their fitness level's information. We must take decisions like managers, scientists and engineers would do. As the world is becoming much complex and competitive in nature, making a decision must be performed correctly. The process of decision making comprises of the following steps explained in Figure 5.1.

- **Formulate the problem:** In the first step, the decision for an issue is identified. Later the initial statement is framed, which might not be precise. The internal and external factors along with objectives related to the issue arrive. Most decision makers would take part in it.

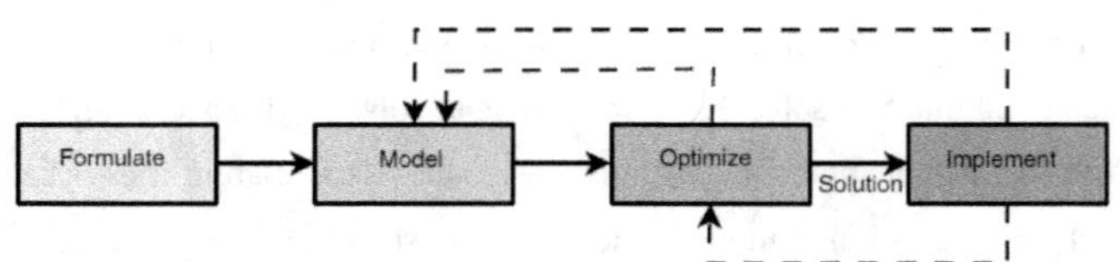

Figure 5.1: The Classical Process in Decision Making

- **Model the problem:** This step causes the abstract mathematical model to be constructed. Many literature models can be used as inspiration by the modeler. This would decrease the issue too well studied optimized models. Generally, the models that we use are simplified, have approximations and few processes are skipped to denote a mathematical model. However, this would cause the occurrence of an interesting query like: Why should you solve real-life optimization issues that are naturally fuzzy?

- **Optimize the problem:** after modeling the issue, the procedure to solve it would be offering the ideal solution to it. This might be optimal or suboptimal in nature. We must notice that we are arriving at a solution for the abstract problem model and not for the ones in real life. Therefore, it is essential to arrive at the solution that is indicative of the performance which makes it an accurate one.

The designer can reuse these algorithms while dealing with similar issues that integrate the knowledge of the specific application of algorithms.

- **Implement a solution:** The solution that is obtained the decision maker is implemented when accepted. Practical knowledge is implemented by the solution and if it is unacceptable, the model and decision-making process is revised.

During practice, this process might be reiterated to enhance the optimization model or the algorithm. Problems related to dynamic optimization would pose a real challenge in applications based in real life. The input elements of the dynamic optimization issue change from time to time. This is explained below:

$$f_{dynamic}(x) = f_t(x)$$

Where t refers to the time during which evaluation of the objective function is performed. This means the optimal solution to the problem would also differ. Unlike uncertain optimization, the **f** or function is the same. At the given time, multiple evaluations regarding the objective function would offer similar values.

The main issues in overcoming the dynamic optimization issues are:

- Identify the change in the surroundings while it happens. Most of the problems that occur in real life would be changing in a smooth way than in a drastic way.
- Respond to the environmental change to monitor the optimal solution globally.

Therefore, the search process must change quickly with the objective function as the aim is to track the optimal solution with the close ratio.

The big challenge is to reuse data about the last searches to adapt to the issue instead of solving it again from the start. Other strategies of the forecast would also be employed to predict future scenarios. So, the population can rely on better areas of the solution in the search space. The important classes of optimization algorithms that were based on population are:

1. GI or Genetic Algorithm
2. ACO or Ant colony optimization
3. ABC or Artificial Bee Colony

The present section focused on GA and rests are presented in the respective chapters. Recently, fresh paradigms founded on evolutionary calculation have emerged to substitute the usual, mathematically founded approaches to optimization (Ashlock 2006). Most powerful of these happens to be a Genetic Algorithm (or GA) that are encouraged by natural selection, & genetic programming.

Genetic Algorithms happen to be among some Artificial Intelligence tools/apparatuses used problem like optimization, data fitting, scheduling, trend spotting, clustering, &pathfinding. Great deals of endeavor were enforced to develop calculation performance of GAs and evade untimely union of solutions. Structured Genetic Algorithm (or SGA) &Hierarchical Genetic Algorithm (or HGA) have been put forward to crack optimization problems/difficulties even as simultaneously letting alone the problem/difficulty of untimely convergence (Lai & Chang 2004)Hierarchical make-up of chromosomes does enable concurrent optimizations of parameters in diverse parts of chromosome make-ups. Of late, a DNA working out scheme executing GAs has been urbanized (Chen et al., 1999).

Application of the organic model onto an optimization job in the form of evolutionary tactics appears as exceptionally effective in the state of affairs where regular analytical approaches fall short of succeeding.

The hereditary algorithms make allowances for being able to find optima / at any rate, over-averaged answers to multidimensional & multi-modal functions. Hereditary algorithms might also be rightfully used in cooperation with added optimizing techniques.

Heritable algorithms have been applied to an extremely wide variety of practical problems/difficulties, often with important results. A GA does generate a populace of likely solutions set as chromosomes, does evaluate their fitness && does create a new populace by applying hereditary operators which happen to be crossover & mutation. By replicating this procedure over a lot of generations, the hereditary algorithm has 5 fundamental components, which happen to be (Gen & Cheng, 2000).

Among the most primitive GA application is tocontrol a gas pipeline in the steady-state & passing conditions, explained in (Golgberg, 1987). Medeiros et al. (2006), did propose a genetic mining algorithm (or GMA) that makes use of genetic operators in overcoming such shortcomings.

GMAs develop a population of graph-based procedure models towards a procedure model that can fulfill the fitness criterion, the procedure model man does age to play again all of the behaviors viewed in the occasion that log does not let the added ones.

A heuristic search method made use of in calculating and Artificial Intelligence for finding optimized solutions to the search problems/difficulties using methods motivated by evolutionary biology: Mutation, Selection, Reproduction [or inheritance] and Recombination

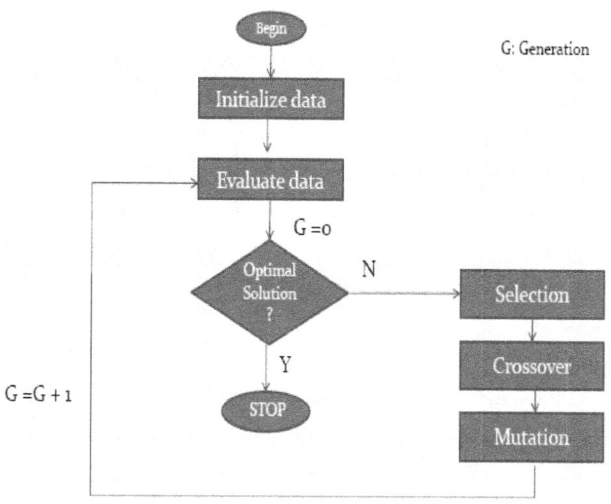

Figure 5.2: GA Algorithm

Refer Appendix 2, for an outline of the Basic Genetic Algorithm and Basic Cos and Pros.

5.1.2. Applications of GA

GA happens to be simple to put into practice. The basic GA algorithm having been implemented, there's a need to just write a fresh chromosome (just a single object) to resolve a different problem/difficulty. With the identical encoding, we just alter the fitness function - & done. Nevertheless, for a few problems/difficulties, selecting & implementation of the encoding & fitness function is able to be tricky.

5.1.3. Outline of the Basic Genetic Algorithm

1. **[Start]** Generate a random population of n chromosomes (suitable solutions for the problem)
2. **[Fitness]** Evaluate the fitness $f(x)$ of each chromosome x in the population
3. **[New population]** Create a new population by repeating the following steps until the new population is complete
    a. **[Selection]** Select two parent chromosomes from a population according to their fitness (the better fitness, the bigger chance to be selected)

b. **[Crossover]** With a crossover probability cross over the parents to form a new offspring (children). If no crossover was performed, offspring is an exact copy of parents.

c. **[Mutation]** With a mutation probability mutate new offspring at each locus (position in the chromosome).

d. **[Accepting]** Place new offspring in a new population

4. **[Replace]** Use newly generated population for a further run of the algorithm

5. **[Test]** If the end condition is satisfied, **stop**, and return the best solution in the current population

6. **[Loop]** Go to step **2**

Every process of iteration is known as a *generation*. The iteration of GA can range anywhere from 50 – 500 or even much more generations. The whole generations set is known as a run. At the last of every run, there are one or more chromosomes which are fit among the rest in the population. As randomness has a big role to play in every run, 2 runs of various numbers of seeds at random would offer detailedbehavior. Researchers of GA reveal that a run with the best level of fitness along with perfect generation of an individual with similar fitness levels was found at an average with so many runs of GA regarding the same issue.

5.1.4. Implementation

An individual representation at every point during the process of search maintained is called as a generation with individuals. Every individual found in the data structure denotes the "genetic structure" of a hypothesis or the best solution. An individual's genetic structure is described similar to a chromosome with the help of a fixed or a finite alphabet. Alphabet like 0 and 1 are used in GAs, which is considered as a solution that we are aiming at, to solve.

5.1.5. Population Initialization

Population initialization stands for a set of individuals who are customers, patients or candidates, whom we would be handling. The population tends to differ based on business needs.

The profile of the Bank account holders and the details of Diseases like cancer are considered by me in this study. After initialization of population, we have to segregate the massive data we have collected to clear off all unwanted data and lower the data set's redundancy levels. Then we will have the base ready for initiation the process of optimization.

The individual representing a population would be preset at 1000 as an element vector.

[*X1, X2, X3, ..., X1000*] where α-, β-, and γ- are the constraintsof an individual, while, *X1, X2, ..., X100,* which isthe sub-corresponds to a candidate, who is the solution to the optimization issue. The initial individuals' population is generated in a random manner.

Thus, Xi = (*X1, X2, X3, ...,X1000*) where i= 1,2,3 1000   (1)

5.1.6. Fitness Calculation

The population of GA is available as bit strings with chromosomes' locus points in 0 and 1. Every chromosome is assumed as a solution for the candidate search in every search space. The processes of GA would replace the population effectively. It needs the perfect level of fitness to identify the chromosome from the population. Let us assume a population with 1000 number and constraints as 5.

Maximize $F(X_i) = \sum(Y_j)$, where 1<= i <=1000&1<= j <= 5   (2)

Where Fitness Function stands for $F(X_i)$ and Objective function is denoted by Y_j which features the constraints' number. Every constraint has a definite set of variables.

The constraints have Action Rules like:

1. Criteria of Age
2. Criteria of Income
3. Maintenance of Average Quarterly Balance or AQB
4. Cibil Score – Good / Bad
5. Credit Card – Yes /No

If the constraints are satisfactory then the result would be 1 or else it would be 0. The table given below would illustrate it well.

Table 5.1: Illustration of the Fitness

Xi	Y1	Y2	Y3	Y4	Y5	F(Xi)
23	1	0	1	1	1	4
19	1	1	1	0	0	3
89	0	1	1	0	0	2
78	1	1	1	1	1	5
....	...	...	...	...	...	...
92	0	0	0	0	0	0

Where the Xi is the number of population, initially calculate the fitness.

5.1.7. Selection Methods

In GA, the whole population is perceived as an element with single reproduction using which a selection is made at a random level.

The method of reproduction involves ranking method, the selection at a random level by population, assessment of reproduction by individuals based on their ranks. While using the ranking method [6], the sorting of individuals is performed based on the levels of fitness. Then each individual is offered a rank based on the population with a central value. The ranks are assigned to find the fittest and least fit individuals to find the best candidates even if there is a problem in the search at any time. The individuals with a high level of fitness are reserved and the least fit ones are identified.

Roulette Wheel Selection

It is one among the common strategy that is equivalent in offering the circular roulette wheels slice to the individual when it comes to their fitness levels. This would offer an individual the probability of selecting the ones based on their fitness levels. This probability proportion is performed by:

$$p_i = \frac{\mathcal{F}_i}{\sum_{i=1}^{n} \mathcal{F}_i}$$

The pie features a roulette wheel at the outer area. The μ individual selection is done by roulette wheel's μ spins. Every spin of the wheel would offer an individual. The ones with a better fitness record would have good space.

$$\overline{\mathcal{F}} = \sum_{i=1}^{n} \mathcal{F}_i$$

When using the selection using roulette wheel the individuals might experience a bias at the initial stage which can trigger diversity loss and convergence at a premature level. While many individuals are fit, the strategy to select would not offer too much pressure on them.

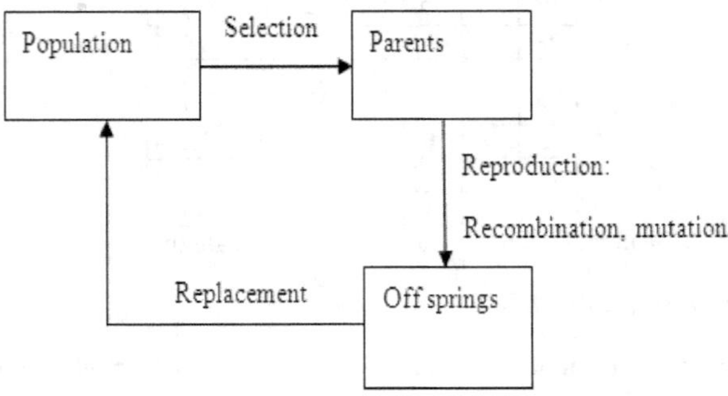

Figure 5.3: A generation in Evolutionary Algorithms

Genetic Operators

The decision to implement a genetic algorithm is similar to the ones used by genetic operators. This decision relies greatly on the strategy of encoding.

Crossover

The aim of crossover operators is to achieve a few characteristics of the parents to produce better offspring. The crossover operators design relies on the representation used by the mutation operator. Crossover is the distinguishing feature of GA. A single point crossover is a simple form that is selected at a random level, two parents can deliver two offspring through this crossover. The idea behind this is to re-blend the schemas or building blocks on various strings. There is only one drawback regarding single point crossover, which is that it might not combine all possible building blocks. Also, those schemas with high defined lengths would be destroyed in Single-point crossover.

This is termed as "positional bias" by Eshelman, Caruana, and Schaffer (1989): the cross over creates or destroys the schemas that rely on the location strongly based on chromosome bits. Single point crossover makes an assumption that schemas with short and low order are functional strings but how the group would function is not known, which the aim of the inversion operator is. To lower the bias of the position and effect of the endpoint, practitioners of GA make sure that they make use of 2 point cross over where the positions are chosen and segmented randomly. 2 point cross over is not advisable for schemas with defined lengths and to blend well then the single point crossover. 2–point crossover becomes less as likely to the disruption schemas along with the concerned lengths prevailing with large definition and gets combined with more schemas other than a single–pointed crossover. Additionally, the segments which get exchanged don't necessarily contain those endpoints for the strings. Other than this, there are certain schemas which 2–point crossover can never for the combination. The failure or success of the particular operator for a crossover which depends along complicated ways with the particular function for fitness, encoding, &several details of GA.

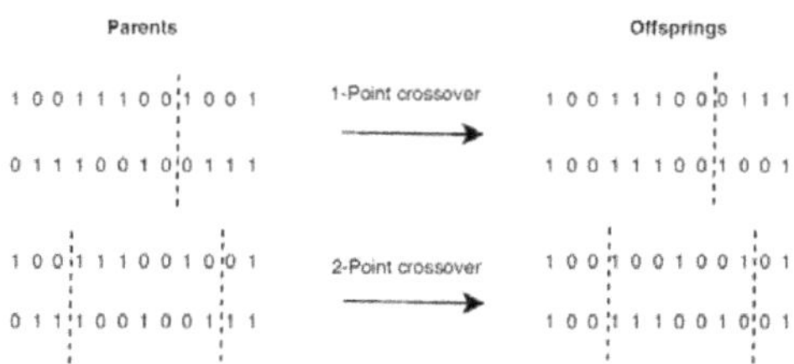

Figure 5.4: Point and n-Point Crossover Operators

```java
Candidate[] childs = new Childs(w1, w2);
            child1 = childs[0];
            child2 = childs[1];


            double mutatePercent = 0.01;
            boolean m1 = rand.nextFloat() <= mutatePercent;
            boolean m2 = rand.nextFloat() <= mutatePercent;


            if (m1)
                    mutate(child1);
            if (m2)
                    mutate(child2);


            boolean isChild1Good = child1.fitness() >= w1.fitness();
            boolean isChild2Good = child2.fitness() >= w2.fitness();


            newpopulation.add(isChild1Good ? child1 : w1);
            newpopulation.add(isChild2Good ? child2 : w2);
    }


    // add top percent parent
    int j = (int) (populationSize * parentUsePercent / 100.0);
    for (int i = 0; i < j; i++) {
            newpopulation.add(population.get(i));
    }


    population = newpopulation;
    Collections.sort(population);

}
```

Figure 5.5: (Continued)

```java
// one-point crossover random pivot
    Candidate newChild(Candidate c1, Candidate c2, int pivot) {
        Candidate child = new Candidate();

        for (int i = 0; i < pivot; i++) {
            child.genotype[i] = c1.genotype[i];
        }
        for (int j = pivot; j < Candidate.SIZE; j++) {
            child.genotype[j] = c2.genotype[j];
        }

        return child;
    }
```

```java
// Uniform crossover
    Candidate[] newChilds(Candidate c1, Candidate c2) {
        Candidate child1 = new Candidate();
        Candidate child2 = new Candidate();

        for (int i = 0; i < Candidate.SIZE; i++) {
            boolean b = rand.nextFloat() >= 0.5;
            if (b) {
                child1.genotype[i] = c1.genotype[i];
                child2.genotype[i] = c2.genotype[i];
            } else {
                child1.genotype[i] = c2.genotype[i];
                child2.genotype[i] = c1.genotype[i];
            }
        }

        return new Candidate[] { child1, child2 };
    }
```

Figure 5.5: Coding of Genetic Algorithm

Mutation

Crossover remains to be a major instrument for innovation and innovation along GAs, with the mutation which insures population against the permanent fixation for any of the particular loci& thus plays more of the background role. It finally differs from those traditional positions along with other of the methods for evolutionary computation, like evolutionary programming & earlier versions of the evolution strategies, which the random mutation remains to be the only source for variation.

```
void mutate(Candidate c) {
        int i = rand.nextInt(Candidate.SIZE);
        c.genotype[i] = !c.genotype[i]; // flip
    }
```

Figure 5.5: Coding of Genetic Algorithm - Continued

Implemented in Coding

Along with coding space, there are 'n' – no of populations, it's not necessary that all population setsmust go along feasible area. Considerably some of the population might be illegal, not being eligible for those Solution areas& some will remain eligible for that Solution areas¬ being eligible for those feasible areas. Since optimization remains based along the population which comes come along those feasible areas.

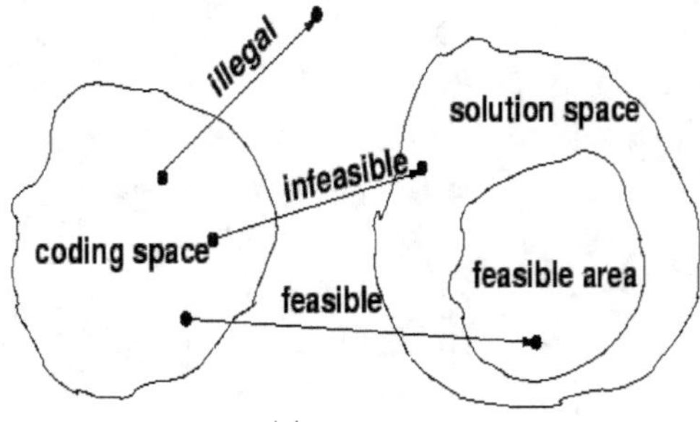

Figure 5.6: Implementation in Coding

Every Population gets selected along the below-given criteria for Cross over, Selection& mutation remains optional, where it either or never happen. Finally, replacement of the sustaining population along with the new set of population sustains.

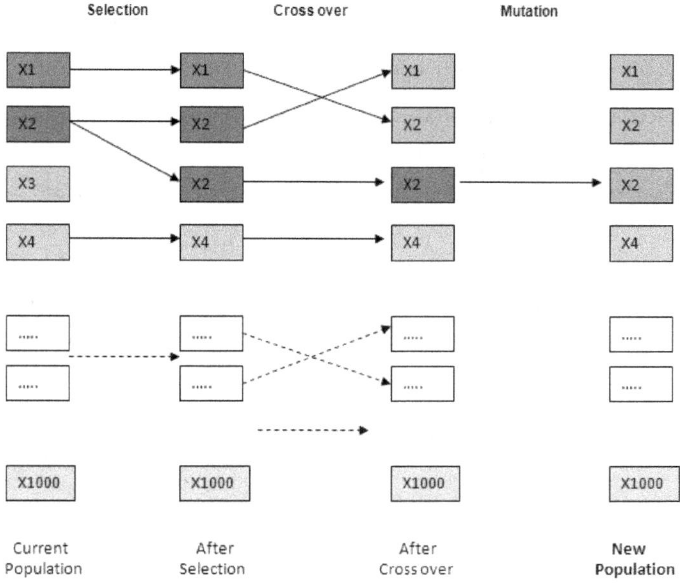

Figure 5.7: Overall Concept of Genetic Algorithm

5.1.8. Experimental Results

The existing genetic algorithm proposed for decision support functionality was implemented in the MATLAB platform (version 7.10) and it is evaluated using the cancer data and data obtained from DST.

In the concerned section, we usually focus along the decision which supports the functionality of the GA algorithm. Particularly, we usually show how the GA solution gets the usage in selecting the target point being best where expected profit gets maximized. We usually consider two varied strategies for 1 case targeting the customers being under the age group of 25-40 years, having income ranging between 25001-40,000 &AQB ranging from 10001-25,000. Hence, we usually made 3 common assumptions for ordering the run of the analysis &the identification of the optimal customers under the concerned lists of 1 million prospects for the target. We usually showed our experimental results along the Figure.

5.1.9. Performance Evaluation

The ROC or receiver operating characteristics curve that gets calculated along the area given under ROC curve remains to be the best model for performance in the study.

The ROC curves became the standard tool for the assessment of the accuracy for the model of predictions along the field of the medical diagnosis and becoming used increasingly along the financial environment and machine learning.

The concerned TP rate gets plotted along the Y-axis while the FP rate gets plotted along the X-axis. Further, the performance of the method was examined using Precision, Recall and F-measure (Larsen and Aone 1999; Steinbach, Karypis and Kumar 2000) subsequently these values are compared with the Precision, Recall and F measure values of conventional algorithms. Precision, Recall, and F-measure were used as described in (Larsen and Aone 1999; Steinbach, Karypis and Kumar 2000) to evaluate the performance of the proposed approach.

$$Precision\ (i,j) = M_{ij} \,/\, M_j \tag{38}$$

$$Recall\ (i,j) = M_{ij} \,/\, M_i \tag{39}$$

$$\mathbf{F-measure}\ (i,j) = \frac{2 * Recall\ (i,j) * Precision\ (i,j)}{Precision\ (i,j) + Recall\ (i,j)} \tag{40}$$

where M_{ij} is the number of members of genes i in the cluster j, M_j is the number of members of the cluster j and M_i is the number of members of genes i. Precision and recall values of the clusters obtained by the proposed technique are given in Table 5.4. Precision and recall values of the clusters obtained by the conventional clustering are given in comparison Chapter. Further, ROC

- Sensitivity or True Positive Rate:
  - TPR = TP / P = TP/ (TP+FN)
- False Positive Rate:
  - FPR = FP / N = FP/ (FP+TN)
- Accuracy:
  - ACC = (TP+TN) / (P+N)
- Specificity or True Negative Rate:
  - SPC = TN / N = TN / (FP+TN) = 1-FPR
- Positive Predictive Value:
  - PPV = TP / (TP+FP)

A, B & C are Manual Decision Making with the experience of 3, 2 & fresher respectively; D is ABO decision Making.

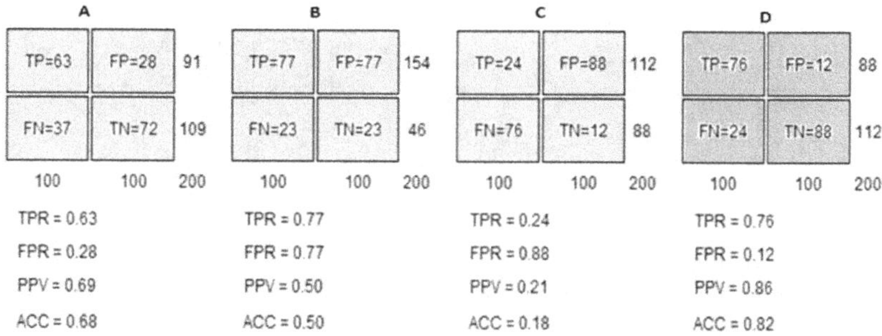

Figure 5.8: Manual decision Making – Pictorial Representation

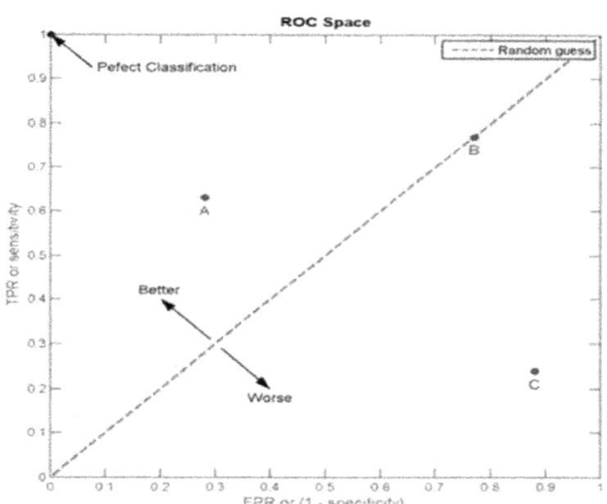

Figure 5.9: Manual Decision Making – ROC Curve

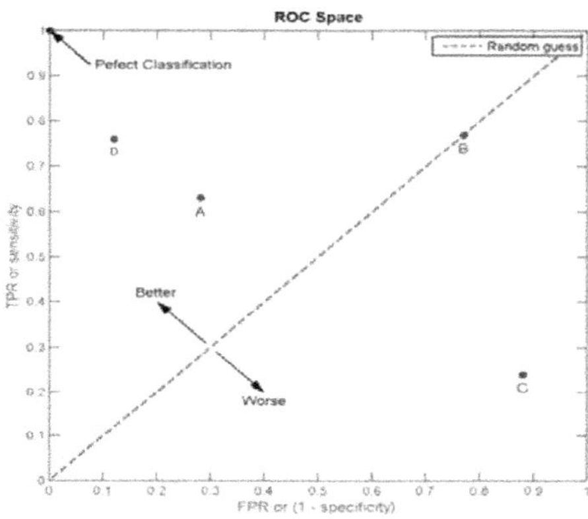

Figure 5.10: Manual Vs ABO Decision Making – ROC Curve

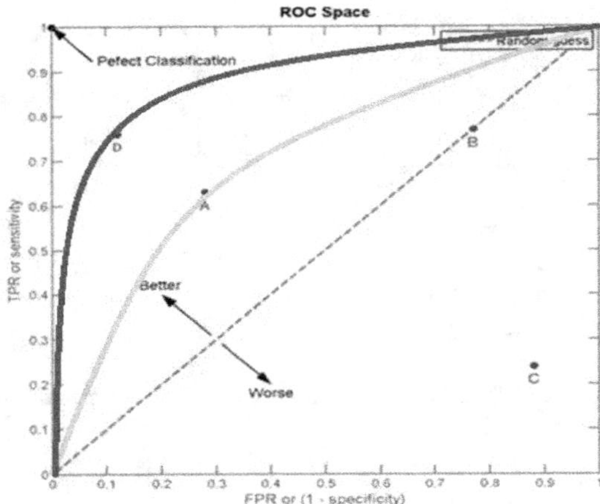

Figure 5.11: A decision Plot can be Shown to Help in Choosing Optimum Decision Levels in Terms of Sensitivity (True Positive Rate) and Specificity (True Negative Rate)

5.1.10. Results

The ROC curve plots the true positive (sensitivity) versus false positive (1-specificity) for a binary classifier system as its discrimination threshold is varied. The graph below shows that GA performs at par with manual decision making. The above ROC Analysis shows that GA performs well with 0.48. Although this predictive ability is better than manual decision making, the ROC of 0.48 indicates that the value has low discriminatory power.

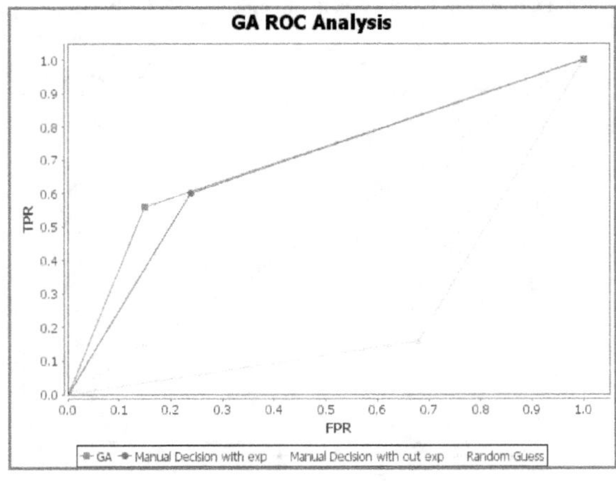

Figure 5.12: GA ROC Cut-Off Values

Table 5.2: GA Values

Analysis variables/Techniques	GA
True Positive	233
True Negative	256
False positive	237
False Negative	274
True positive rate	0.47
False positive rate	0.18
Positive predicted value	0.49
AZ value	0.48

The TP of GA was 0.47 while FPR was 0.18. This illustrates that the accuracy of diagnoses of predicted customers targeted for bankers to market, the GA failed to accurately predict the numbers. The value of 0.90 was found to be excellent prediction ability while GA was found to be 0.50-0.60 which indicates that the prediction was failed to predict. This area measures discrimination. For the comparison of the traditional algorithms along the accuracy of the classification being 0.79 for the ABO, this was poor in the case of GA, ACO and ABC. This gets implied with the proposed algorithm being better than those of previous algorithms.

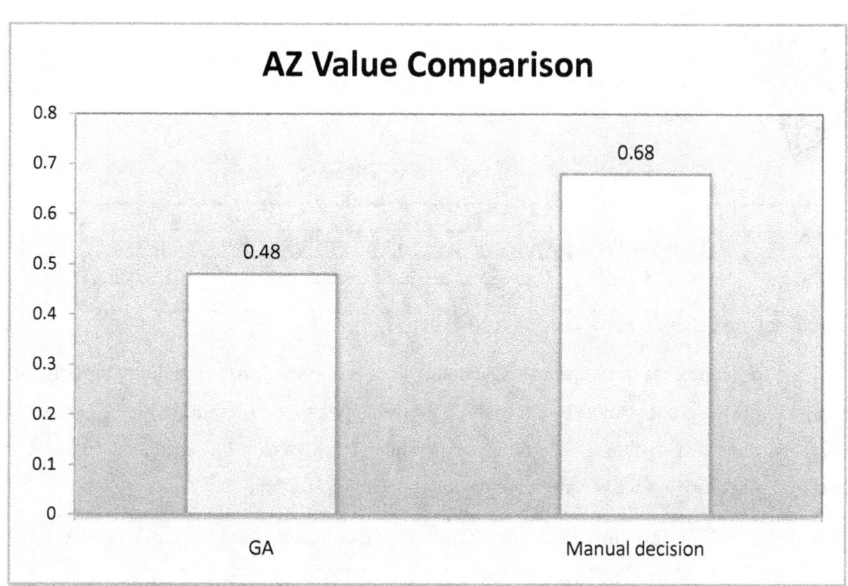

Figure 5.13: AZ Value Comparison

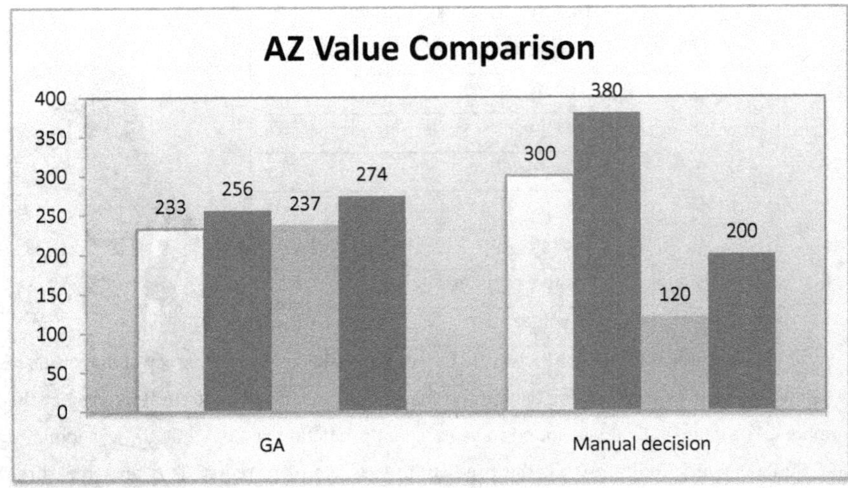

Figure 5.14: Comparison of Algorithms with ROC Attributes

As based along the above-given analysis, it is said ABO being a competitive classifier, under the comparison of traditional algorithms which precisely gets the prediction of optimized customers. The Statistical Significance along the experiments provides the result of the significant findings under ABO having higher true positivity as compared to other algorithms.

Table 5.3: Relationship between Grouping and Type

Grouping	Type				Total
	True positive	True negative	False positive	False negative	
GA	233	256	237	274	1000
	21.5%	21.1%	30.5%	29.7%	25.0%

Chi-square value-276.606, p-value-0.00<0.01;

The table compares the Grouping (GA) and type. It is observed that 25% of the participants belong to the GA group. Majority of the false positive belong to the GA group (30.5%). From the observed chi-square value of 276.606 and p-value of 0.00 which is less than 0.01 so it is declared that there is an association between the Grouping (GA) and type.

Table 5.4: Performance Evaluation of GA for Banking Customer Profile and Cancer

Dataset	Precision	Recall	F-measure
Banking Customer profile	0.49574	0.48302	0.4893
Cancer	0.43333	0.54082	0.48115

Table 5.4 represents the Precision, Recall and F-Measure comparison graph for the proposed clustering technique with the cancer data set. The Table shows that customer profile data set had poor precision, recall, and F-measures. The same was depicted in the Figure5.13.

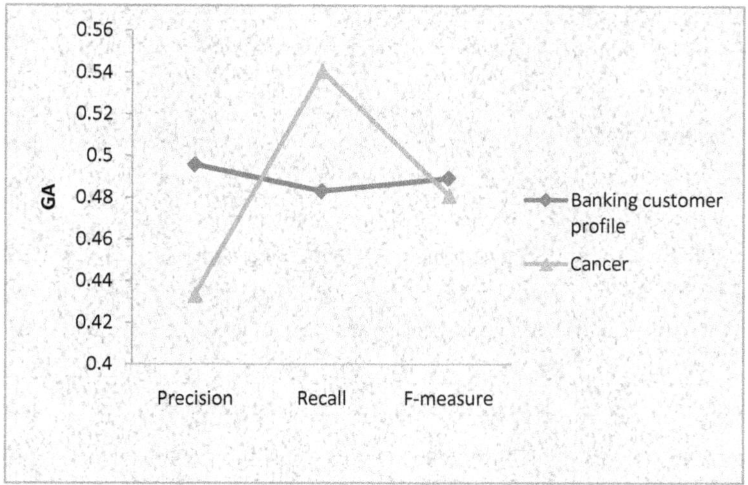

Figure 5.15: Performance Evaluation of GA for Banking Customer Profile and Cancer

5.1.11. Summary of this Work

The analytical results showed that the GA algorithm showed poor discriminatory power (0.48) and had lower precision, recall and f-measure values of 0.49, 0.48 and 0.49% respectively and this algorithm works par with the manual decision-making method. The decision making the performance of the proposed technique was visualized by implementing it in MATLAB. Experimental results on real-life datasets proved that the decision-making tool using Genetic Algorithm is not effective than manual decision making.

5.2. Efficiency of Ant Colony Optimization with Manual Decision Making

5.2.1. Introduction

Ant Colonies are social insect societies and havethe ability to accomplish complex tasks. Researchers have moreover utilized ant optimization algorithm for developing a hybrid routing modus operandi like works by Rajgopalan& Shen, 2006, Baras & Mehta, 2003, & Camara and Loureiro (2000) amongst others. Likewise, HBMO has been productively applied to answer problems/difficulties like partitioning & design of the embedded systems (Koudil et al., 2007) & cluster examination (Fathian, et. al., 2007), only to name some.

Such algorithms have found countless industrial applications. For instance, US maker of American Air Liquids has accomplished significant monetary savings by employing a computer model founded on algorithms encouraged by the foraging actions of ants to analyze each combination of plant scheduling, gas costs, and weather & truck movements. Additional applications consist of telecoms data routing & delivery vehicle armada scheduling (Bogue, 2008).

5.2.2. *Experimental Results*

In the concerned section, we usually focus along the decision which supports the functionality of the ACO algorithm. Particularly, we usually show how the GA solution gets the usage in selecting the target point being best where expected profit gets maximized. We usually consider two varied strategies for 1 case targeting the customers being under the age group of 25-40 years, having income ranging between 25001-40,000 &AQB ranging from 10001-25,000.

Hence, we usually made 3 common assumptions for ordering the run of the analysis &the identification of the optimal customers under the concerned lists of 1 million prospects for the target.

We usually showed our experimental results along the Figure. The ROC or receiver operating characteristics curve that gets calculated along the area given under ROC curve remains to be the best model for performance in the study. The ROC curves became the standard tool for the assessment of the accuracy for the model of predictions along the field of the medical diagnosis & becoming used increasingly along the financial environment and machine learning.

The concerned TP rate gets plotted along the Y-axis while the FP rate gets plotted along the X-axis.

5.2.3. *Results*

The ROC curve plots the true positive (sensitivity) versus false positive (1-specificity) for a binary classifier system as its discrimination threshold is varied. The graph below shows that ACO performs better than manual decision making.

The above ROC Analysis shows that ACO performs well with 0.50. Although this predictive ability is better than manual decision making, the ROC of 0.50 indicates that the value has low discriminatory power.

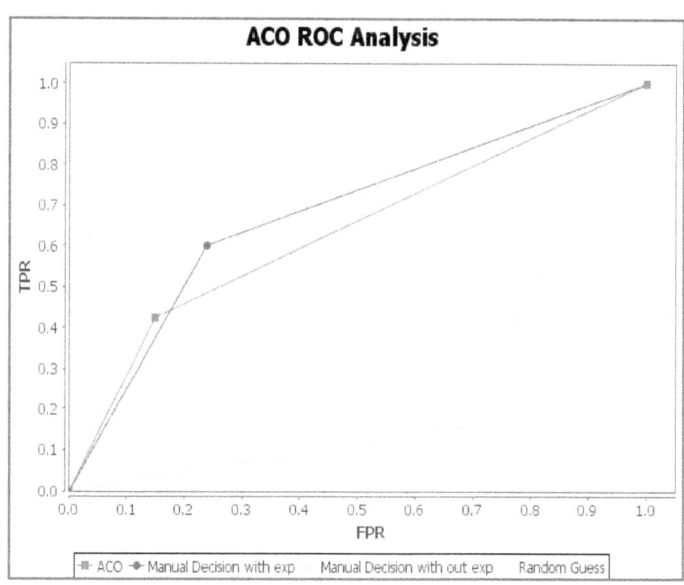

Figure 5.16: ACO ROC Analysis

The above ROC Analysis shows that ACO performs well with 0.50. Although this predictive ability is better than manual decision making, the ROC of 0.48 indicates that the value has low discriminatory power.

Table 5.5: ACO Analysis

Analysis variables/Techniques	ACO
True Positive	241
True Negative	264
False positive	240
False Negative	255
True positive rate	0.48
False positive rate	0.47
Positive predicted value	0.5
AZ value	0.5

For the comparison of the traditional algorithms along the accuracy of the classification being 0.79 for the ABO, this was poor in the case of GA, ACO and ABC. This gets implied with the proposed algorithm being better than those of previous algorithms.

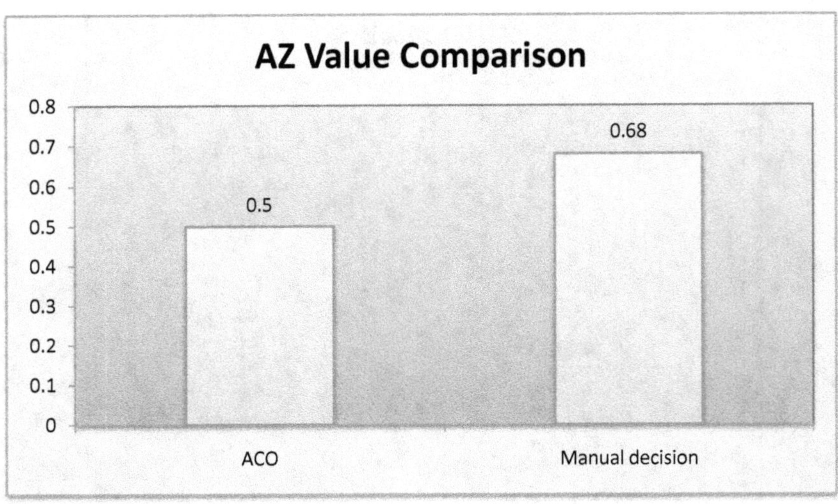

Figure 5.17: AZ Value Comparison

AZ Value Comparison Across the Algorithms

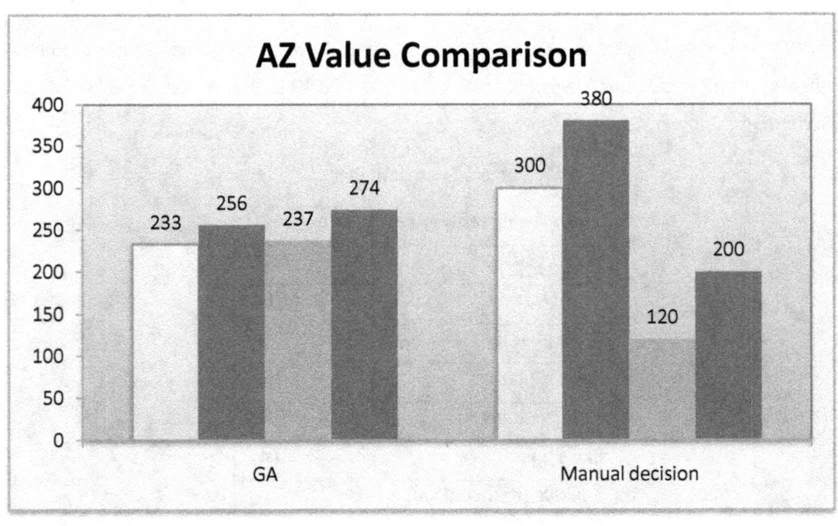

Figure 5.18: Comparison of the Algorithms with ROC Attributes

As based along the above-given analysis, it is said ABO being a competitive classifier, under the comparison of traditional algorithms which precisely gets the prediction of optimized customers.

The Statistical Significance along the experiments provides the result of the significant findings under ABO having higher true positivity as compared to other algorithms.

Table 5.6: Relationship between Grouping and Type

| Grouping | Type | | | | Total |
	True positive	True negative	False positive	False negative	
ACO	241	264	240	255	1000
	22.2%	21.7%	30.9%	27.7%	25.0%

Chi-square value-276.606, p-value-0.00<0.01;

The table compares the Grouping (ACO) and type. It is observed that 25% of the participants belong to the ACO group. Majority of the false positive belong to ACO group (30.9%). From the observed chi-square value of 276.606 and p-value of 0.00 which is less than 0.01 so it is declared that there is an association between the Grouping (ACO) and type.

Table 5.7: Performance Evaluation of ACO for Banking Customer Profile and Cancer

Dataset	Precision	Recall	F-measure
Banking Customer profile	0.50104	0.50867	0.50483
Cancer	0.55252	0.54962	0.55107

Table5.7 represents the Precision, Recall and F-Measure comparison graph for the proposed clustering technique with the cancer data set. The Table shows that customer profile data set had poor precision, recall, and F-measures. The same was depicted in the Figure5.18.

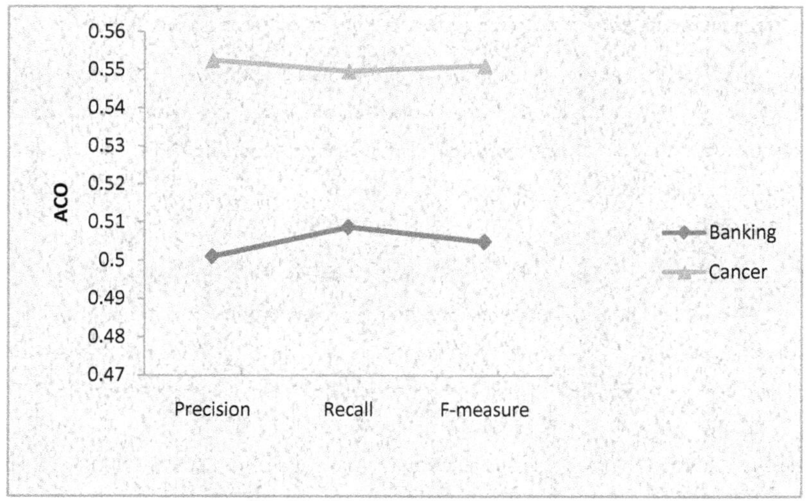

Figure 5.19: Performance Evaluation of ACO for Banking Customer Profile and Cancer

5.2.4. *Summary of this work*

The analytical results showed that the ACO algorithm showed poor discriminatory power (0.48) and had lower precision, recall and f-measure values of 0.50, 0.50 and 0.50% respectively and this algorithm works par with the manual decision-making method. The decision making the performance of the proposed technique was visualized by implementing it in MATLAB. Experimental results on real-life datasets proved that the decision-making tool using Genetic Algorithm is not effective than manual decision making.

5.3. Efficiency of the Artificial Bee Colony [Abc] with Manual Decision Making

5.3.1. *Introduction*

Artificial bee colony (or ABC) algorithm that was put forward by Karaboga is a narrative nature motivated algorithm founded on the foraging actions of a honeybee swarm (Karboga, 2005).ABC algorithm is a fresh meta-heuristic approach motivated by smart foraging actions of honeybee swarm. We've compared the performance of the ABC approach of ours with the finest approaches accounted in the literature. Calculation results show the pre-eminence of the fresh ABC approach over every other approach. The fresh approach did obtain superior quality solutions in briefer time (Singh, 2009). The optimization method employed in the study work of this book happens to be the Artificial Bee Colony (or ABC) Algorithm that's an optimization algorithm founded on the smart behavior of a honey bee group (Karboga, 2005).

Lately, Karaboga has developed a fresh optimization algorithm referred to as the Artificial Bee Colony (or ABC) algorithm (Karboga, 2005). ABC algorithm was initially introduced for arithmetical optimization difficulties/problems founded on foraging actions of a honey bee group. Additional improvements of the ABC algorithm have been done by Karaboga & Basturk (Karaboga & Basturk, 2007).

This model has the foraging bees classified into 3 different kinds: employed bees, onlookers & scouts. A bee that's found a foodstuff source to use is known as an employed bee. Bystanders are the ones waiting inside the hive to obtain the information on the food sources from the employed bees and Scouts are the bees which are randomly searching for new food supplies about the hive. Many types of research did a study and apply the Artificial Bee Colony on numerous study cases varying from usual equations to structural design difficulties/problems. Karaboga & Basturk put forward the key outlines of the ABC algorithm (Karaboga & Basturk, 2008).

Afterward, Akay & Karaboga (Akay &Karaboga, 2009) did apply ABC algorithm on arithmetical test functions & did compare results with renowned algorithms like the GA, Particle Swarm Optimization (or PSO) & HS. ABC algorithm happens to be swarm founded meta-heuristic algorithm.

Set up by Dervis Karaboga in the year of 2005 for optimization numeric difficulty/problem. Diverse suitable applications of ABC algorithm have been stated in the literature like optimization of the steel trusses in (Hadidi & Kazemzadeh, 2010). The settlement of artificial bees includes 3 classes of bees: employed bees, bystanders & scouts. The primary half of the settlement includes the working artificial bees & the 2nd half consists of the bystanders. For each food supply, there is just one working bee. Basically, the figure for working bees is the same as the figure of food reserves about the hive. The working bee whose food supply has been finished by the bees does become a scout. (Karboga, 2005)

The settlement of artificial bees includes 3 classes of bees:

- *Employed/working bees* linked with precise food reserves
- *Onlooker/bystander bees* observing the dance of the employed/working bees inside the hive to select a food supply
- *Scout bees* hunting for food sources haphazardly

Both bystanders/onlookers & scouts are moreover, mentioned as unemployed bees. Firstly, all food supply positions are found out by the scout bees. The nectars of the food reserves are utilized by employed bees & onlooker bees & this continual utilization will eventually exhaust them. The employed bee having been exhausted of food source turns into a scout bee. The place of a food supply represents a likely solution to the problem/difficulty & the nectar quantity of a food supply signifies the quality (or fitness) of the linked solution. The figure of employed bees is equivalent to the figure of food reserves (or solutions) since all employed bees are connected to one & just one food reserve.

In the ABC algorithm, while onlookers/bystanders & employed bees perform the utilization procedure in the search space, scouts are in charge of the utilization procedure. In the event of genuine honey bees, the staffing rate does represent a "determination" of how fast the bee horde locates & utilizes the recently discovered food reserve. Artificial staffing procedure could likewise signify the "determination" of the pace at which the possible solutions / the most favorable solutions of the tricky optimization problems/difficulties can be determined. The survival & advancement of the actual bee swarm depends on the fast finding and competent utilization of the most excellent food reserves (Karaboga & Basturk, 2008).

- The settlement of artificial bees includes three categories of bees:
  - *Employed/working bees* linked with precise food reserves
  - *Onlooker/bystander bees* observing the dance of the employed/working bees inside the hive to select a food supply
  - *Scout bees* hunting for food sources haphazardly
- Both onlookers/bystanders & scouts are moreover, mentioned as unemployed bees.
- At first, all food supply places are found out by the scout bees.
- The nectar of the food reserves are utilized by employed bees & onlooker bees & this continual utilization will eventually exhaust them.
- The employed/working bee having been exhausted of a food source turns into a scout bee.
- The place of a food supply represents a likely solution to the difficulty/problem & the nectar quantity of a food supply signifies the quality (or fitness) of the linked solution.
- The figure of employed/working bees is equivalent to the figure of food reserves (or solutions) since every employed bee is linked with one & just one food reserve.

Detailed of Pseudo of ABC Algorithm Refer Appendix 2

5.3.2. Experimental Results

In the concerned section, we usually focus along the decision which supports the functionality of the ABC algorithm. Particularly, we usually show how the ABC solution gets the usage in selecting the target point being best where expected profit gets maximized. We usually consider two varied strategies for 1 case targeting the customers being under the age group of 25-40 years, having income ranging between 25001-40,000 &AQB ranging from 10001-25,000.

Hence, we usually made 3 common assumptions for ordering the run of the analysis &the identification of the optimal customers under the concerned lists of 1 million prospects for the target. We usually showed our experimental results along the Figure. The ROC or receiver operating characteristics curve that gets calculated along the area given under ROC curve remains to be the best model for performance in the study.

The ROC curves became the standard tool for the assessment of the accuracy for the model of predictions along the field of the medical diagnosis & becoming used increasingly along the financial environment and machine learning. The concerned TP rate gets plotted along the Y-axis while the FP rate gets plotted along the X-axis.

5.3.3. Results

The ROC curve plots the true positive (sensitivity) versus false positive (1-specificity) for a binary classifier system as its discrimination threshold is varied. The graph below shows that ACO performs better than manual decision making. The above ROC Analysis shows that ABC performs well with 0.50. Although this predictive ability is better than manual decision making, the ROC of 0.50 indicates that the value has low discriminatory power.

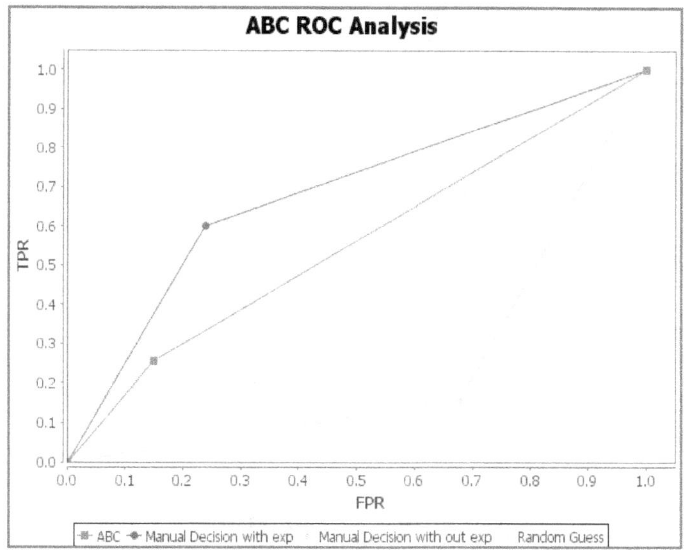

Figure 5.20: ABC ROC Analysis

The above ROC Analysis shows that ACO performs well with 0.48. Although this predictive ability is better than manual decision making, the ROC of 0.48 indicates that the value has low discriminatory power.

Table 5.8: ABC Analysis

Analysis variables/Techniques	ABC
True Positive	237
True Negative	272
False positive	225
False Negative	266
True positive rate	0.47
False positive rate	0.45
Positive predicted value	0.51
AZ value	0.5

129

For the comparison of the traditional algorithms along the accuracy of the classification being 0.5 for the ABC, this was poor in comparison to a manual decision.

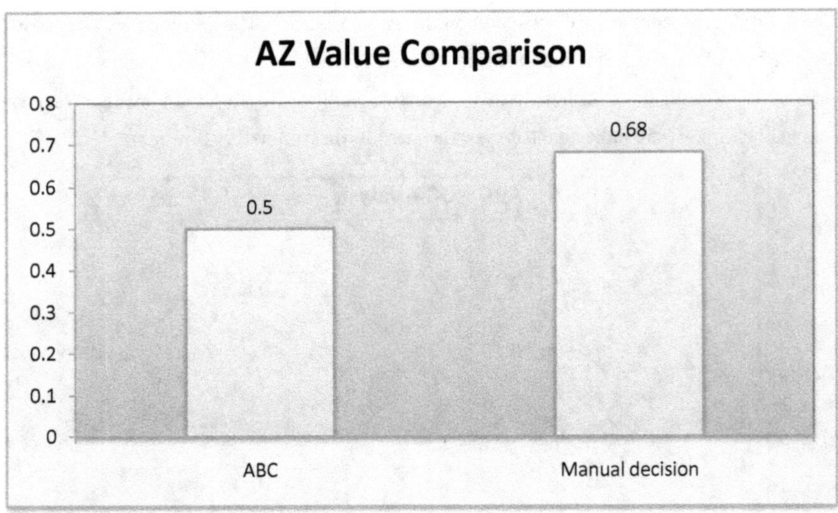

Figure 5.21: AZ Value Comparison

AZ Value Comparison Across the Algorithms

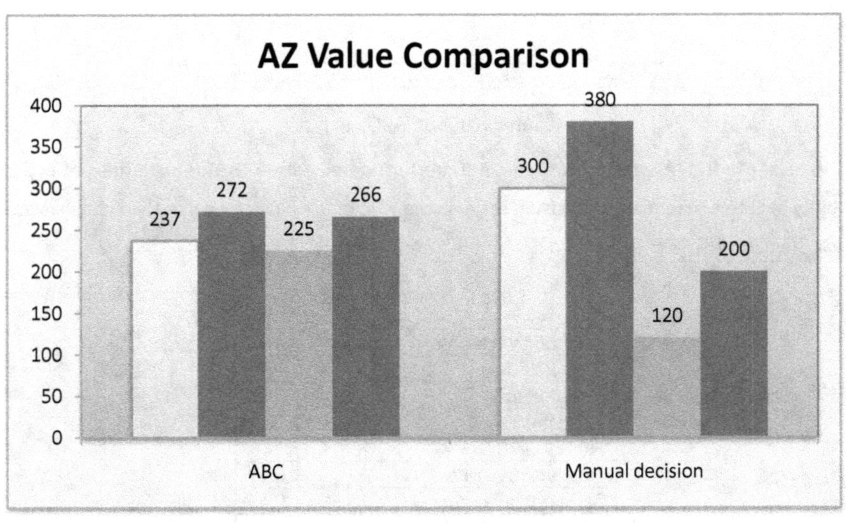

Figure 5.22: Comparison of the Algorithms with ROC Attributes

As based along the above-given analysis, it is said ABO being a competitive classifier, under the comparison of traditional algorithms which precisely gets the prediction of optimized customers. The Statistical Significance along the experiments provides the result of the significant findings under ABO having higher true positivity as compared to other algorithms

Table 5.9: Relationship between Grouping and Type

Grouping	Type				Total
	True positive	True negative	False positive	False negative	
ABC	237	272	225	266	1000
	21.8%	22.4%	29.0%	28.9%	25.0%

Chi-square value-276.606, p-value-0.00<0.01;

Table 5.10: Performance Evaluation of ABC for Banking Customer Profile and Cancer

Dataset	Precision	Recall	F-measure
Banking Customer profile	0.51299	0.50558	0.50925
Cancer	0.43154	0.70449	0.53523

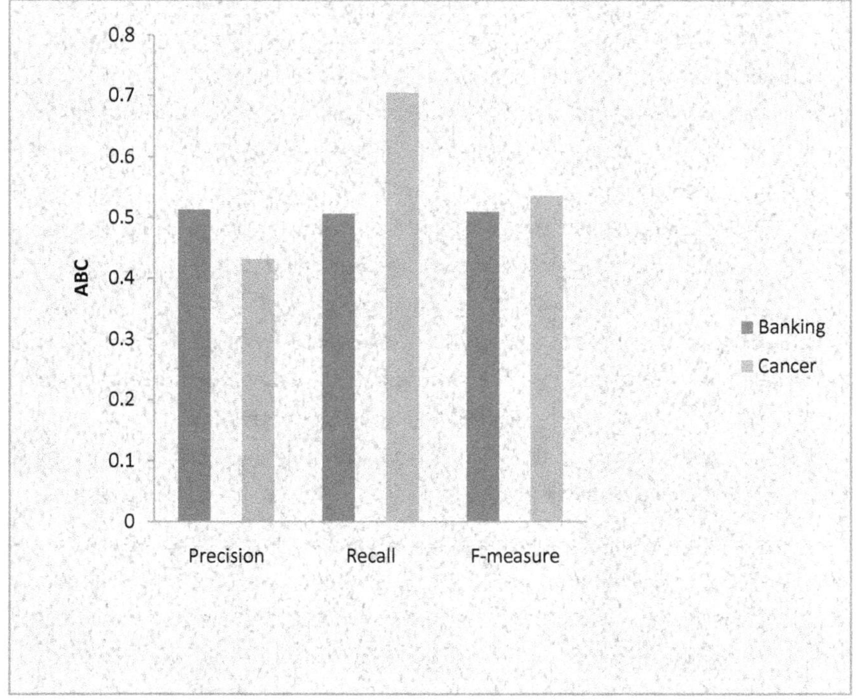

Figure 5.23: Performance Evaluation of ABC for Banking Customer Profile and Cancer

5.3.4. *Summary of this Work*

The analytical results showed that the ABC algorithm showed poor discriminatory power (0.51) and had lower precision, recall and f-measure values of 0.51, 0.50 and 0.50% respectively and this algorithm works par with the manual decision-making method. The decision making the performance of the proposed technique was visualized by implementing it in MATLAB. Experimental results on real-life datasets proved that the decision-making tool using Genetic Algorithm is not effective than manual decision making.

5.4. Proposed Work: Artificial Bear Optimization (ABO)

5.4.1. *Introduction*

Every algorithm for meta-heuristic inspired by nature. Hence, before this gets applied along with the existing algorithm for meta-heuristic, the algorithms are required to besatisfied with the below-given questions for proceeding along with those respective methodologies:

- Does the concerned functionality for the algorithm providea solution to the problem?
- Though it provides the solution, we require checking the solution as given along the complex functions that help for understanding and deriving the functionality?

In the implementation of the concerned NEW algorithm along with inspiration for Nature, that remains differed from smelling the sense of BEAR to the dynamic and optimalsystems for decision making under the current business world.The concerned question remains with designing the meta-heuristic of the problems for dynamic optimization is what the information requires during the concerned search which must get memorized & how the information gets used towards the guide in searching and maintainingthe adaptability towards changes. Along several optimization problems, concernedenvironmental variables or the decision variablesgets subjected or perturbed that changes after the final solution gets implemented and obtained for the concerned problem. Thus, for solving the problem it is required to be taken into account which the solution requires to be acceptable along the respect with slight changes for the values of decision variable.

Bears sustain a sense of smell due to the area of the along their brain which manages the concerned sense of smell, known as olfactory bulb, remains to be five times larger thansimilar area along human brains being the bear's brain is 1/3rd the size.Thebears can smell much better than any of the animals on earth, due to the region of olfactory bulb present in the brain. The surface area of the bear's nose has aroundhundred times more the sense of smell receptors than the human nose. The sense of smell which the bear remains 2,100 times much better than the humans.

The acute sense of smell they have helps them to track their concerned cubs, in finding food, mates along with keeping a tab on the other competing bears. Hundreds of tiny muscles alongwith their nose help them to control smell.

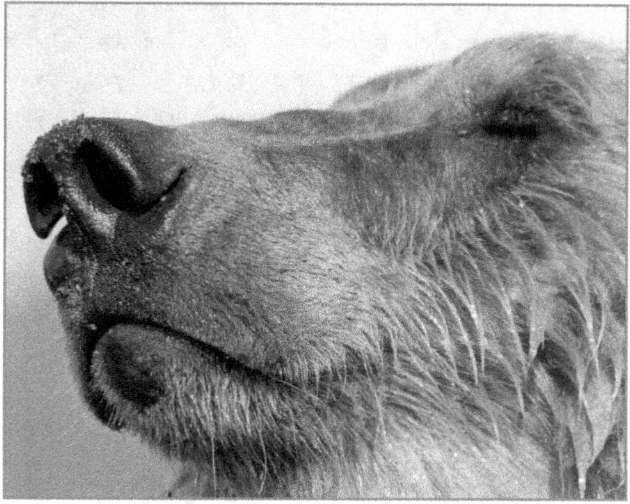

Figure 5.24: Grizzly Bear

The skull of the bear showed the higher cavity of nasal for the grizzly bear. Along the cavity of nasal the vast network of the tissue which looks similar to honeycomb. The concerned tissues get created along the immense amount of the surface area under the processing of the scent information.The bears are generally robust and bulky animals having relatively shorter legs. The eyes of the bearsalong with ears are usually small being a bigger animal. But the snout and nose of the bearare large. Grizzlies depend on their concerned sense of smell in finding the food. Smelling remains to be bear's one of the sharpest sense. The grizzly bear often smells the flesh or carrion of the dead animal, from distantplaces. Some scientists described that the bears can smell the carrion from a distance of 18 miles away. The Grizzlies are about and out during both day & night. They often seem to becomemore active during dusk or dawn, however. Along with this, the places with people around, the bears remain to be nocturnal.

The adult bear usually has individual territory. The part of the territory remains to be the exclusive domain of the bear, but it gets shared with the other bears. These territories usually comprised of varied smaller areas being a food source as connected with travel lanes. Generally, the female bears have the home ranging between 6.5 and 26 square kilometers, while the males normally have the home range being 26 to 124 square kilometers.

Their acute sense of smell usually helps them in tracking their cubs, finding food, and mating along with keeping a tab on the competing bears. The bears can often detect the dead animal at a distance of 20 miles, thanks to the keen smelling power they have. The bears can smell often better than the other animal on earth, due to the region of the olfactory bulb. This remains to be surprised where the size of the brain is just 1/3rd of humans. Hence, if you ever visit the nature parks for camping, it remains difficult to keep the bears away from the food. The smelling power of the bear is around 2,100 times much better than that of humans.

The bears are often thought to be one of the best animals having the smelling power animal on earth. For instance, the average of the smelling power of the dogs remains to be100 times much better than humans. The blood houndremains better than 300 times. The bears usually have higher developed noses which contain 100 of the tiny muscles & let them manipulate them along the similar dexterity similar to people's fingers. The concerned surface area as inside their nine inches noses has around100 times more of the surface area & receptors than that of human's.

5.4.2. Bear's Nasal Cavity

Figure5.25: Bear's Nasal Cavity

It is believed that Grizzly bears possess a strong smelling sense, which is stronger than the human by 100000 times.

The skull of the bear shows that the nasal cavity has a wide tissue network which makes it look like a honeycomb. These well-knit tissues develop a huge area to process the information regarding the scent.

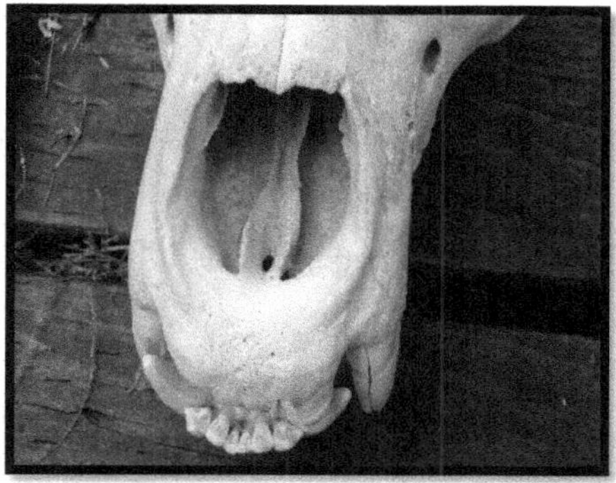

Figure 5.26: Top View of a Grizzly Bear Skull

Grizzly bears utilize their smelling sense to find the clams hidden under the sand, which makes the bears an expert in digging clam. Their smelling ability is acute which makes them find the fish under the water.

- Smell receptors would collect and transmit information about the smell.
- The olfactory bulb area of the brain acts and processes the data regarding the smell.
- The vast amount of network in the nasal cavity offers information about the smell.

5.4.3. *Artificial Bear ABO Gist*

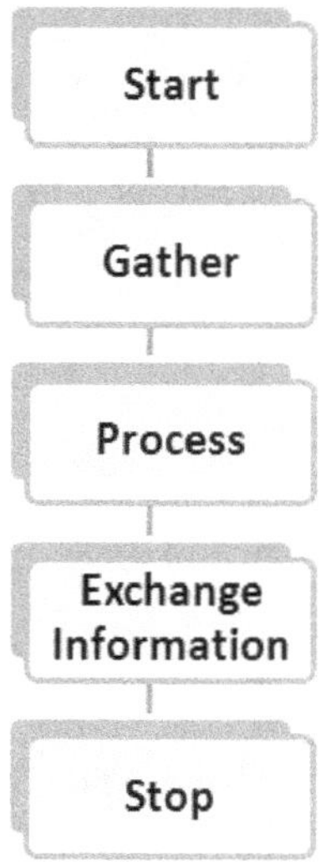

Figure 5.27: ABO Gist

Algorithm

Step 1: Collect the 'n' number of data about the smell in a given area.

Step 2: Evaluate the data about the smell [Decide on which smell is needed and evaluate it from the rest of it]

Step 3: To arrive at the data regarding the value of fitness for each smell.(i.e : f(n))

Step 4: To remember the best smell data through its fitness value and store it in the given area S(n).

Step 5: Repeat Step 3 and 4 again, until the data regarding the smell is complete.

Step 6: Exchange the data of smell in the given area [S (n)] to determine the optimal decision making.

Pseudo-Algorithm

- Initializing of population; x_i= 1,2,...,n
- Determine the fitness function with the help of constraints or objective function (y_j)

$$f(x_i) = \sum f(y_j) \text{ where } j = 1,2,3$$

- Cycle = 1
    - Compare between x_1 and x_2 ; if $f(x_1) > f(x_2)$, then $f(x_1)$ must be considered as the best solution. [Local Maxima]
    - Similarly, $f(x_1)$ must be compared with the remaining population.
    - Determine the suitable solution, anda perfect set of the population is derived Z_i . [Global Maxima]
    - Remove the perfect solution from set x_i.
- Cycle = cycle +1

    Until all the needs are met

Implementation

- Initializing of population:

    X_i= 1,2,3....,200

- Calculation of Fitness:

    Let us Assume,

    No. of Constraints = 3

    1st constraint's value – Age (y_1) = 1 if 25<= y1 <=45

    = 0 or

    2nd constraint's value – Income (y_2) = 1 if 25000<= y2 <=60000

$$= 0 \text{ or}$$

3rd constraint's value – Vintage years $(y_3) = 1$ if $3 <= y3 <= 5$

$$= 0 \text{ or}$$

When there are 3 constraints for a customer, then the level of fitness is maximum.

$f(x_1) = 3$
$f(x_2) = 2$
$f(x_3) = 0$
$f(x_4) = 1$
$f(x_5) = 3$

.

.

.

.

$f(1000) = 2$

Compare between $f(x_1)$ & $f(x_2)$ and the respective values are 3 & 2.

To maximize $f(x_1)=3$

Compare between $f(x_1)$ & $f(x_3)$ and the respective values obtained are 3 & 0.

To maximize $f(x_1)=3$

Compare between $f(x_1)$ & $f(x_4)$ and the respective values obtained are 3 & 1.

To maximize $f(x_1)=3$

Compare between $f(x_1)$ & $f(x_5)$ and the respective values obtained are 3 & 3.

To maximize $f(x_1)=3$ & $f(x_2)=3$

Similarly, compare the local maxima values up to 1000.

Remember the final set population:

$Z_i = f(x_1)$ & $f(x_5)$.

Deduct the $f(x_1)$ & $f(x_5)$ from the population set x_i.

Now the population is x=2,3,4,..................,1000

Compare between $f(x_2)$ & $f(x_3)$ and the respective values derived are 2 & 0.

To maximize $f(x_2)=2$

Compare between $f(x_2)$ & $f(x_4)$ and the respective values derived are 2 & 1.

To maximize $f(x_2)=2$

Likewise, compare the local maxima. values up to 1000.

Remember the final set population:

$Z_i = f(x_1)$, $f(x_5)$, $f(x_2)$

Subtract the $f(x_2)$ from the population set x_i.

Finally, we would derive the new population set Z_i. The new population set would be fitness valuein descending order from maximum to minimum. Then find out the best n customer to find the valued customer.

5.4.4. *Merits of ABO*

- It can eradicate the chances of guessing within the firm.
- To respond faster to initiate changes in the financial sector and preferences of the customer.
- To initiate quick decision making through quick action, the right information before the competitors in the business would do to offer the best performance than the rest.
- Perform clickstream data analysis to boost the strategies of e-commerce.
- Initiate more rates of profit for insurance premiums.
- To determine the objectives to optimize the business quickly with a low amount of risk, low cost and effective strategy of information.
- Improve the power of decision making, enhance productivity and efficiency through the environment where timely data which is accurate, reliable and actionable is offered to track and enhance the performance.
- To be flexible and agile.
- To prevent the manual processes that are prone to errors.
- To gain the maximum advantage of loyalty economics by boosting the retention.
- Lowers the risk.
- Perform action-oriented and accurate decisions faster.

Table 5.11: Factor Analysis

Factors	Component					Squared Loadings % of Variance
	1	2	3	4	5	
Profession	.815					64.5%
Years of familiarity	.758					
Aliment details	.732					
Additional Asset info	.645					
Rental or owned residence		.789				69.5%
Standard Quarterly balance ought		.654				
A cheque does not return		.582				
Verification of the last six-month wage credited			.856			72.3%
Motor vehicle details			.785			
Place				.756		75.4%
Family reliant				.696		
Age					.764	80.3%
Income					.654	

Table 5.11 presents the results of the factor analysis and a detailed description of each item for each of the five main factors. Factor loadings ranged from .86 to 0.64. All the factors accounted for 65-80% of the variance.

5.4.5. Performance Evaluation

Any of the assessment for diagnostic performance seemed with the requirement of some comparison for the diagnostic decisions along with "truth."The Performance remains to be the test's ability in correctly identifying the negative and positive cases. ROC or *Receiver operating characteristic* curve charts usually allows the user in visually evaluating the accuracy for the classifier & the comparison of the different models for classification.

The ROC chart remains to be2-dimensional plot along with the proportion for false positives or"fp"along horizontal axis & the proportion for true positives or "tp" along the vertical axis. The individual levels of decision levels get evaluatedwith the usage of Qualitative (Sensitivity or Specificity). The sequence of the concerned confusion matrices along with theallowed the ideal trade-off in between the no of correctly classified positive observations and the number of negative observations being incorrectly classified required the assessment.

The diagonal effectively divides ROC space. The points as given above the concerned diagonal represent the good result for classification, the points below the results along line poor. The ideal curve climbs quickly toward the concerned top-left which means the test gets correctly identified cases. The approach effectively focuses the attention along the issues as involved along the diagnostic evaluation & the decision makingdiagnostic. During the machine learning, ROC curve gets used along the evaluation of discriminative performance for binary classifiers. This primarily gets obtained along the plotting forthe concerned curve in the rate of true positive versus the rate of false positive for binary classifier by as varied along the threshold discrimination.

5.4.6. Proposed Algorithm

Figure 1.1 represented the overall application as proposed for finding the varied optimal population.

GA or Genetic Algorithm, ACO or Ant Colony Optimization & ABC or Artificial Bee Colony algorithms as implemented with finding the resultant set of database set along with the evaluation of the performance for ROC curve.

The concerned flow chart represents the proposed algorithm along ABO or Artificial Bear Optimization in Figure 5.28.

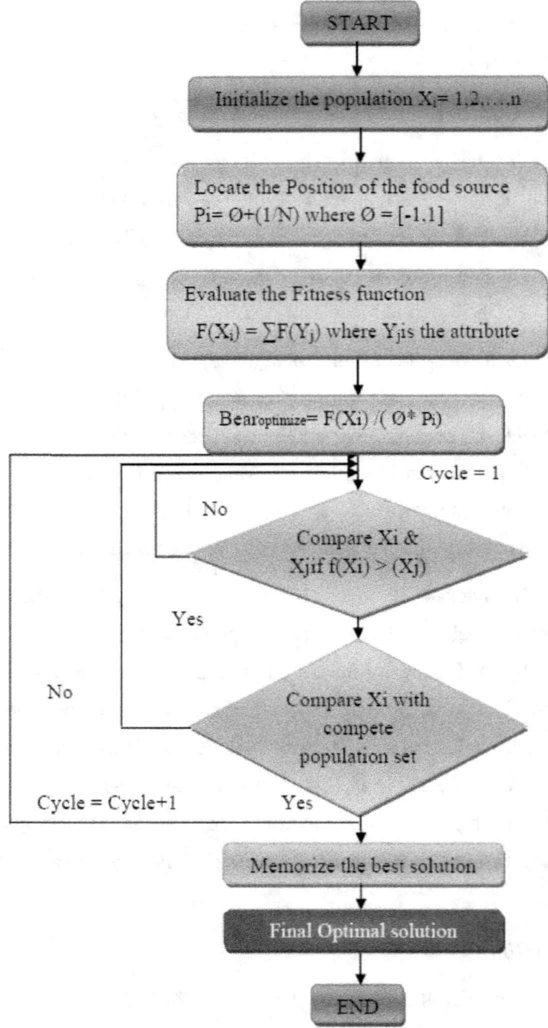

Figure 5.28: Artificial Bear Optimization: Pseudo Code Algorithm

The application gets produced along the implementation for the algorithms & results remained shown under the database & ROC analysis along with the algorithms as comparative Study takes place with the Intelligence concept having the implementation for forecasting customer performance along the Back Propagation of algorithm.

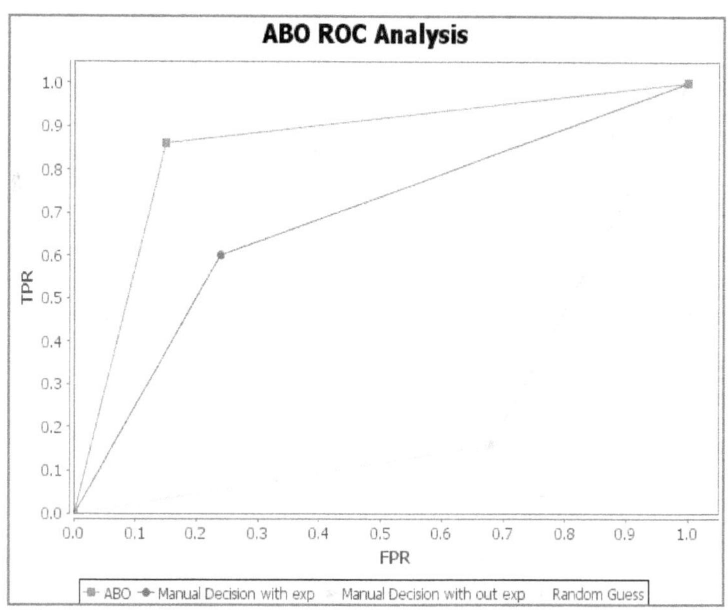

Figure 5.29: ABO - ROC Analysis

Table 5.12: ABO Algorithm

Analysis variables/Techniques	ABO
True Positive	374
True Negative	424
False positive	75
False Negative	127
True positive rate	0.74
False positive rate	0.15
Positive predicted value	0.83
AZ value	0.79

Table 5.13: Comparative study of ABO with Manual decision making

Analysis of variables/techniques	Manual decision making with experience	A manual decision without experience	Artificial bear algorithm
True positive	300	80	430
True negative	380	160	424
False positive	120	340	76
False Negative	200	420	70
True positive rate	0.6	0.16	0.86
False positive	0.24	0.68	0.15
Positive predicted value	0.71	0.19	0.85
AZ value	0.68	0.24	0.85

Table 5.14: Relationship between Grouping and Type

Grouping	Type				Total
	True positive	True negative	False positive	False negative	
ABO	374	424	75	127	1000
	34.5%	34.9%	9.7%	13.8%	25.0%
Total	1085	1216	777	922	4000
	100.0%	100.0%	100.0%	100.0%	100.0%

Chi-square value-276.606, p-value-0.00<0.01;

The table compares the Grouping (ABO) and type. It is observed that 25% of the participants belong to the ABO group. Majority of the True negative belong ABO group (34.9%). From the observed chi-square value of 276.606 and p-value of 0.00 which is less than 0.01 so it is declared that there is an association between the Grouping (ABO) and type.

Table 5.15: Performance Evaluation of ABO for Banking Customer Profile and Cancer

Dataset	Precision	Recall	F-measure
Banking Customer profile	0.83296	0.76951	0.79998
Cancer	0.87611	0.82299	0.84872

Table 5.15 represents the Precision, Recall and F-Measure comparison graph for the proposed clustering technique with the cancer data set. The Table shows that customer profile data set had poor precision, recall, and F-measures. The same was depicted in Figure5.30.

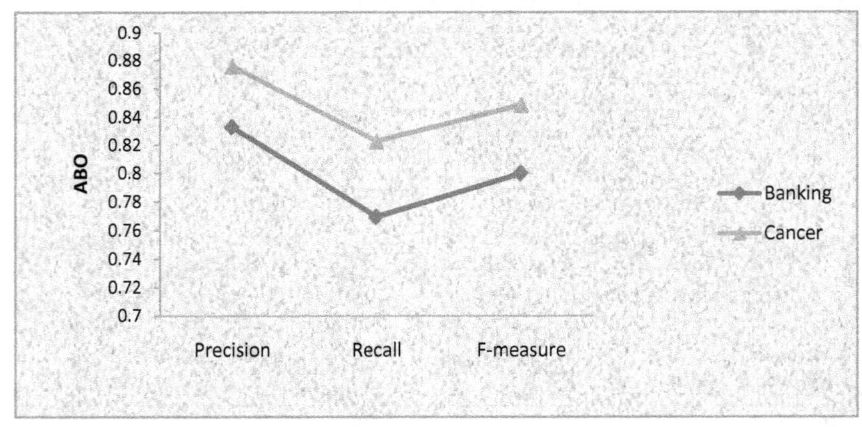

Figure 5.30: Performance evaluation of ABO for banking customer profile and cancer

The analytical results showed that the ABO algorithm showed good (excellent) discriminatory power (0.74) and had higher precision, recall and f-measure values of 0.83, 0.76 and 0.79% respectively and this algorithm works better than the manual decision-making method.

The decision making the performance of the proposed technique was visualized by implementing it in MATLAB. Experimental results on real-life datasets proved that the decision-making tool using Genetic Algorithm is not effective than manual decision making.

5.5. Predictive Analysis: Back Propagation Algorithm in Neural Networks

5.5.1. Introduction

The operational for the Back networks of propagation neural gets divided into 2 steps: feed forward & Back propagation. Along the step of feedforward, the input pattern gets applied along the input layer &the concerned effect propagates, under layer to layer, through the effective network until the output gets produced. The concerned concept for the output valve along the network gets compared for the output as expected, along with the error signal as computed along each of the concerned output nodes. This process gets repeated, aa layer to layer, till each node of the network gets received under the error signal as described along the relative contribution for the overall error as processed under the network having multi-layer neural as employing with *backpropagation* algorithm. For the illustration of the concerned process under3 layer of the network for neural with 2 inputs and 1 output, that is showed in the below-given picture, gets used:

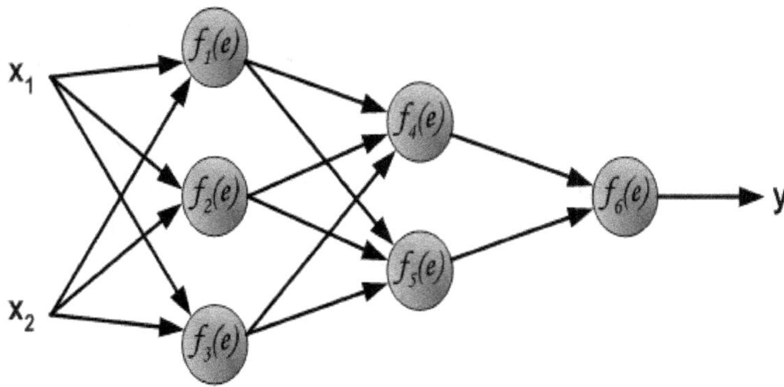

Figure 5.31: Multi-Layer Back Propagation Algorithm

Every neuron gets the composition of two units. The 1stt unit has an addition to the products of the weights coefficients & input signals. 2nd unit realized the nonlinear function, known as the function for neuron activation. The signal remains the output signal, &y = $f(e)$remains as the output signal for the nonlinear element. The Signal remains to be the output signal for the neuron.

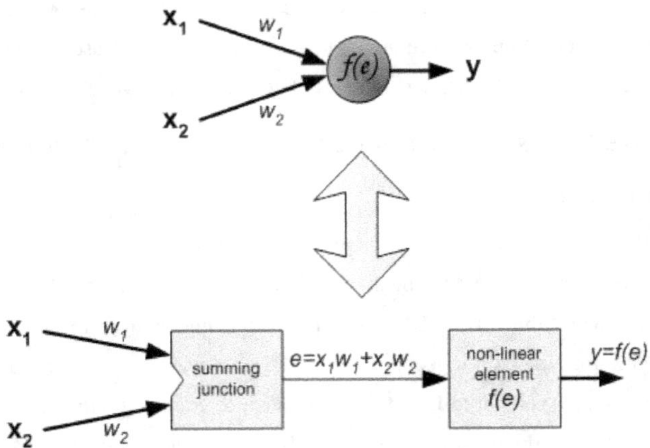

Figure 5.32: Working of the Back Propagation

For teaching the neural network it is needed to have the set of training data. The set of training data consists of the input signals as assigned along with the corresponding target z. The training for the network remains to be one of the iterative processes. In every iteration coefficient of weights of the nodes, they are modified with the usage of new data along the sets of training data. The modification gets calculated with the usage of the algorithm as described below: Every teaching step gets started with the force of both the input signals along the sets of training. After the concerned stages, we determine the values of output signals for every neuron in every network layer. The pictures below gets illustrated as for how the signal gets propagated through the concerned network, the Symbols $w_{(xm)n}$ gets represented along the weights of the connections in between the network input x_m & neuron n along the input layer. The Symbols y_n gets represented as the output signal for neuron n.

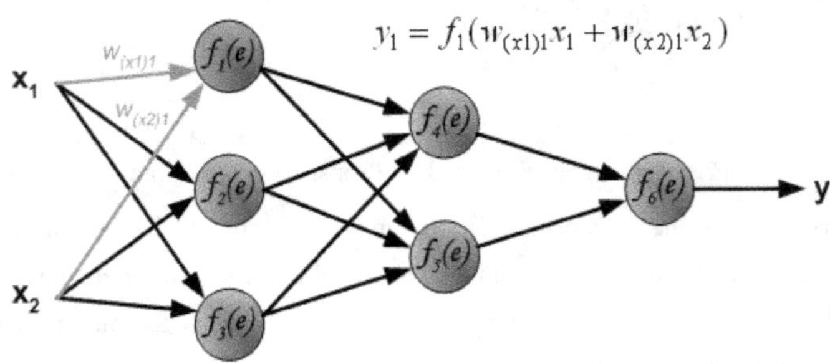

Figure 5.33: First Attribute Calculation of Back Propagation

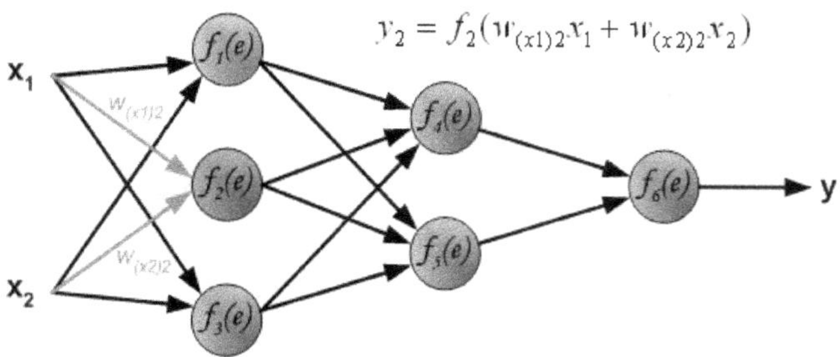

Figure 5.34: Second Attribute Calculation of Back Propagation

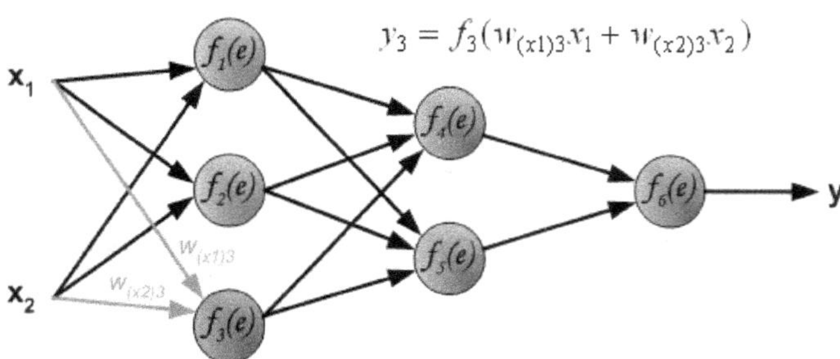

Figure 5.35: Third Attribute Calculation of Back Propagation

The propagation for the signals along the concerned hidden layer with the Symbols w_{mn} as represented with the weights of the connections in between the output of the neuron m & input of the neuron n along the next layer.

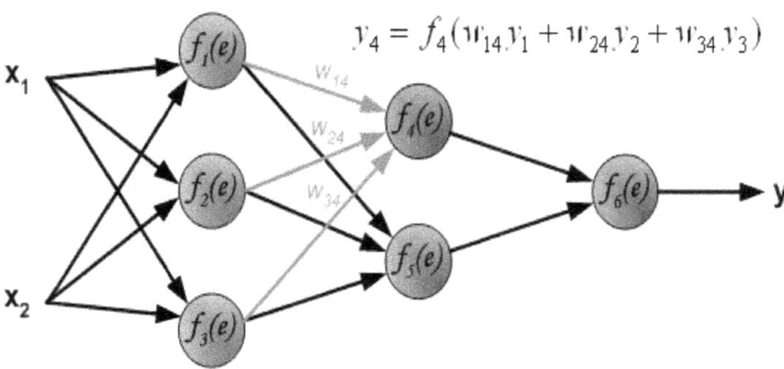

Figure 5.36: Fourth Attribute Calculation of Back Propagation

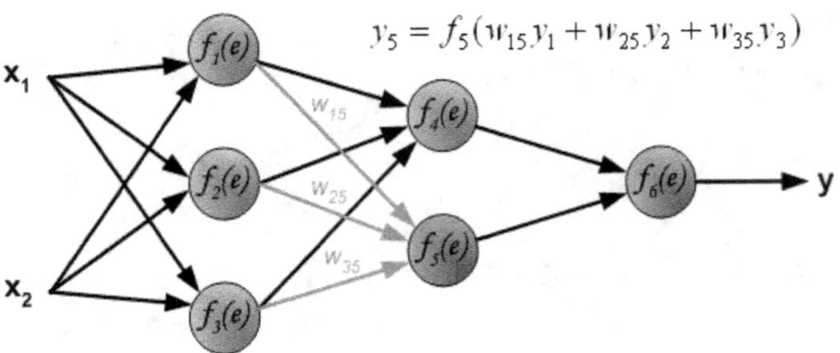

$$y_5 = f_5(W_{15}.y_1 + W_{25}.y_2 + W_{35}.y_3)$$

Figure 5.37: Fifth Attribute Calculation of Back Propagation

The propagation of the signals along the layer of output

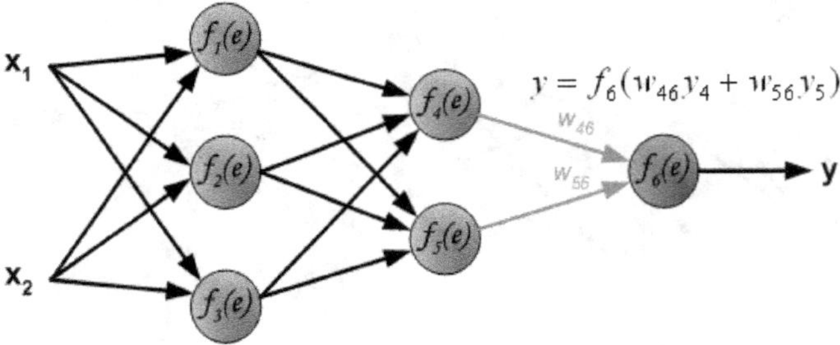

$$y = f_6(W_{46}.y_4 + W_{56}.y_5)$$

Figure 5.38: Output Signal of Back Propagation

Along the next step for an algorithm with the signal of the output signal with the network y gets compared along the desired value of output that is found along the sets of training data. The difference gets the name of the error signal for the neuron at the output layer.

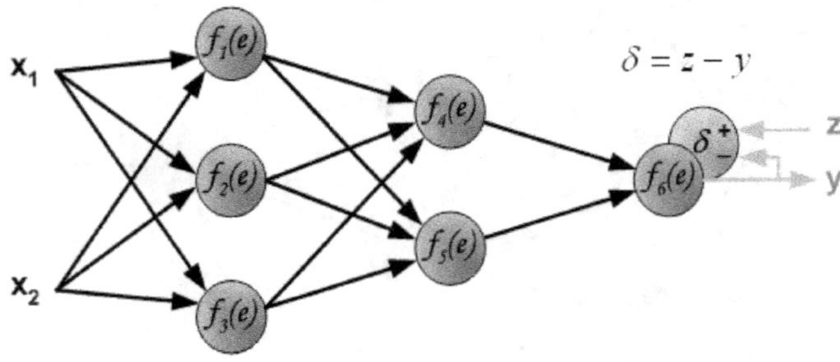

$$\delta = z - y$$

Figure 5.39: Computation of Error Signal

This is impossible for the computation of the error signal of the direct internal neurons, due to the output values for these neurons as unknown. For several years effective methods for the networks of training multiplayer remained unknown. Only along the middle of the 80s, the backpropagation of the algorithm got worked out. The idea remains to propagate the error signal back to every neuron that the output signals remained to be the input of the discussed neuron.

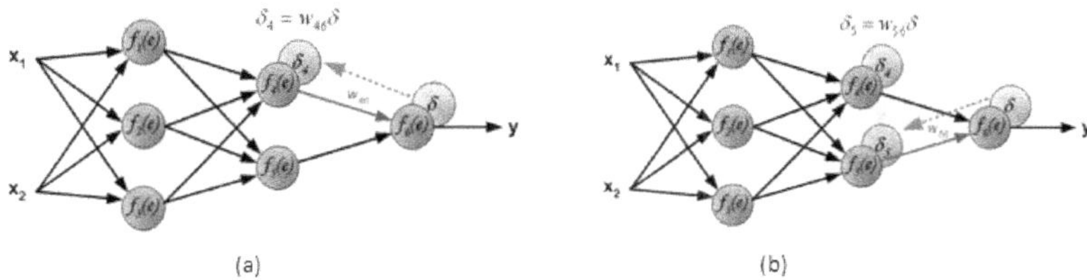

(a)   (b)

Figure 5.40: Signal Back to the Nodes

Weights' coefficients w_{mn} has the usage of the propagation of the errors back as equal to the usage of computing the output value. Hence, only for the direction of the data flow gets changed. The concerned technique gets the usage of all the network layers. For the propagation of the errors came from some neurons which get added. The concerned illustration is given below:

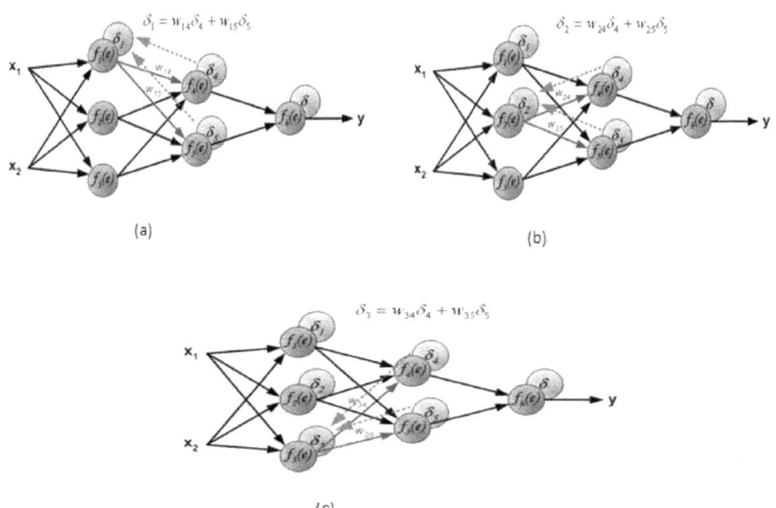

(a)   (b)

(c)

Figure 5.41: Directions of the Data Flow in Back Propagation

When the signal of error for every neuron gets computed, the coefficient weights for every node of neuron input get modified. Along the formulas, as given below *df (e) or de* represents the derivative of the function for neutron activation

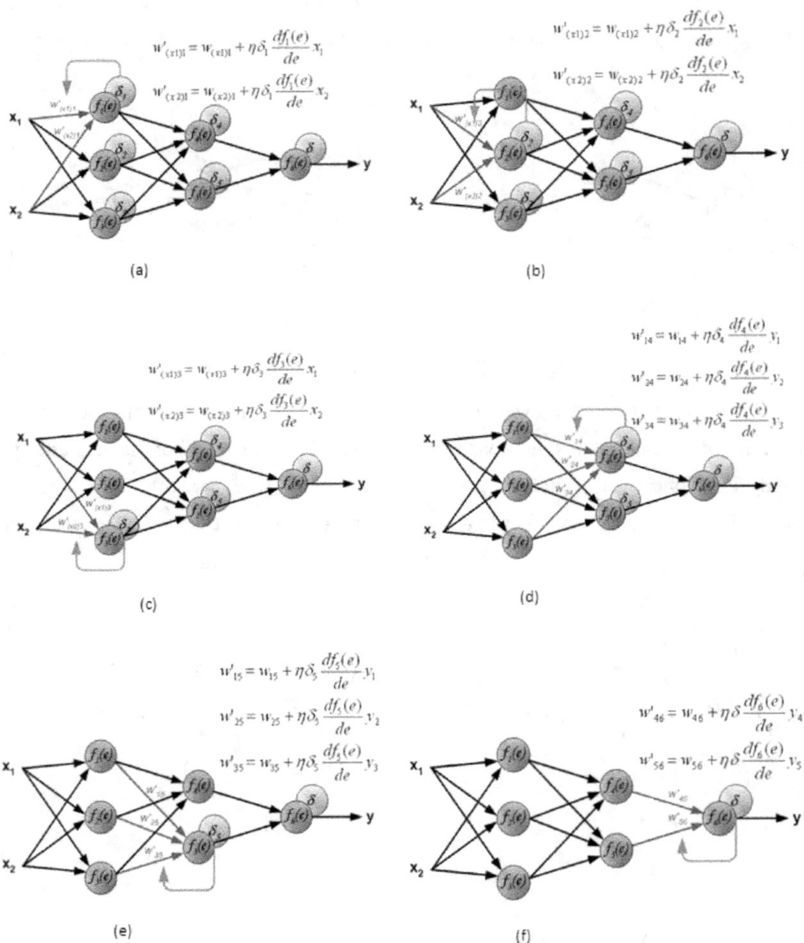

Figure 5.42: Calculating the Coefficient Weights of Each Node

The coefficient affects the teaching speed of network teaching. There seem to be some techniques that select the following parameter. The 1st method sustains with starting the process of teaching process under a larger value of this parameter. While the weights coefficients get established along the parameter that gradually decreases.

The 2ndremains to be more complicated, method gets started for teaching along the smaller value of the parameter. For the process of teaching the parameter increases during the teaching gets advanced & then it gets decreased again along the final stage. For starting the process of teaching along the low value of parameter enables the determination of the signs of weights coefficients.

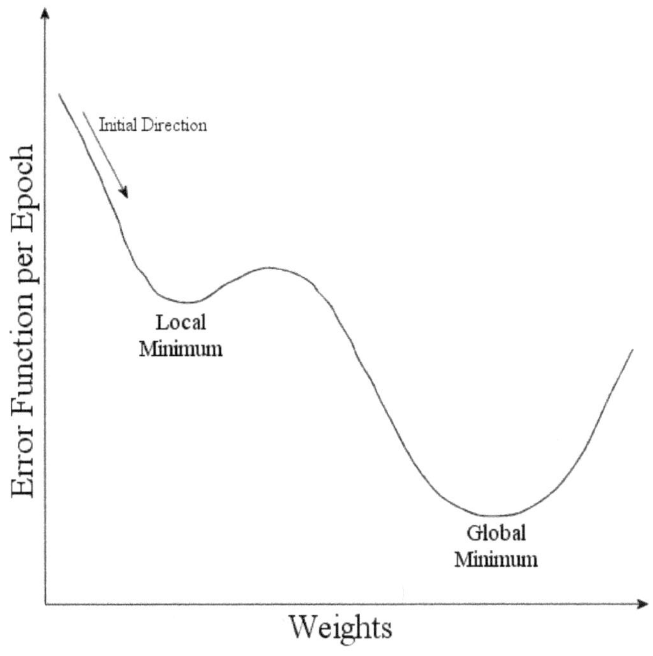

Figure 5.43: Global and Local Minima of Error Function

5.5.2. Experimental Results

In order to evaluate the performance of our proposed algorithm, we have conducted experiments using the back-propagation learning algorithm was performed to measure in terms of mean square error. Two error measures were used in evaluating the performance of both algorithms. The first is the classification error, while this measure reports the percentage of incorrectly classified examples. The second measures are the squared error percentage. The following shows the results of Backpropagation Classification Algorithm for generating optimum customer prediction.

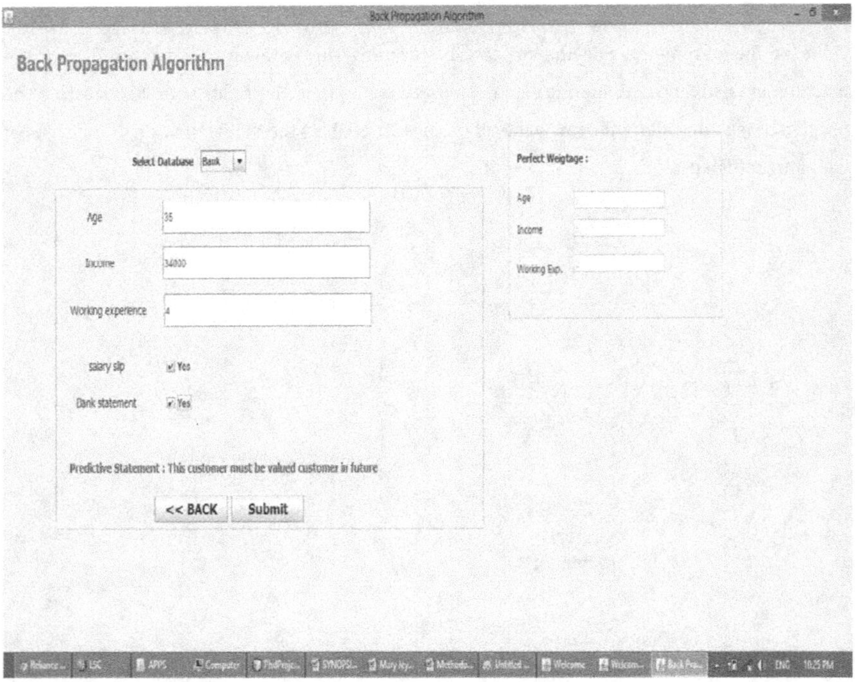

Figure 5.44: Customer Profile Updation

The validation error was only used to indicate which of the 10 replications for each algorithm and problem generated the best solution. In almost every case, over the 10 replications for each algorithm and 3 architectures, the ABO found 10 out of 10 superior classification errors compared to other algorithms. The ABO also found superior error percentages for all 10 problems. Table 5.16 shows the average of the ten replications for each algorithm, and problem across all architectures. The mean classification error percentage for the ABO is significantly below the mean for backpropagation at the 1% level for every problem. Not only is the mean lower but the variation of the solutions is typically smaller for the ABO.

Table 5.16: Average Classification Error and Squared Error Percentage

Algorithms	Classification Error Percentage		Squared error percentage	
	Mean	SD	Mean	SD
GA	2.55	1.12	1.50	0.42
ACO	2.51	1.12	1.96	0.96
ABC	2.52	1.12	1.48	0.38
ABO	1.95	0.98	0.98	0.24

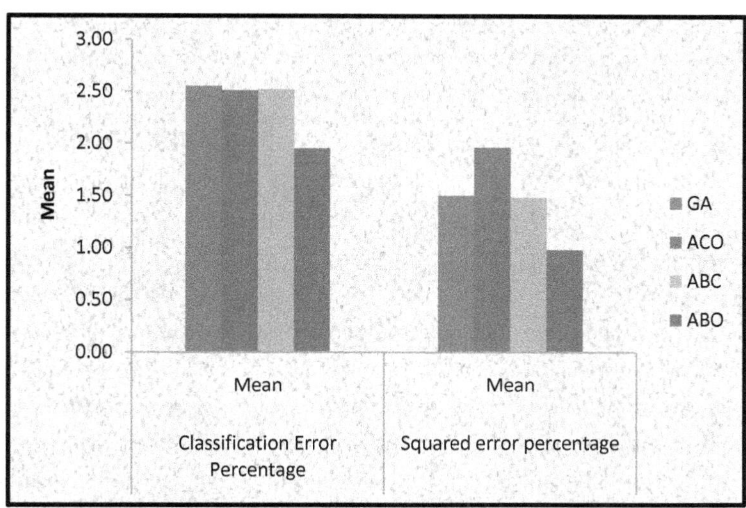

Figure 5.45: Average Classification Error and Square Error Percentage (Mean) by Algorithms

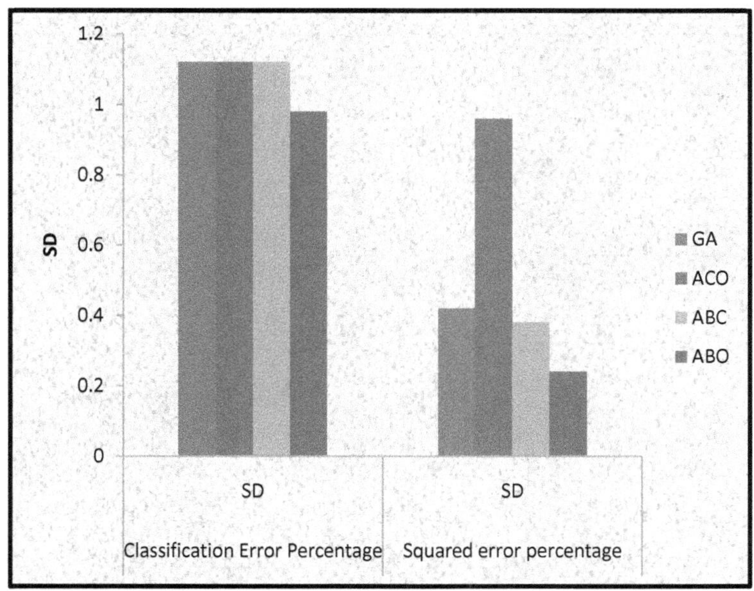

Figure 5.46: Average Classification Error and Square Error Percentage (SD) by Algorithms

A ranking of each algorithm and their different architectures was also tabulated to illustrate the average best to worst algorithm and architecture for each problem, shown in Table 5.17.

The ranking was based on classification error percentage, using the squared error percentage to break any ties between the solutions for each problem. It can be seen in Table 5.17 that the ABO found the best three solutions for all problem rose.

Table 5.17: Ranking of Algorithms for Best Average Classification Error Percentage

	Rank			
Data	GA	ABC	ACO	ABO
Customer (DST)	2	3	1	4
Cancer	2	1	4	3

Tables 23 and 24 show how well each algorithm does on average over the 10 replications, giving an indication of the robustness of each algorithm. Tables 23 and 24 show the best-found solution for each algorithm instead of their averages. As mentioned earlier, the best solution was determined by the smallest classification error percentage of the validation data set. Once the best weights were determined the test set errors were then calculated and compared. As can be seen in Table 5.17, the ABO found the best solution for every problem. This table also shows that the ABO found all 10 of the best solutions, with respect to the squared error percentage.

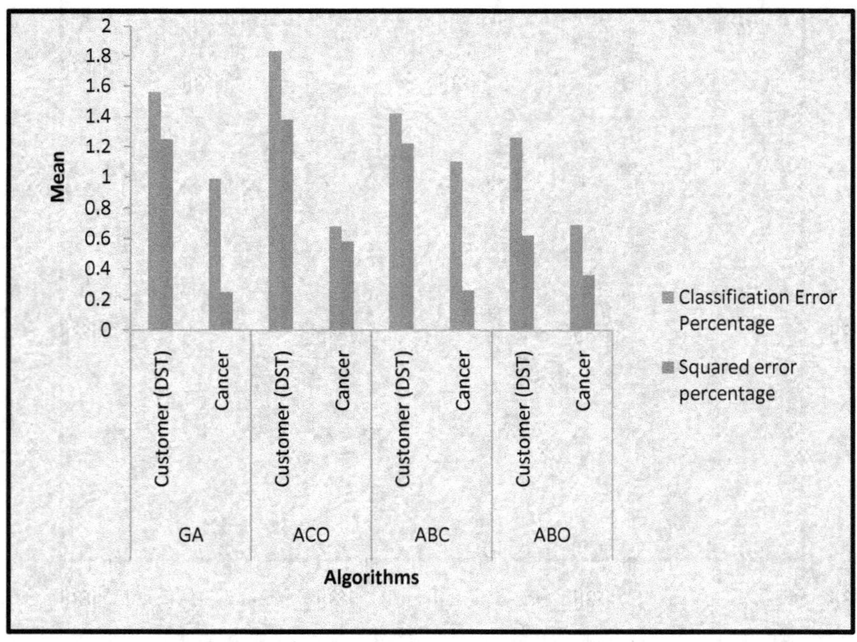

Figure 5.47: Best Classification Error and Squared Error Percentage

A ranking of each algorithm and their different architectures was also tabulated to illustrate the best to worst algorithm and architecture for each problem, shown in Table 5.17. The ranking was based on classification error percentage, using the squared error percentage to break any ties between the solutions for each problem. The ABO found all 10 of the best solutions, 9 out of 10 second best solutions, and 8 out of 10 third-best solutions. Comparing the performance of the best model found with each algorithm, a Wilcoxon Sign test finds that the ABO model forecasts for out-of-sample data have a smaller error than the other algorithms model at the 1% level for each of the data sets. A comparison of CPU time and a number of epochs trained was also tabulated in Figure5.48.

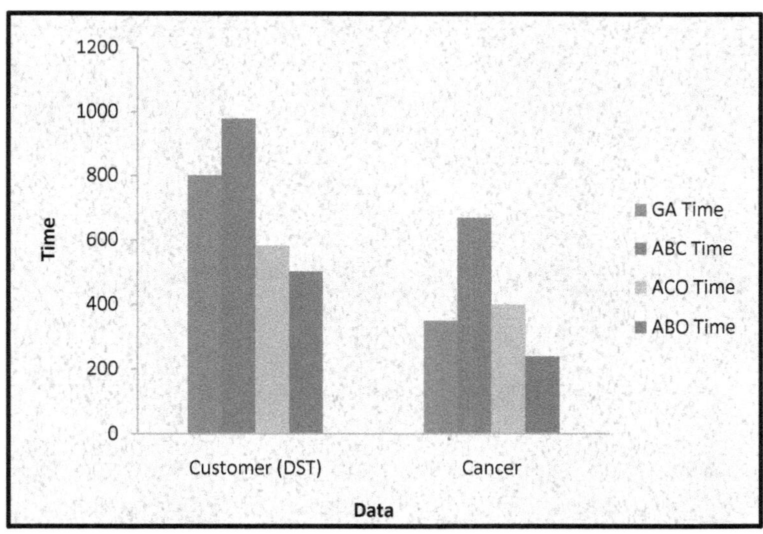

Figure 5.48: Average CPU Time for all Algorithms

As mention earlier, all algorithms were allowed to train until validation error ceased to decrease, or when a maximum of 10 million epochs were reached. The ABO was terminated before fully converging upon a solution at 36,000 epochs. Although the ABO trained with far fewer epochs than others, it converged much slower than others such as GA, per epoch of training. While the ABO does take more time for each epoch of training, it found superior solutions in a shorter amount of time in 5 out of the 10 problems. The value of converging upon a poorer solution faster has to be weighed for the problem being estimated. In the case of these and most other classification problems, the extra time needed for finding more consistent and predictable solutions is minimal.

Figure 5.49 (a): Visual Slides of Back Propagation Algorithm

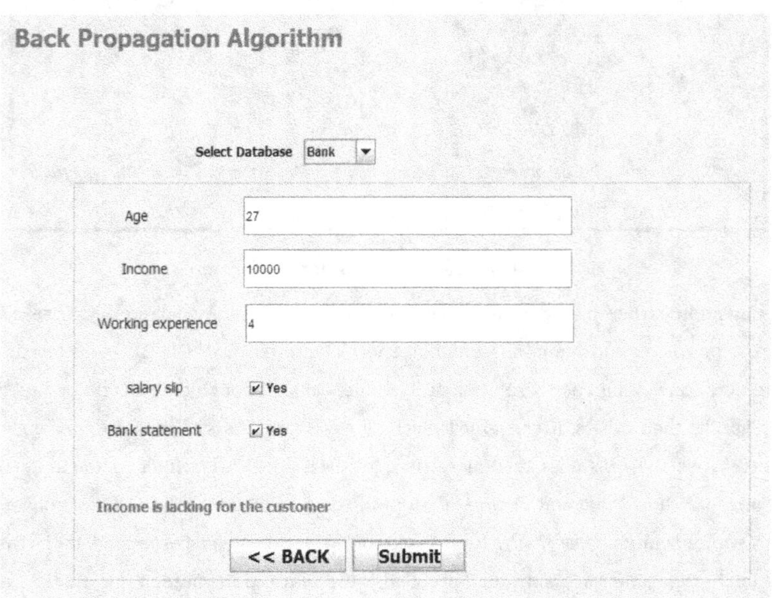

Figure 5.49: (b) Visual Slides of Back Propagation Algorithm

Back Propagation Algorithm

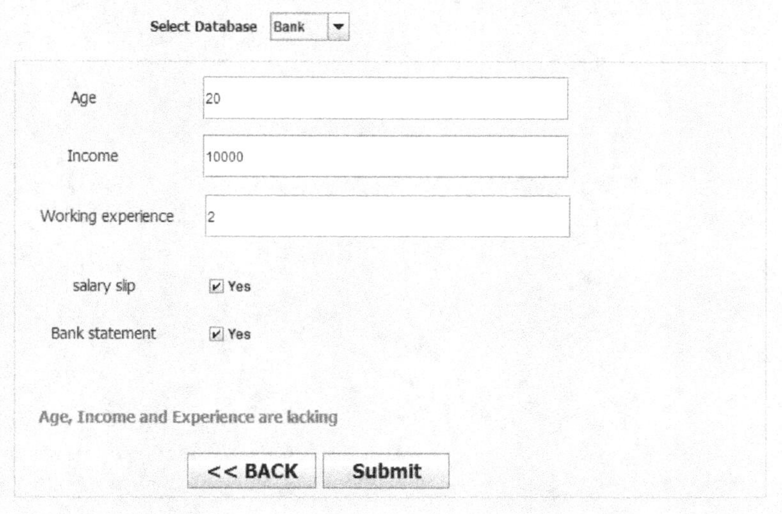

Figure 5.49: (c) Visual Slides of Back Propagation Algorithm

CHAPTER 6

Performance Evaluation

6.1. Introduction

It is argued by (Weideman ET AL., 1995) that several of the renowned algorithms often generate the classifiers for comparable quality. Though, it remains clear as what the assumptions are required for such comparisons. For example, the method or type of evaluation never gets mentioned orthe configurations for the inclusion of the algorithms as used and their effective determination. Along the application domains for the induction algorithms, with the goals that vary significantly. In the section, the goal getsidentified as how far this proposed algorithm gets capable of the generation of the reasonably better classifier along with the minimum tuning of the parameter. For different problems, it isimportant to choose the algorithm being capable of producing the classifier along with the best possible classification accuracy, with the varied possibility of drawbacksfor getting worse results.

A systematic presentation is featured between GA, AO and ABC algorithms along the proposed algorithm. 1 rationale staying behind the study is the investigation of the impact along the classifier performance for the algorithm choice as compared to that of the configuration for algorithms. Other than just finding those algorithmsfor generating the maximum accurate classifier along withsome data, it requires to be important in looking at the varied performance, or the sensitivity of the proposed. Though obviously it remains to be a complex issue and it is argued that no algorithm remains superior alongevery possible problem for induction (Schaffer, 1994). It is often argued that along the particular configuration of the algorithm remains good as others taken possible problems. For investigating this issue, the quantifiers of the performance along withseveral systematic ways in comparing the algorithm & algorithm configurations as needed.

The paper presents 2 quality attributes along the algorithm assessment; classification performance and sensitivity.

The study showedthe2 attributes as reflected withvaried aspects of the quality as related to the learning problems &the existing varied metrics of the possible candidate for the assessment of quality attributes.

Along the next section, it is described that quality attributes along with the metrics are used for their access.

The concerned experiment procedure & the results get presented & this gets followed with the discussion being quality attributes as how they are used related toalgorithm selection along the systematic way. The final sections featured the related work along with the pointers and conclusions for future work.

It is argued by (Weideman et al., 1995) that several of those well-known algorithms get generated along the classifiers of the comparable quality. Though, it is never always made effectively clear as what the assumptions required to be made in the concerned comparisons. For instance, the type or method of the concerned evaluation, being mentioned along with the varied configurations, under the inclusions of the algorithms used is being determined. Along the application of domains for the induction algorithms, the goals often vary significantly. In the concerned section, the goal gets the identification as for how far the proposed algorithm remains capable in generating the reasonably good classifier along with the minimum tuning of the parameter. For varied problems, it gets more important in choosing the algorithm is capable of the production of the classifier along with the enhanced classification of the accuracy possible, along with the concerned possible drawback for getting the worse results.

It is presentedunder the systematic comparison between GA, ACO & ABC algorithms along that of the proposed algorithm. Being, 1 rationale behind the study in investigating the impact for the classifier performance, the choice of the algorithm gets compared to the concerned configurationfor algorithms. Other than just finding the concerned algorithm which generates the accurate classifier along some data, it gets important to have a look towards the variety of performance, or the sensitivity for the proposed algorithm. Primarily, the complex issue faced the argument; theoretically, none of the algorithms gets superior along the possible problems of induction (Schaffer, 1994).

It is often argued as any of the particular configurations for an algorithm remainsgood as compared tothe other along varied possible problems. For the investigation ofthe issue, for quantifiers of the performance withseveral systematic ways as compared algorithm & the algorithm configurations as per needed. The concerned paper gets the presentation for2 varied quality attributes along the sensitivity, algorithm assessment; & the classification performance. The study usually showedthe following2 attributes reflecting the different aspects of quality as related to the learning problems & there existing metrics of thevaried possible candidates for the assessment of the quality of the attributes.

Along the next concerned section, it is described that the quality attributes along with the metrics for the usage in the assessment.

Hence, the procedure of experiment with the results as presented along with the discussion as followed about having the quality attributes & how they get the usage for the algorithm selection under the systematic way. The final sections featuredthe related work along with the pointers and conclusions for future work.

6.2.   Algorithm Outline

The recent algorithm has an abstract view (Figure 1.1). Being at the1st step, the model searches the local solutions as optimized under the specific points of the target. The local solution being best remains to be the optimal solution as the firm thoroughly targets best i % of customers as based alongthe estimated probability for responding towards the solicitation letter. ABO component along our algorithm has the usage in finding the local solution. While every localsolution is discovered, the combination is doneinto the final model. Every local solution remains to be the model of the neural network as built with the usage of the featured subset specifics towards the target point. The estimation along the performance for the local solution bestgets optimized along the target point $i.$ being, ABO having the return of the highest of the hit rate for all the concerned target points as compared to varied algorithms.

6.3.   Structure of ABO Model

The concerned structure for ABO works in finding the local solutions asgiven in Figure 5.28 (Refer in Section 5.4.4).

First, ABO effectively searches the concerned exponential space for featuring the subsets & learning the concerned patterns. The ABO once learned the effective data patterns, & returning2 evaluation metrics, being $F_{accuracy}$& $F_{Complexity}$. The 2 evaluation metrics gets the combinationalong the equal weight under1 fitness value. As based along the fitness value, the ABO biases the search direction in maximizing the combination of the objectives.

Among varied models, the best model gets selected along the terms of the fitness value by the comparedmethods of traditional evaluation.

The model is used in rankingthose potential customers while descending, as ordered by the concerned probability for eligibility, that finally gets selected along the top i% of those prospects under the evaluation sets& the evaluation of the accuracy of the model.

6.4.   Application

The ABO methodology as proposed gets applied along the prediction for the bank customers under predicting customers having high value.

For the benchmark, the concerned procedure gets compared with the proposed algorithm along3varied traditional algorithms like GA, ACO and ABC and additionally, it is compared along the results having the manual process of decision making. Resultant showed the data set having the evaluation of the performance along ROC curve. Hence, the newly proposed algorithm gets the implementation. The application gets produced along the implementation for algorithms & the results showingthe database & the analysis of ROC & among the comparative study of the algorithms taking the place & the Intelligence concept under the implementation forecasting the concerned customer performance along the Back Propagation of algorithm.

6.5. Data Description

The optimization gets done with 2 different sets of data. The concerned objective of the datasets remains ensuredwith the proposed algorithms having the capability with the classification of the sets of data as given under varied features. Every business is completely related to data irrespective of the field and the intelligence is the necessary and important steps to adhere the same. The first data sets related to that of the customers, being the data as obtained from DST or Direct Sales Team, where the concerned team gets related to that of the CRM or customer relationship management. The recent study sampled around 1000 randomly selected of the customers. 2nd, cancer sets ofdata got obtained from http://www.broadinstitute.org/cancer/software/genepattern/datasets/& the performance of concerned proposed technique during the clustering ground as per their symptoms gets based on 1000 randomly selected sets of data. In segmenting, the customer data, DST as provided along 1000 pieces of the historical customer data under, Table 1.1 has, thelist of the customer distribution.

The customer dataset has the considered attributes: AGE, VINTAGE, SALARY, CIBIL, EXPERIENCE, DESIGNATION, AQB& CREDIT CARD.

However, the sets of cancer, the variables get chosen to be the symptoms that include AGE, FEVER, VOMITING, PAIN& SWELLING.

The data including cancer information gets the usage in calibrating the model & the estimationfor the hit rate as expected along the concerned evaluation set. Of the XXX patients along the data sets of cancer, XXX had concerned cancer, as resultedalong the hit rate being XXX/1000=X.X%. From the perspective of the manager, this remains to be hit rate whichgets obtained during the solicitation as gets send randomly towards the consumers along the concerned firm's database.

Table 6.1: Description of the Dataset Used for Experiments

Feature ID	Feature Description
1	Account No as presented
2	Name of the person
3	Salary in actual (rupees)
4	Vintage
5	Cibil (categorical variable) Y/N
6	Designation (categorical variable)
7	Experience
8	AQB
9	Credit card (categorical variables)

Further, Table 6.1 shows the description of the dataset used for experiments

Table 6.2: Bank Customer Details

DST	N	Mean±SD	Max-Min
Age	1000	31.44±8.78	56-18
Salary	1000	32692.60±42648.02	230080-5050
Vintage	1000	11.99±2.18	31-5
Experience	1000	1.13±0.57	4-1
AQB	1000	2585.00±2410.52	17000-2000
		N	%
Cibil	Yes	63	6.3
	No	937	93.7
	Total	1000	100.0
Designation	1	946	94.6
	2	18	1.8
	4	36	3.6
	Total	1000	100.0
Credit card	Yes	63	6.3
	No	937	93.7
	Total	1000	100.0

Table 6.3: Cancer Details

Cancer class		N	%
Vomiting	Low	312	31.2
	Medium	312	31.2
	High	376	37.6
	Total	1000	100.0
Fever	Low	376	37.6
	Medium	250	25.0
	High	374	37.4
	Total	1000	100.0
Pain	Low	313	31.3
	Medium	312	31.2
	High	375	37.5
	Total	1000	100.0
Swelling	Yes	600	60.0
	No	400	40.0
	Total	1000	100.0
	N	Mean±SD	Max-Min
Age	1000	30.58±7.76	56-18

6.6. Experimental Results

6.6.1. Sensitivity Analysis

In the concerned section, we usually focus along the decision which supports the functionality of the ABO algorithm. Particularly, we usually show how the ABO solution gets the usagein selecting the target point being best where expected profit gets maximized. We usually consider two varied strategies for 1 case targeting the customers beingunder the age group of 25-40 years, having income ranging between 25001-40,000 &AQB ranging from 10001-25,000. Hence, we usually made 3 common assumptions for orderingthe run of the analysis &the identification of the optimal customers under the concerned lists of 1 million prospects for the target. We usually showed our experimental results along the Figure.

The ROC or receiver operating characteristics curvethat gets calculated along the area given under ROC curve remains to be the best model for performance in the study. The ROC curves became the standard tool for the assessmentof the accuracy for the model of predictions along the field of the medical diagnosis & becoming used increasingly along the financial environment and machine learning. The concerned TP rate gets plotted along the Y-axis while the FP rate gets plotted along the X-axis.

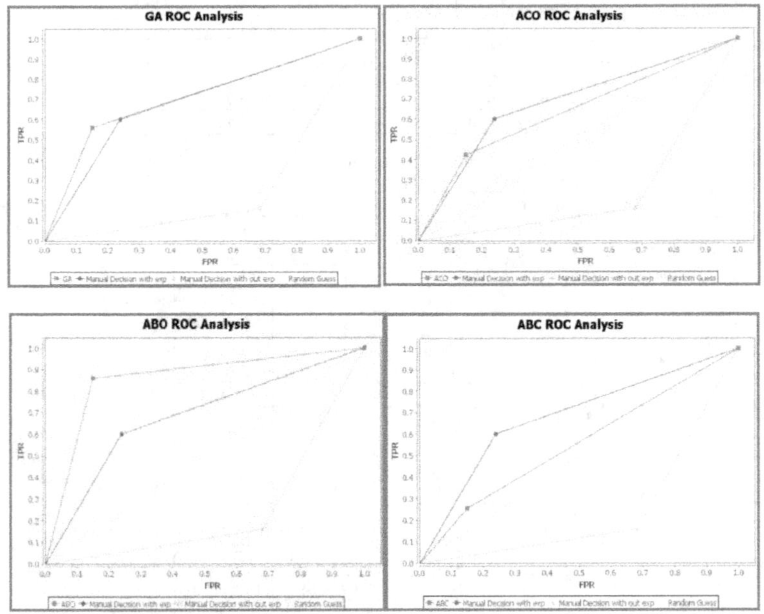

Figure 6.1: GA, ACO, ABC& ABO – ROC Analysis

From the higher sets of the customer, we require theidentification of the optimal customer.

As based along the experiments having the performance, being found for the concerned data set, the accuracy remains better than the manual process of decision with the experiments, following the random guess (Figure A). Other than this, the false rate of predictiveremains greater than around 70%. Additionally, the manual process of decision leaving the experiment showed a higher false rate of predictive. Along the case for ABC, the trend gets similar to the ABO (Figure X). Along the case of the GA, the accuracy of the process of manual decision along with GA performs similar as compared to the ACO (Figure53), as the manual decision performs better accuracy. The concerned GA showed a lower rate of true predictive compared to the higher rate of false predictive.

The proposed algorithm gets compared to the manual process of decision making, which shows the ABO performing better than being greater than in 85% of accuracy as compared to the manual process of decision making where the experiment is 65%. Though, manual process of decision differed from experiment & random guess usually had a lower prediction.

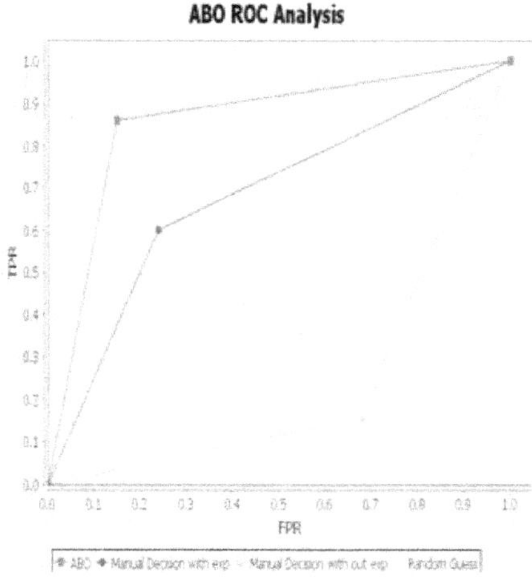

Figure 6.2: Meta-heuristic Algorithms (GA, ACO, ABC) with Proposed Algorithm (ABO) Comparison of ABO ROC Analysis with Manual Decision Making

Along the statistical and empirical tests, it is focused on the effective comparison between our proposed and traditional algorithms. The comparison of varied versions of algorithms like GA, ABC & ACO and the decision making being manual &the predictive capability as presented below.

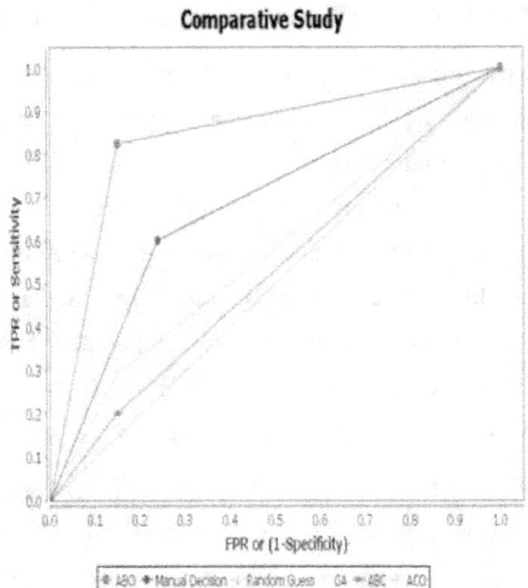

Figure 6.3: Comparative Study

Table 6.4: Comparative Study of ABO with Manual Decision Making

Analysis of variables/techniques	Manual decision making with experience	A manual decision without experience	Artificial bear algorithm
True positive	300	80	430
True negative	380	160	424
False positive	120	340	76
False Negative	200	420	70
True positive rate	0.6	0.16	0.86
False positive	0.24	0.68	0.15
Positive predicted value	0.71	0.19	0.85
AZ value	0.68	0.24	0.85

The above findings as shown along the comparison for the decision making being manual with & without the experience, the rate of true positive (0.86) being higher with the lower false positive being (0.15). Additionally, it is recorded the higher accuracy being 85%. This finally leads to a conclusion, where it result in the accuracy being more when closer to ABO.

Table 6.5: Comparison of ABO with GA, ACO, ABC

Analysis variables/Techniques	GA	ACO	ABC	ABO
True Positive	233	241	237	374
True Negative	256	264	272	424
False positive	237	240	225	75
False Negative	274	255	266	127
True positive rate	0.47	0.48	0.47	0.74
False positive rate	0.18	0.47	0.45	0.15
Positive predicted value	0.49	0.5	0.51	0.83
AZ value	0.48	0.5	0.5	0.79

For the comparison of the traditional algorithms along the accuracy of the classification being 0.79 for the ABO, this was poor in the case of GA, ACO and ABC. This gets implied with the proposed algorithm being better than those of previous algorithms.

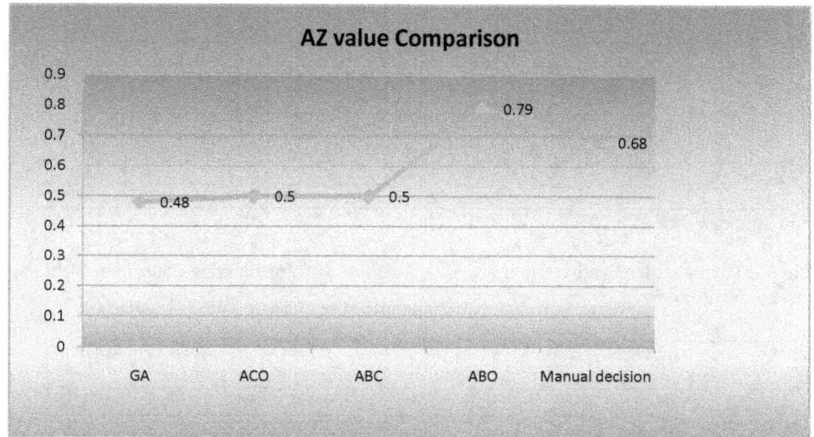

Figure 6.4: AZ Value Comparison Across the Algorithms

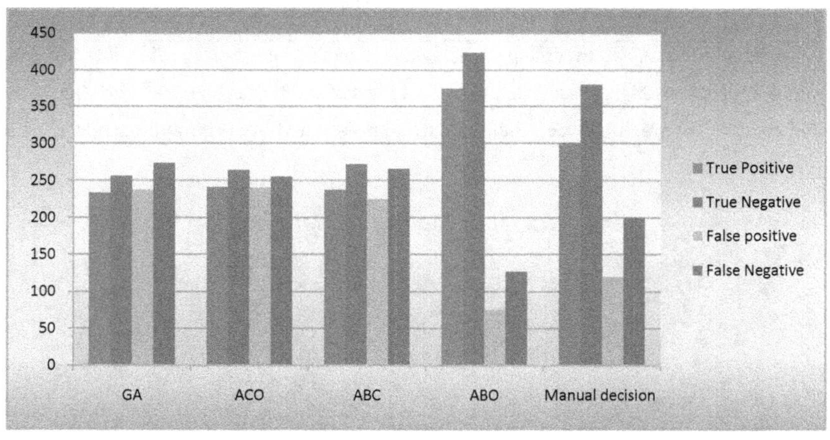

Figure 6.5: Comparison of the Algorithms with ROC Attributes

As based along the above-given analysis, it is said ABO being a competitive classifier, under the comparison of traditional algorithms which precisely gets the prediction of optimized customers. The Statistical Significance along the experiments provides the resultof the significant findings under ABO having higher true positivity as compared to other algorithms.

Table 6.6: Relationship between Grouping and Type

Grouping	Type				Total
	True positive	True negative	False positive	False negative	
GA	233	256	237	274	1000
	21.5%	21.1%	30.5%	29.7%	25.0%
ACO	241	264	240	255	1000
	22.2%	21.7%	30.9%	27.7%	25.0%
ABC	237	272	225	266	1000
	21.8%	22.4%	29.0%	28.9%	25.0%
ABO	374	424	75	127	1000
	34.5%	34.9%	9.7%	13.8%	25.0%
Total	1085	1216	777	922	4000
	100.0%	100.0%	100.0%	100.0%	100.0%

Chi-square value-276.606, p-value-0.00<0.01;

Table 6.7: Performance Evaluation of GA, ACO, ABC and ABO for Banking Customer Profile and
Cancer

Dataset	Analysis variables/Techniques	GA	ACO	ABC	ABO
Banking Customer profile	Precision	0.49574	0.50104	0.51299	0.83296
	Recall	0.48302	0.50867	0.50558	0.76951
	F-measure	0.4893	0.50483	0.50925	0.79998
Cancer	Precision	0.43333	0.55252	0.43154	0.87611
	Recall	0.54082	0.54962	0.70449	0.82299
	F-measure	0.48115	0.55107	0.53523	0.84872

As per table, it is shown that the precision value of banking customer profile obtained from the ABO approach is higher than the precision values of clusters in the prior technique. The Recall comparison graph between the proposed approach and the prior approach is given in Figure 57.

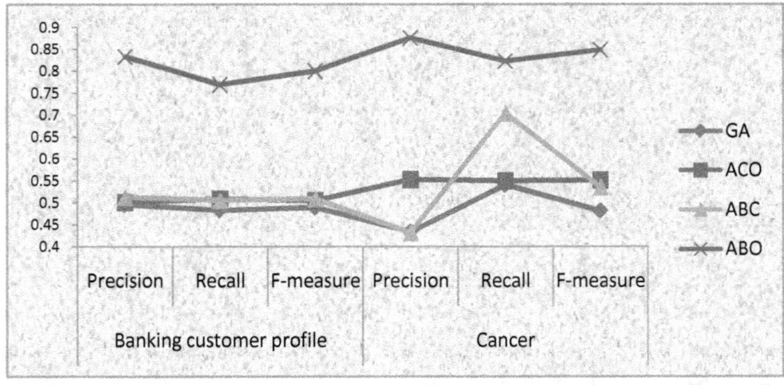

Figure 6.6: Performance Evaluation of GA, ACO, ABC and ABO for Banking Customer Profile and
Cancer

Table 6.8: Comparison of Statistical Metrics for Banking Customer Profile

Analysis variables/Techniques	Precision	Recall	F-measure
GA	0.495745	0.483019	0.489299
ACO	0.50104	0.508671	0.504826
ABC	0.512987	0.505576	0.509255
ABO	0.832962	0.76951	0.79998
Mean (μ)	0.585683	0.566694	0.57584
SD (σ	0.16501	0.135693	0.149671
Minimum	0.5	0.5	0.5
Maximum	0.8	0.8	0.8

Table 6.9: Comparison of Statistical Metrics for Cancer

Analysis variables/Techniques	Precision	Recall	F-measure
GA	0.433333	0.540816	0.481145
ACO	0.552521	0.549618	0.551066
ABC	0.431542	0.704492	0.535227
ABO	0.876106	0.822993	0.848719
Mean (μ)	0.573376	0.65448	0.604039
SD (σ	0.20961	0.13517	0.165844
Minimum	0.4	0.5	0.5
Maximum	0.9	0.8	0.8

The analytical results showed that the ABO algorithm showed excellent discriminatory power and had higher precision, recall and f-measure values of 0.83, 0.76 and 0.79% respectively and this algorithm works better than the manual decision-making method. The decision making the performance of the proposed technique was visualized by implementing it in MATLAB. Experimental results on real-life datasets proved that the decision-making tool using Genetic Algorithm is not effective than manual decision making.

CHAPTER 7

Summary

The main purpose of the research is to find out how much is the algorithm proposed is capable of providing a best classifier with low tuning of the parameter. It is very important to select an algorithm that can produce the best classifier with better accuracy level with the help of better parameters. It must also have the possible disadvantages of experiencing poor results when the care is taken is much lower. In this backdrop, the current study features a new algorithm with the help of the attributed of bear technique. It also makes a systematic comparison with BBO proposal using ABC, AO, and GA algorithms.

The study was held in various stages and according to our sources; this is a unique study as many studies were conducted to create an algorithm to maximize the database of the customer specified in the bank applications.

Even today, most of the banks make use of Excel or other applications of lower end level to find out about the best customer. This study would throw light upon the issue where the proposed algorithm would be utilized as an application for those bankers to make use of decision making on day to day basis.

First, the researchers involved in the study created an algorithm that took in to account the limitations of those ANN or genetic models of the current scenario. Also, the proposed model was developed with a sense of smell of the bear. (The algorithm is not depicted but the framework is shown in the Introduction chapter - Section 1). The information from the banks wasacquired at a random pace to make the proposed algorithm. The five stages were applied to optimize customer such as:

1. The first stage: preparation of database and Normalization of the data.
2. The second stage: Applying the Metaheuristics algorithms that are existing separately.
3. The third stage: Application of the proposed new algorithms.
4. The fourth stage: Compare and analyze with the Metaheuristics algorithms that are existing with the latest algorithm.
5. The fifth stage: Implementation of the intelligence concept using Backpropagation algorithm.

With the existing dataset, the evaluation was made to make a comparison of the new Meta heuristics algorithms that are existing such as GA, ACO and ABA. However, no studies were performed using various methodologies to a single network.

There are 2 different strategies involved in the study such as one that targets participants of age 25-40 years, have an income of 25001-40,000 and AQB 10001-25,000. Thus, 3 major assumptions were made to perform the analysis and to find the best ones from the millions.

With the experiments as the base, it is found out that the accuracy of the data is 85%which shows is better than the manual decisions. The false rate of prediction is 70% or more. In ABC case, it was identical to the ABO trend. The manual decision according to GA was similar to ACO which showed manual decision had better accuracy. GA showed low true value in prediction and higher rate in the false prediction rate. In a nutshell, the study findings showed that 0.86 was the true positive rate while 0.15 low false positive rate. This shows ABO is more accurate.

When the proposed algorithm is compared with the decision-making process performed manually, it depicted that ABO was better in performance as it had 85% accuracy while comparing with the manual process of 65%. When compared with the ancient algorithm, ABO had 0.79 which was very poor for ABC, GA, and ACO. This depicts ABO as a competitive option when compared to the old proposed algorithm methods as it shows the optimized customers. The significant findings of the study were derived by the statistical significance which showed that ABO had a high true positive rate.

The finding also made a classification about the error based on the performance of finding the best customer with the given data. The mean error of percentage for ABO classification was much below the backpropagation level at 1% for all issues. In addition, the percentage of error for mean classification is much lower than the mean propagation level of 1%. This also indicates that the solution variation is very small for ABO. The base for ranking of classification error percentage was derived by the squared error percentage to sever all between the problem's solutions.

Table 2 shows that ABO offered the best 3 solutions for all the issues. ABO also offered the best answer to all problems and study reveals that ABO had the best 10 solutions, 9 of best 10 and 8 of best 10 respectively.

Therefore, in this book, optimization techniques with varied algorithms like ACO GA and ABC were used to obtain the best results for the customers. Artificial Bear Optimization (ABO) derived the results of using proposed algorithms over traditional ones while the ROC curve offered AZ value to denote the performance. At the current business scenario, CRM driven MIS is essential to cater to the latest needs. The paper has a presentation of an evolving framework that focuses on an MIS that utilizes data mining and knowledge classification.

Data mining offers technology to make an analysis of huge data volume and to reveal hidden data issues to secure valuable information. The paper focuses on Customer Relation Management which is related to data mining using Backpropagation technique.

To maintain discipline about strategic financial model, implementation of meta-heuristic algorithm and forecasting strategies were done. The experiments of the results show that the manual decision making's view and the meta-heuristic algorithm and ABO algorithm proposal. To make a performance forecast, the attributes were analyzed using Back Propagation algorithm along with weight strategy. The GA approach's AZ value offers 0.48, ACO approach offers 0.50, ABC approach offers 0.50, the method of Manual decision making offers 0.68 and the proposed ABO approach offers 0.79. It was revealed that the performance of the proposed ABO algorithm was best than the rest of the traditional ones. The research work has made a contribution to algorithm learning theory. This offers enhanced speed in learning, better behavior and a good amount of training. The limitations of these algorithms are that the new schemes have no guarantee of global minima. However much more studyhas to perform in future on Bear Algorithm to determine its performance.

APPENDIX 1

Definitions of BI

1. As per Okkonen et al (2002), it is defined as the process of business information gathering and analyzing from internal and external sources.

2. BI is architecture, neither a product nor a system, which provided the access to business data to the business community in an easy way through a collection of integrated operations as well as databases and decision-support applications. (Moss & Atre, 2003)

3. A general term provided for the tools, platforms, applications, and technologies, which support the exploration of business data, trends and data relationship is Business Intelligence which paves the businessman or women to know more information with accuracy in a timely manner to make the real-time business decisions(Raisinghani, 2004).

4. English, in the year 2005 stated that most of the BI definitions defined only about the software or technology components in an organization leaving the core component that is a better understanding of organizational happening, the environment in order to take appropriate action to achieve the organizational goals.

5. As per Lonnqvist & Pirttimaki (2006, p.32), Business intelligence is a systematically organized process through which the information is acquired, analyzed and disseminated by the organizations from the intricate and extricate source, which is important for business activities and makes a decision.

6. Decisions and actions taken in a key business process through a set of business information and business analysis are Business Intelligence. To be specific, BI meant to be leveraging information assets inside the prominent business processes to accomplish business performance improvement (Williams & Williams, 2007).

7. Wells (2008) defined Business Intelligence as an organization's ability for planning, precise and futuristic thinking, problem-solving, comprehend, efficient and effective actions which in turn help the organization to achieve its goals, rather than data, processes, and technologies such as tools and applications.

Data Mining

The systems could find meaningful relationships, which might be taking years in order to find the conventional techniques. Data mining is the interdisciplinary field, which uses the methods of different areas of research in order to extract the high knowledge of the practical datasets. It is an essential part: discovering knowledge from the databases that include several methods of preprocessing in order to prepare data for mining of data as well as methods for post-processing for refining & improving the information that has been discovered. The Three characteristics of data mining have been mentioned as follows:

- Discovering comprehensible knowledge;
- Integrating with the databases;
- High degrees of autonomy that are needed for extracting knowledge that was previously unknown;

APPENDIX 2

The Advantages of Modeling

The advantages of utilizing modeling are: (Turban et al., 2001; Mallach 1994)

- The expenditure of modeling is lesser than the expenses incurred to carry out experiments with a real system.
- Models permit for years of working to be replicated in seconds on a computer.
- Operating the model is effortless as compared to operating the actual scheme: Experiments are done effortlessly and the daily routine on the enterprise is not disturbed.
- The loss of committing mistakes at the time of a trial-and-error test is comparatively less while utilizing models than utilizing the actual scheme.
- Models permit the estimation of risks, in particular activities: Experiments can be carried out in fields that incorporate substantial ambiguity.
- Numerical modeling permits the assessment of outcomes providing an extensive amount of options.
- Modeling improves as well as strengthens learning and backs training.

It is simpler to retrieve as well as operate a prototype while looking for options rather than apply the options, in reality: Numerous decision alternatives could be examined through computerized models.

Outline of the basic Genetic Algorithm

1. **[Start]** produce arbitrary populace of n chromosomes (appropriate answers to the problem/difficulty)
2. **[Fitness]** assess the fitness $f(x)$ of every chromosome x inside the populace

3. **[New population]** make a fresh populace by replicating subsequent steps until the fresh populace is complete

   e. **[Selection]** Select a couple of parent chromosomes from a populace in accordance with their vigor (the better vigor, the bigger possibility of being picked)

   f. **[Crossover]** With a crossover likelihood cross over parents to form a fresh offspring (or children). In the event of no crossover being performed, offspring are a precise copy of the parents.

   g. **[Mutation]** With a mutation odd mutate fresh offspring at every locus (place in the chromosome).

   h. **[Accepting]** Place fresh offspring in a fresh population

4. **[Replace]** make use of the freshly generated populace for an additional run of the algorithm

5. **[Test]** On the end condition being satisfied, **stop**, & return the most excellent solution in the present population

6. **[Loop]** stop at step **2**

Every iteration of this procedure is referred to as a *generation*. A GA's naturally iterated for wherever from 50 - 500 or additional generations. The complete set of generations is referred to as a *run*. At the conclusion of a run, there're frequently one / more extremely fit chromosomes inside the populace. Since chance does play a large part in every run, a couple of runs with diverse random–number seeds are generally going to produce diverse detailed behaviors. The GA researchers repeatedly report information (like the most excellent fitness come across in a run & the age group at which the person having that most excellent fitness happened to be determined) averaged over a lot of different runs of GA on the identical problem/difficulty.

Pros & Cons of Genetic Algorithms

At the conclusion of the discussion on genetic algorithm developments, we'll list a number of the attractive pros & also some cons of genetic algorithms:

Pros

- It is able to solve all optimization problems/difficulties that are able to be explained with chromosome encoding.
- It does solve problems/difficulties with manifold solutions.

- Because the genetic algorithm carrying out method technique isn't dependent on error surface, we're able to solve the multi-dimensional, non-continuous, non-differential, & even non-parametrical difficulties/problems.

- The structural genetic algorithm provides us with the possibility to resolve the solution structure & solution parameter difficulties/problems concurrently with a genetic algorithm.

- A genetic algorithm is a technique that's very simple to comprehend & it practically doesn't demand knowledge of mathematics.

- Hereditary/Genetic algorithms are transferred with no difficulty to existing simulations & models.

Cons

- Definite optimization difficulties/problems (they're called variant difficulties /problems) are not solvable with genetic algorithms. This occurs because of poorly understood fitness functions that produce bad chromosome blocks despite the fact that just the first-rate chromosome blocks cross-over.

- There's no complete guarantee that a genetic algorithm would be finding a global optimum. It does happen very frequently when populaces have many subjects.

- Like additional artificial intelligence methods, the genetic algorithm is unable to guarantee continuous optimization response times. Moreover, the difference between the shortest & longest optimization response time's a lot larger than by means of conventional gradient techniques. This unlucky genetic algorithm property does limit the genetic algorithms' employment in real-time applications.

- The genetic algorithm applications in controls that are performed in real-time are restricted owing to random solutions & convergence, basically, this implies that the whole populace's improving, but this isn't able to be said for a person inside this population. Thus, it's unreasonable to employ genetic/hereditary algorithms for on-line controls in the real systems while not first testing them on simulation models.

- The fitness of every one of the models might be similar and thus convergence is slow.

GA - Demerits

- GAs performs most excellent at the time that solution vectors happen to be binary.

- On the difficulty/problem having in excess of a single variable, a multi-variable codings put up by concatenating as a lot of single variables coding as the figure of variables in the difficulty/problem.

- All real life problems/difficulties are active & as a result, their behaviors are a great deal complex, Genetic programming does suffer from grave weakness.

- GAs performs most excellent at the time that solution vectors happen to be binary. It solves difficulties/problems with manifold solutions.

- The populace considered for the fruition ought to be a moderate / appropriate one for the difficulty/problem (normally 20 to 30 / 50 to100)

- There's no complete pledge that a genetic/hereditary algorithm would be finding a global optimum. It does happen very frequently when populaces have many subjects.

- Like additional artificial intelligence methods, the genetic algorithm is unable to guarantee steady optimization response times.

- On the difficulty/problem having more than a single variable, a multi-variable coding's put up by concatenating as a lot of single variables coding as the figure of variables in the difficulty/problem.

- All real-life difficulties/problems are active & so their behaviors are a great deal compound, Genetic programming does suffer from grave weakness.

ABC – Algorithm

- Preliminary food reserves are produced for every employed bee
- REPEAT
  - Every employed bee visits a food reserve in her remembrance & finds out a neighbouringreserve after that evaluates its nectar quantity & dances inside the hive.
  - Every onlooker/bystander witnesses the dance of employed/working bees & selects one of their reserves based on dances and subsequently visits that reserve. Having chosen a neighbor in that region, she assesses its nectar quantity.
  - Deserted food reserves are found out and substituted with the fresh food reserves found out by the scouts.
  - The most excellent food reserve found up to now is registered.
  - UNTIL (needs are met)

The Detailed Pseudo Code of the ABC Algorithm

1. Initialize the population of solutions $x_{i,j}$
2. Evaluate the population
3. Cycle= 1
4. Repeat

5. Produce new solutions (food source positions) $v_{i,j}$ in the neighborhood of $x_{i,j}$ for the employed bees using the formula $v_{i,j=x_{i,j}+\Phi_{i,j}(x_{i,j}-x_{k,j})}$ (K is a solution in the neighborhood of I, Φ is a random number in the range [-1,1] and evaluate them

6. Apply the greedy selection process between x_i and v_i

7. Calculate the probability values P_i for the solution x_i by means of their fitness values using the below equation

$$P_i = \frac{fit_i}{\sum_{n=1}^{SN} fit_n}$$

In order to calculate the fitness values of the solution we employed the following equation

$$fit_i = \left(\begin{array}{l} \frac{1}{1+f_i} \ if \ f_i \geq 0 \\ 1 + abs \ (f_i) \ if \ f_i < 0 \end{array} \right)$$

Normalize P_i values into [0, 1]

- Produce new solutions (new positions) v_i for the onlookers from the solution x_i, selected depending on P_i, and evaluate them

- Apply the greedy selection process for the onlookers between x_i and v_i

- Determine the abandoned solution (source), if exist, and replace it with a new randomly produced solution x_i for the scout using the below equation

$$x_{i,j} = min_j + rand(0,1) * (max_j - min_j)$$

8. Memorize the best food source position (solution) achieved so far

9. cycle = cycle + 1

    Until cycle= Maximum Cycle Number (MCN)

Implementation

1.   Initialization phase:

Consider the optimization problem as follows:

$$f(x) = \sqrt{|x_1^2 - x_2^2|}, \quad 0 < x_1, x_2 > 255$$

The fitness function is defined as below:

$$fit_i = \left(\begin{array}{l} \frac{1}{1+f_i} \ if \ f_i \geq 0 \\ 1 + abs \ (f_i) if \ f_i < 0 \end{array} \right)$$

Calculate the probability values ρ for the solution x by means of their fitness values by using the below formula:

$$P_i = \frac{fit_i}{\sum_{n=1}^{SN} fit_n}$$

Step 2: Move the onlookers: Calculate the probability of selecting a food source by the equation

$$P_i = \frac{fit_i}{\sum_{n=1}^{SN} fit_n}$$

Select a food source to move by roulette wheel selection for every onlooker bees and then determine then nectar amounts of them. The movement of the onlooker follows the equation $v_{ij} = x_{ij} + \phi_{ij}(x_{ij} - x_{kj})$ where fit_i is the fitness value of the solution i which is proportional to the nectar amount of the food source in the position i, SN is the number of food source which is equal to the number of employed bees (BN), $k \in \{1,2,3,..,SN\}$ and $j \in \{1,2,...,D\}$ are randomly chosen indexes. Although k is determined randomly, it has to be different from i. $\varphi_{i,j}$ is a random number between [-1,1]. It control the production of neighbor food sources around $x_{i,j}$ and represents the comparison of two food positions visually by a bee..

Step 3: Move the Scouts: If the fitness values of the employed bees do not be improved by a continuous predetermined number of iteration, which is called "*limit*", those food sources are abandoned, and these employed bees become the scouts. The scouts are moved by the equation

$$x_i^j = x_{min}^j + rand(0,1)(x_{max}^j - x_{min}^j)$$

Step 4. Bring up to date the most excellent Food reserve Found until now: commit to memory the most excellent fitness worth & the places, which are located by bees.

Step 5. Termination scrutiny: verify if the quantity of the iterations does satisfy the termination condition. On the termination condition being satisfied, end the program & output the end results, or else return to Step 2.

Karaboga (2005) does analyze the foraging deeds of honey bee horde and recommends a fresh algorithm simulating these deeds for being able to solve multi-dimensional & multi-modal optimization difficulties/problems, known as Artificial Bee Colony (or ABC). The most important steps of an algorithm are: 1) forward the employed/working bees onto food reserves and find out their nectar quantities; 2) work out the probability worth of the reserves with which they're liked better by the onlooker/bystander bees; 3) discontinue the utilization procedure of the reserves deserted by bees; 4) dispatch the scouts into the search region for discovering fresh food reserves, arbitrarily; 5) commit to memory the most excellent food reserve found thus far.

In the algorithm, a non-natural bee colony includes 3 classes of bees: employed/working bees, onlookers/bystanders & scouts. Employed bees are connected to a particular food reserve which they're currently utilizing.

They bear the information regarding this particular reserve and split this info with a certain odds by waggle dance. Unemployed bees look for a food reserve to exploit. There're 3 kinds of unemployed bees: scouts & onlookers/bystanders. Scouts explore the environment for fresh food reserves with no guidance. Seldom, the scouts are able to accidentally find out rich, wholly unfamiliar food reserves.

Then again, onlookers/bystanders view the waggle dance & thus are placed on the food reserves by making use of a probability founded selection procedure. With the nectar quantity of a food reserve increasing, the probability worth with which the food reserve is favored by onlookers/bystanders increases, also. In ABC algorithm the 1st half of the settlement includes the employed bees & the 2nd half consists of the onlookers/bystanders. For each food reserve, there's just a single employed bee. One more issue that's considered in the algorithm's that the employed/working bee whose food reserve has been drained by the bees turns into a scout. Basically, on a solution signified a food reserve not being better by a fixed figure of trials the food reserve is deserted by its employed/working bee & the employed bee's transformed into a scout. The algorithm's tested on 3 renowned test functions. From simulation end results, it's wrapped up that the projected algorithm is able to be employed for being able to solve uni-modal & multi-model arithmetical optimization.

Table A 2.1: Optimization Performance

Method	Human Readability	Automatic selection of Variables	Automatic Integration of data types	Non – Unear Relation
Statistical Analysis	Yes	Limited	No	Limited
Cluster analysis	Yes	No	No	No
Support Vector Machine	No	No	No	Yes
Neural Networks	No	No	No	Yes
Genetic Programming	Yes	Yes	Yes	Yes

Advantages

- It can help to solve each issue of optimization that can be explained using chromosome ends.
- It solves issues using multiple outcomes.

- The execution technique of genetic algorithm is not dependant on errors as we can solve issues that are non-parametrical, non- continuous, multi-dimensional and non-differential.

- The structure of the genetic algorithm offers the possibility to arrive at the solution to overcome the parameters of the problems with the help of a genetic algorithm.

- The method of the genetic algorithm is very simple to understand which indicates that there is no need to have any prior mathematics knowledge.

- The genetic algorithm can be transferred with great ease to simulations and models that exist at present.

Demerits in GA

- The performance of GAs turns best during the solution vectors gets binary.

- While the problem remains along more than 1 variable, the coding under multi-variable gets constructed with concatenating becoming several coding with single variables as the no of variables gets in the problem.

- Each problem in real life are dynamic, hence their behaviorsremain much complex, serious weakness is suffered by Genetic programming.

- The performance of GA gets best during the solution vectors gets binary. The problem gets multiple solutions.

- The population gets considered for evolution that should be suitable or moderate 1 for the concerned problem (generally 20-30 / 50-100)

- Some optimizations problems cannot be get solved by the means of algorithms for genetic. This happens due to the poorly known functions for fitness that generates blocks of bad chromosome though being the fact were only good blocks of chromosome cross-over.

- There remains no absolute assurance along the genetic algorithm finding the global optimum. This happens quite often during the populations sustains with several subjects.

- Similar to the techniques of artificial intelligence, the algorithms related to genetic cannot assure constant the response times of optimization. Even more, the difference in between the longest and the shortest response time of optimization remains much larger compared to the conventional methods of the gradient. This unfortunate algorithm of genetic property restrains the algorithms for genetic for the usage along the applications for real time.

- The application for genetic algorithm under the controls which has the performance in the real-time gets limited due to random convergence and solutions, other than this, it has the meaning of the entire population is improving, but it couldn't be said to an individual along the concerned population. Hence, it remains unreasonable to have the usage of genetic algorithms remaining on-line controls along real systems leaving the testing for the simulation model.

ANN Research

Research of the applications of the neural network will increase with significance in future based on the publication rates of the past and its increase of interest in a particular area.

1. The major portion of the articles that are reviewed related to the self-organizing map i.e., 21.88% that is 14 articles & 34.38% that is 22 articles have been related to the common algorithms of the neural network.

2. The Systems of the journal Expert with the applications that are related to the expert & intelligence systems in the industry, the government & the university across the world contains about 29 articles that contribute the 45.31% of the total of the selected 64 articles. The Rest journals published are more or less the same amount of the articles with a count of 1-3. Therefore, the trend of the research of ANN to the segmentation has been more obviously from the various articles that are published in kind of the journal that has been related to the development of the expert system.

3. The articles could be providing insights to the strategists of the organization on the practices of the neural network that have been used in terms of market segmentation. Of the 64 numbers of articles, the highest amount of journals that is 8 has been in the domain of the management/marketing & IT & computer sciences, respectively.

But the total number of articles that are published in the highest in terms of the later domains of information/expert system that is 60%. There are relatively fewer amounts of articles with meta-heuristic, data mining, ART2, fuzzy algorithms & Genetic Algorithm. Despite the articles that relate to the category of the l neural network applications to the market segmentation, it doesn't mean that the application of the artificial network of neural in such aspect is lesser matured than the others. The Applications of these algorithms in the other domains, like clustering & classification, might also apply in the segmentation if they have possession of the same purpose of the analyzing of the customers & market's distinctiveness.

4. For partitioning of a larger market into some smaller groups and the clusters of customers most commonly apply the clustering model that is k-means in the

segmentation. This doesn't surprise as the classification modeling that could be of use in order to find t the similarities of each segment in order to predict the effectiveness of the similar purchase behavior of the customers.

5. With respect for the findings of the research, we do suggest that more researches could be conducted in terms of the domain of market segmentation. For maximizing the profits of the organizers through the segmentation, the strategists would have to segment the market, therefore, increasing the ability of profit of the organisation.

The work of the review may have a few limitations. Firstly, the work did survey only the articles that were published between the years 2000 & 2010, which are obtained on the base of the query keyword query of the "market segmentation" & "artificial neural network". The Research papers couldn't be extracted, which mentions the applications of the techniques of the artificial neural network in the segmentation, without the index of any keyword. Secondly, the work is restricted to the search for the articles to about 7 repositories online. Presence of the other journals related to the academics might be able in order to provide a little more representation of articles that are related to applications of the artificial neural network in the segmentation. Lastly, non-English publications weren't studied. We do believe that the researches regarding applications of the techniques of the artificial neural network are also discussed & published in other languages.

Table A 2.2: Distribution of Articles by Journal Name, Title, ANN Tools Used, Author and Year of Publication

Year of Publication	Journal Name	Title	ANN Used	Tools Authors
2001	European Journal of Economic and Social Systems	Buying behavior study with a basket analysis: pre-clustering with a Kohonen map	SOM	Pierre Desmet
2001	European Journal of Marketing	Neural market structure analysis: Novel topology-sensitive methodology	VQ	Josef A. Mazanec
2001	Expert Systems with Applications	Mining association rules procedure to support online recommendation by customers and products fragmentation	SOM	S. Wesley Changchien and Tzu-Chuen Lu
2001	International Journal of Intelligent Systems	Knowledge discovery in a direct marketing case using least squares support vector machines	SVM	S. Viaene, B. Baesens, T. Van Gestel, J. A. K. Suykens, D. Van den Poel, J. Vanthienen, B. De Moor, G. Dedene
2001	Journal of International Consumer Marketing	Micro-Market Segmentation Using a Neural Network Model Approach	BPNN	Jafar Ali, C. P. Rao
2001	Neural Computing & Applications	Identification of Residential Property Sub-Markets using Evolutionary and Neural Computing Techniques	SOM	O.M. Lewis, J.A. Ware, and D.H. Jenkins

Table A2.2 (Continued)

Year of Publication	Journal Name	Title	ANN Used	Tools Authors
2002	Advanced Engineering Informatics,	A strategy for acquiring a customer requirement patterns using laddering technique and ART2 neural network	ART2	Chun-Hsien Chen, Li Pheng Khoo, Wei Yan
2002	Computer & Industrial Engineering	Cluster analysis in the industrial market segmentation through artificial neural network	SOM & K-means	R. J. Kuo, L. M. Ho, C. M. Hu
2002	Computers &Operations Research	Integration of self-organizing feature map and K-means algorithm for market segmentation	SOM	R. J. Kuo, L. M. Ho, C. M. Hu
2002	European Journal of Operational Research	Bayesian neural network learning for repeat purchase modelling in direct marketing	BNN	Bart Baesens, Stijn Viaene, Dirk Van den Poel, Jan Vanthienen, Guido Dedene
2002	Housing Studies	Capturing Housing Market Segmentation: An Alternative Approach based on Neural Network Modelling	NN	Tom Kauko, Pieter Hooimeijer, Jacco Hakfoort
2002	International Journal of Research in Marketing	Retail segmentation using artificial neural networks	Hopefiss	Derrick S. Boone, Michelle Roehm
2002	Journal of Interactive Marketing	Retail segmentation using artificial neural networks	NN	DS Boone, M Roehm
2002	Tourism Management	Determinants of guest loyalty to international tourist hotels—a neural network approach	ANN	Sheng-Hshiung Tsaura, Yi-Chang Chiu, and Chung-Huei Huang

Table A 2.2: (Continued)

Year of Publication	Journal Name	Title	ANN Used	Tools Authors
2003	Tourism Management	Segmenting the market of West Australian senior tourists using an artificial neural network	NN	Jaesoo Kim, Sherrie Weia and Hein Ruys
2004	Decision Support Systems	An intelligent system for customer targeting: a data mining approach	GA	Yong Seog Kim and W. Nick Street
2004	Expert Systems with Applications	An integrated data mining and behavioral scoring model for analyzing bank customers	SOM	Nan-Chen Hsieh
2004	Expert Systems with Applications	Segmentation of stock trading customers according to potential value	fuzzy k-means	H.W. Shin, S.Y. Sohn
2004	Expert Systems with Applications	A cross-national market segmentation of online game industry using SOM	SOM	Sang Chul Lee, Yung Ho Suh, Jae Kyeong Kim, Kyoung Jun Lee
2004	Expert Systems with Applications	Joint optimization of customer segmentation and marketing policy to maximize long-term profitability	MH	Jedid-Jah Jonker, Nanda Piersma and Dirk Van den Poel
2004	Expert Systems with Applications	A purchase-based market segmentation methodology	GA	C.-Y. Tsai, C.-C. Chiu
2004	International Journal of Industrial Ergonomics	Predicting automobile seat comfort using a neural network	ANN	M. Kolich

Year of Publication	Journal Name	Title	ANN Used	Tools Authors
2004	Journal of Business Research	Using an artificial neural network trained with a genetic algorithm to model brand share	GA	Kelly E. Fisha, John D. Johnson, Robert E. Dorsey and Jeffery G. Blodgett
2004	Journal of Organizational Computing and Electronic Commerce	Using an artificial neural network trained with a genetic algorithm to model brand share	SOM & GA	R. J. Kuo; K. Chang; S. Y. Chien
2004	Tourism Management	Tourist market segmentation with linear and non-linear techniques	SOM	Jonathan Z. Bloom
2005	Annals of Tourism Research	MARKET SEGMENTATION: A Neural Network Application	SOM	Jonathan Z. Bloom
2005	Computers & Operations Research	A neural network application to consumer classification to improve the timing of direct marketing activities	ANN	Frederick Kaefer, Carrie M. Heilman, and Samuel D. Ramenofsky
2005	Data analysis and decision support system	The Number of Clusters in Market Segmentation	SOM	Ralf Wagner, Sören W. Scholz and Reinhold Decker
2005	Expert Systems with Applications	The Number of Clusters in Market Segmentation	DM	Anita Prinzie, Dirk Van den Poel
2005	Management science	Customer Targeting: A Neural Network Approach Guided by Genetic Algorithms	GA	W. Nick Street, Filippo Menczer, Gary J. Russell

Table A 2.2: (Continued)

Year of Publication	Journal Name	Title	ANN Used	Tools Authors
2005	The International Review of Retail, Distribution and Consumer Research	Market Basket Analysis by Means of a Growing Neural Network	ANN	Prof. Dr Reinhold Decker
2006	Decision Support Systems	An extended self-organizing map network for market segmentation—a telecommunication example	SOM	Melody Y. Kiang, Michael Y. Hu, Dorothy M. Fisher
2006	Expert Systems with Applications	Integration of self-organizing feature maps neural network and genetic K-means algorithm for market segmentation	SOM	R.J. Kuo, Y.L. An, H.S. Wang, W.J. Chung
2006	Expert Systems with Applications	means algorithm for market segmentation	SOM	R.J. Kuo, Y.L. An, H.S. Wang and W.J. Chung
2007	Computational Statistics &Data Analysis	The effect of sample size on the extended self-organizing map network—A market segmentation application	SOM	Melody Y. Kianga, Michael Y. Hub, Dorothy M. Fisher
2007	Computers & Operations Research	Neural networks in business: techniques and applications for the operations researcher	NN	KA Smith, JND Gupta
2007	Expert Systems with Applications	Marketing segmentation using support vector clustering	SVM	Jih-Jeng Huang, Gwo-Hshiung Tzeng, Chorng-Shyong Ong

Table A 2.2: (Continued)

Year of Publication	Journal Name	Title	ANN Used	Tools Authors
2007	Journal of Engineering Design	Market segmentation for product family positioning based on fuzzy clustering	fuzzyclustering	Yiyang Zhang Jianxin (Roger) Jiao; Yongsheng Ma
2008	Decision Support Systems	Modeling consumer situational choice of long distance communication with neural	NN	Michael Y. Hu, Murali Shanker, G. Peter Zhang, Ming S. Hung
2008	Expert Systems with Applications	Market segmentation based on hierarchical self-organizing map for markets of multimedia on demand	SOM C	Chihli Hung, Chih-Fong Tsai
2008	Expert Systems with Applications	Market segmentation based on hierarchical self-organizing map for markets of multimedia on demand	GA & K-means	K Kim, H Ahn
2008	Expert Systems with Applications	Variable selection in clustering for marketing segmentation using genetic algorithms	GA	Hsiang-Hsi Liu, Chorng-Shyong Ong
2008	Expert Systems with Applications	The exploration of consumers' behavior in choosing hospital by the application of neural network	BPNN	Wan-I Lee, Bih-Yaw Shih, Yi-Shun Chung
2008	Expert Systems with Applications	Intelligent value-based customer segmentation method for campaign management: A case study of automobile retailer	GA	Chu Chai Henry Chan

Table A 2.2: (Continued)

Year of Publication	Journal Name	Title	ANN Used	Tools Authors
2008	Expert Systems with Applications	Selecting the right MBA schools – An application of self-organizing map networks	SOM	Melody Y. Kiang and Dorothy M. Fisher
2008	Neural Computing & Applications	Mature market segmentation: a comparison of artificial neural networks and traditional methods	SOM	Melody Y. Kiang and Dorothy M. Fisher
2008	Neuro computing	Temporal self-organizing maps for telecommunications market segmentation	SOM	Pierpaolo D'Ursoa, and Livia De Giovanni
2009	European Journal of Operational Research	Quantitative models for direct marketing: A review from systems perspective	NN & stat	Indranil Bose, Xi Chen
2009	Expert Systems with Applications	Applying artificial immune system and an algorithm in air-conditioner market segmentation	ant algo	Chui-Yu Chiu, I-Ting Kuo, Chia-Hao Lin
2009	Expert Systems with Applications	Application of data mining techniques in customer relationship management: A literature review and classification	DM	EWT Ngai, L Xiu, DCK Chau
2009	Expert Systems with Applications	An intelligent market segmentation system using k-means and particle swarm optimization	swarm & k-means	Chui-Yu Chiu, Yi-Feng Chen, I-Ting Kuo, He Chun Ku

Table A 2.2: (Continued)

Year of Publication	Journal Name	Title	ANN Used	Tools Authors
2009	Expert Systems with Applications	Neural networks and statistical techniques: A review of applications	NN	Mukta Paliwal, Usha A. Kuma
2009	Expert Systems with Applications	Outlier identification and market segmentation using kernel-based clustering techniques	ybridNN	Chih-Hsuan Wang
2009	International Journal of Nonprofit and Voluntary Sector Marketing	Outlier identification and market segmentation using kernel-based clustering techniques	SOM	Mohamed M. Mostafa
2010	Annals of Information Systems	Predicting Customer Loyalty Labels in a Large Retail Database: A Case Study in Chile	MLP	Cristián J. Figueroa
2010	Electronic Commerce Research and Applications	Identifying influential reviewers for word-of-mouth marketing	NN	Yung-Ming Li, Chia-Hao Lin, Cheng-Yang Lai
2010	Expert Systems with Applications	Visualizing market segmentation using self-organizing maps and Fuzzy Delphi method – ADSL market of a telecommunication company	SOM & fuzzy	Payam Hanafizadeh, Meysam Mirzazadeh
2010	Expert Systems with Applications	Apply robust segmentation to the service industry using kernel induced fuzzy clustering techniques	Hybrid FUZZY	Chih-Hsuan Wang

Table A2.2 (Continued)

Year of Publication	Journal Name	Title	ANN Used	Tools Authors
2010	Expert Systems with Applications	A two-stage clustering approach for multi-region segmentation	SOM	Jiahui Mo, Melody Y. Kiang, Peng Zou, Yijun Li
2010	Expert Systems with Applications	An expert system for perfume selection using artificial neural network	BPNN	Payam Hanafizadeh, Ahad Zare Ravasan and Hesam Ramazanpour Khaki
2010	Expert Systems with Applications	An expert system for perfume selection using artificial neural network	fuzzy delphi& bpn	Payam Hanafizadeh, Ahad Zare Ravasan and Hesam Ramazanpour Khaki
2010	Expert Systems with Applications	Bayesian variable selection for binary response models and direct marketing forecasting	BayesianNN	Geng Cui, Man Leung Wong, Guichang Zhang
2010	Expert Systems with Applications	Cosmetics purchasing behavior – An analysis using association reasoning neural networks	ARNN	I-Cheng Yeh, Che-hui Lien, Tao-Ming Ting, Yi-Yun Wang, ChinMing Tu
2010	Expert Systems with Applications	Application of a 3NN+1 based CBR system to segmentation of the notebook computers market	GA	YanKwang Chen, Cheng-Yi Wang, Yuan-Yao Feng

REFERENCES

[1]   Aaker, DA 2001,'Strategic market management', John Wiley and Son, New York, 2001.

[2]   Abbass, H.A. "Marriage in honeybees optimization (MBO): A haplometrosis polygynous swarming approach", in The Congress on Evolutionary Computation, CEC2001, Seoul, Korea, pp. 207–214, 2001a.

[3]   Abbass, H.A. "A monogenous MBO approach to satisfiability', In: The International Conference on Computational Intelligence for Modelling, Control and Automation, CIMCA, Las Vegas, NV, USA, 2001b.

[4]   Acan, A. and Gunay, A. 'Enhanced particle swarm optimization through external memory support', in Proceedings of the Congress on Evolutionary Computation, Vol. 2, pp. 1875–1882, 2005.

[5]   Acan, A. and Gunay, A. "Enhanced particle swarm optimization through external memory support, in Proceedings of the Congress on Evolutionary Computation", Vol. 2, pp. 1875–1882, 2005.

[6]   AIIMS. AIMMS Modeling Guide - Formulating Optimization Models, Available at: http://www.aimms.com/aimms/download/manuals/aimms3om_formulatingoptimiz ationmodels.pdf, 2012.

[7]   Akay, B. and Karaboga, D. "A comparative study of Artificial Bee Colony Algorithm", Applied Mathematics and Computation, Vol. 214, pp. 108-132, 2009.

[8]   Alter, S. Decision Support Systems: Current Practice and Continuing Challenges, Addison-Wesley, Inc., Reading, Mass, 1980.

[9]   Alves, A.K. and Medeiros, D. Genetic Process Mining, PhD thesis, Technische Universiteit Eindhoven, Eindhoven, The Netherlands, 2006.

[10]   Arnott, D. and Pervan, G. (2005) "A critical analysis of decision support systems Research", Journal of Information Technology, Vol. 20, No. 2, pp. 67-87.

[11]   Ashlock, D. Evolutionary Computation for Modeling and Optimization, Springer, 2006.

[12]   Baesens, B., Viaene, S., Poel, D. V., DenVanthienen, J. and Dedene, G. (2002) "Bayesian neural network learning for repeat purchase modelling in direct marketing", European Journal of Operational Research, Vol. 138, No. 1/1, pp. 191-211.

[13]   Baras, J. and Mehta, H. "A Probabilistic Emergent Routing Algorithm for Mobile Ad-hoc Networks", In: Proceedings of WiOpt '03: Modeling and Optimization in Mobile, Ad-Hoc, and Wireless Networks, 2003.

[14] Bhattacharyya, S. "Evolutionary algorithms in data mining: Multi-objective performance modeling for direct marketing", in Proc. 6th Internat, Conf. Knowledge Discovery Data Mining (KDD-00), ACM, New York, 2000.

[15] Bigné, E., Manzano, A. J., Küster, I. and Vila, N. 'Mature market segmentation: a comparison of artificial neural networks and traditional methods', Neural Computing & Applications, Vol. 19, No. 1, pp.1-11, 2008.

[16] Bolstad, B.M., Irizarry R.A., Astrand, M. and Speed, T. P. (2003) "A Comparison of Normalization Methods for High Density Oligonucleotide Array Data Based on Bias and Variance", Bioinformaticsi, Vol. 19, No. 2, pp. 185-193, 2003.

[17] Bonczek, R.H., Holsapple, C.W. and Whinston, A.B. 'The Evolving Roles of Models in Decision Support Systems', Decision Sciences, Vol. 11, No. 2, pp. 111-139, 1981.

[18] Boone, D. S. and Roehm, M. "Retail segmentation using artificial neural networks", International Journal of Research in Marketing, Vol.19, No.3, pp.287-301, 2002.

[19] Boztug, Y. and Reutterer, T. A Combined Approach for Segment-Specific Analysis of Market Basket Data, Humboldt, Universität zu Berlin, 2006.

[20] Brits, R., Engelbrecht, A. P. and Van den Bergh, F. "Locating multiple optima using particle swarm optimization", Applied Mathematics and Computation, Vol.189, No.2, pp.1859–1883, 2007.

[21] Brits, R., Engelbrecht, A. P. and VandenBergh, F. "Solving systems of unconstrained equations using particle swarm optimizers", In: Proceedings ofthe IEEE Conference on Systems, Man and Cybernetics, pp.102–107, 2002.

[22] Brits, R., Engelbrecht, A.P. and van den Bergh, F. "Locating multiple optima using particle swarm optimization", Applied Mathematics and Computation, Vol.189, pp.1859–1883, 2007.

[23] Brits, R., Engelbrecht, A.P. and van den Bergh, F. "A niching particle swarm optimizer", In: Proceedings of the Fourth Asia–Pacific Conference on Simulated Evolution and Learning, pp.692–696, 2002a.

[24] Brust, AGartner releases 2013 BI Magic Quadrant, Available at: http://www.zdnet.com/gartner-releases-2013-bi-magic-quadrant-7000011264, 2013.

[25] Buglione, L. and Abran, A. "Balanced Scorecards and GQM: what are the differences?" In: Proceedings FESMA/AEMES Conference, Madrid, Spain. 2000.

[26] Bult, J. R. and Wansbeek, T. "Optimal selection for direct mail", Marketing Sci, Vol.14, No.4, pp.378–394, 1995.

[27]   Business intelligence. How to build successful BI strategy Prashant Pant, Available at: http://www.loria.fr/~ssidhom/UE909R/1_BI_strategy.pdf, 2009.

[28]   Business Intelligence and Data Warehousing (BIDW). Transform Raw Data into Business Results Sun Microsystems, Inc, Available at: www.sun.com/storage/white-papers/bidw.pdf, 2005.

[29]   Camara, D. and Loureiro, A. "A novel routing algorithm for ad hoc networks", System Sciences journal, Vol.2, pp.35- 40, 2000.

[30]   Carr, L. and Stagnitto, J. Agile data warehouse design: collaborative dimensional modeling from whiteboard to star schema, DecisionOne Press, 2012.

[31]   Carver, A. and Ritacco, M. The Business Value of Business Intelligence, A Framework for Measuring the Benefits of Business Intelligence, Business Objects, 2006.

[32]   Chamoni, P. and Gluchowski, P. "Integration trends in business intelligence systems - An empirical study based on the business intelligence maturity model", Wirtschaftsinformatik, Vol.46, No.2, pp.119-128, 2004.

[33]   Chan, C. C. H. "Online auction customer segmentation using a neural network model", International Journal of Applied Science and Engineering, Vol.3, No.2, pp.101–109, 2005.

[34]   Chan, C. C. H. "Intelligent value-based customer segmentation method for campaign management: A case study of automobile retailer", Expert Systems with Applications, Vol.34, No.4, pp.2754-2762, 2008.

[35]   Chang, H.-J., Hung, L.-P. and Ho, C.L. "An anticipation model of potential customers' purchasing behavior based on clustering analysis and association rules analysis", Expert Syst. Appl, Vol.32, pp.753-764. 2007.

[36]   Changchien, S. W. and Lu, T. "Mining association rules procedure to support on-line recommendation by customers and products fragmentation", Expert Systems with Applications, Vol.20, No.4, pp.325-335, 2001.

[37]   Chattopadhyay. M., Dan, P. K., Majumdar, S. and Chakraborty, P. S. "Application of Artificial Neural Network in Market Segmentation: a review on recent trends", Management Science Letters, Vol.2, pp.425-438, 2012.

[38]   Chaudhuri, S.and Deb, K. "An interactive evolutionary multi-objective optimization and decision making procedure", Appl. Soft Comput, Vol.10, pp.496-511, 2010.

[39]   Chen, C. H., Khoo L. P. and Yan W "A strategy for acquiring customer requirement patterns using laddering technique and ART2 neural network", Advanced Engineering Informatics, Vol.16, No.3, pp.229-240. 2002.

[40]   Chen, J., Antipov, E., Lemieux, B., Cedeno, W. and Wood, D. H. "DNA computing implementing genetic algorithms", In: Proc. DIMACS Workshop on Evolution as Computation, pp.39-51. 1999.

[41]   Chen, Y. K., Wang, C. Y. and Feng, Y. Y. "Application of a 3NN+1 based CBR system to segmentation of the notebook computers market", Expert Systems with Applications, Vol.37, No.1, pp.276-281, 2010.

[42]   Cheng, C. H. and Chen, Y. S. "Classifying the segmentation of customer value viaRFM model and RS theory", Expert Systems with Applications, Vol.36, pp.4176–4184, 2009.

[43]   Chiu, C. Y., Chen, Y. F., Kuo, I. T. and Ku, H. C. "An intelligent market segmentation system using k- means and particle swarm optimization", Expert Systems with Applications, Vol.36, No.3/1, pp.4558-4565, 2009.

[44]   Chuadhuri, S., Dayal, U. and Narasayya, V. "An overview of business intelligence Technology", Communications of the ACM, Vol.5, No.8, pp.88-98, 2011.

[45]   Chung, K. Y., Oh, S. Y.,Kim, S. S. and Han, S. Y. "Three representative market segmentation methodologies for hotel guest room customers", Tourism Management, Vol.25, pp.429–441, 2004.

[46]   Claudia, I. Three Trends in Business Intelligence Technology, Available at: http://www.b-eye-network.com/channels/1127/view/2608, 2006.

[47]   Computerworld How Companies are Implementing Business Intelligence Competency Centers (BICCs),
Available at: http://www.computerworld.com/pdfs/SAS_Intel_BICC.pdf, 2006.

[48]   Davenport, T. H. and Short, J. E. "The New Industrial Engineering: Information Technology And Business Process Redesign", Sloan Management Review, Vol.31, No.4, pp.11-27, 1990.

[49]   Deb, K. Multi objective optimization using evolutionary algorithms, Chichester, Wiley, U.K,(2001)

[50]   Deming, W. E. Out of the Crisis: Quality, Productivity, and Competitive Position, Cambridge University Press, 1986.

[51]   Dewett, T. and Jones, G. R. "The role of information technology in the organization: a review, model, and assessment", Journal of Management, Vol.27, No.3, pp.313-346, 2001.

[52]   Domingos, P. and Richardson, M. "Mining the network value of customers", In: Proceedings of the Seventh ACM SIGKDD International Conference on Knowledge Discovery and Data Mining, San Francisco, CA, ACM Press, 2001.

[53]   Dorgio, M., Maniezzo, V. and Colorni, A. Ant System: An outocatalytic optimizing process, Italy, Politecnico di Milano, 1991.

[54]   Dorigo, M. and Gambardella, L. M. "Ant colonies for the travelling salesman problem", Biosystems, Vol.43, pp.73-81, 1997.

[55]   Dorigo, M. and Gambardella, L. M. A Study of Some Properties of Ant-Q, Paper presented at the Proceedings of the 4th International Conference on Parallel Problem Solving from Nature, 1996.

[56]   Eberhart, R. C., Simpson, P. and Dobbins, R. Computational Intelligence PC Tools, Academic (Chapter 6), pp.212–226, 1996.

[57]   Eberhart, R.C., Simpson, P. and Dobbins, R. Computational Intelligence PC Tools, pp.212–226, 1996.

[58]   Eckerson, W. Beyond the Basics: Accelerating BI to Maturity, TDWI Monograph Series, TDWI Research, The Data Warehousing Institute, 2007.

[59]   Eckerson, W. Business-Driven BIusing new Technologies to Foster self-service Access to Insights, Available at: http://www.lavastorm.com/assets/Lavastorm-BeyeNetwork-Business-Driven-BI-Report.pdf, 2012.

[60]   Elmasri, R. and Navathe, S. Fundamentals of Database Systems, Addison-Wesley, 2004.

[61]   English, L. P. Business Intelligence Defined, Available at: http://www.b-eye-network.com/view/1119, 2005.

[62]   English, L. P. Improving data warehouse and business information quality: methods for reducing costs and increasing profits, John Wiley & Sons, Inc. New York, USA, 1999.

[63]   Enrique, B., Manzano, A. J., Küster, I. and Vila, N. "Mature market segmentation: a comparison of artificial neural networks and traditional methods", Neural Computing & Applications, Vol.19, No.1, pp.1-11, 2008.

[64]   Eppler, M. J. Managing Information Quality: Increasing the Value of Information in Knowledge-Intensive Products and Processes, Springer, 2003.

[65]   Eppler, M. J. "Information oder Konfusion - Neue Kriterien fur die betriebliche Kommunikation", IO Management, No.5, pp.38-41, 1997.

[66]   Fathian, M., Amiri, B. and Maroosi, A. "Application of honey-bee mating optimization algorithm on clustering", Applied Mathematics and Computation, Vol.190, No.2, pp.1502–1513, 2007.

[67]   Fayyad, U. M. "Data mining and knowledge discovery: making sense out of data", IEEE Expert, Vol.11, No.5, pp.20-25, 1996.

[68]   Ferguson, B. and Lim, J. N. W. "Incentives and clinical governance. Journal of Management in Medicine", Vol.15, No.6, pp.463-487, 2001.

[69]   Foley, E. and Manon, G. "What is Business Intelligence?", International Journal of Business Intelligence Research,Vol.1, No.4, pp.1-28, 2010.

[70]   Forslund, H. "Measuring information quality in the order fulfillment process", International Journal of Quality & Reliability Management, Vol.24, No.5, pp.515-524, 2007.

[71]   Frolick, M. N. and Ariyachandra, T. R. "Business Performance Management: One Truth", Information Systems Management, Vol.23, No.1, pp.41-48, 2006.

[72]   Gangadharan, G. and Swami, S. Business Intelligence Systems: Design and Implementation Strategies, 26th International Conference on Information Technology Interfaces ITI 2004, Croatia, pp.139-144, 2004.

[73]   Gangadharan, G.R. Business intelligence systems: design and implementation strategies. Information Technology Interfaces, 26th International Conference, Available at: http://ieeexplore.ieee.org/xpls/abs_all.jsp?arnumber=1372391, 2004.

[74]   Gen, M. and Cheng, R. Genetic Algorithms and Engineering Optimization, Wiley, New York, 2000.

[75]   Ghoshal, S. and Kim, S. K. "Building Effective Intelligence Systems for Competitive Advantage", Sloan Management Review, Vol.28, No.1, pp.49-58, 1986.

[76]   Gilad, B. and Gilad, T. "SMR Forum: Business Intelligence – The Quiet Revolution", Sloan Management Review, Vol.27, No.4, pp.53-61, 1986.

[77]   Golfarelli, M. Beyond Data Warehousing: What's Next in Business Intelligence? Availableat:http://student.bus.olemiss.edu/files/Conlon/Others/Others/BusinessIntelligence/Beyond%20data%20warehousing_whats%20next%20in%20business%20intelligence.pdf, 2004.

[78]   Golgberg, D. Genetic algorithm in search, Optimization and machine learning, Addison Wesely. 1987.

[79]   Gönül, F. and Shi, M. Z. "Optimal mailing of catalogs: A new methodology using estimable structural dynamic programming models", Management Sci,Vol.44, No.9, pp.1249–1262, 1998.

[80]   Gonzales, M. L. IBM Data Warehousing with IBM Business, Intelligence Tools, Wiley, 2003.

[81]   Goonatilake, S. and Khebbal, S. Intelligent Hybrid Systems, John Wiley and Sons. 1995.

[82]   Grotz-Martin, S. Informations-qualitätund Informations-akzeptanz in Entscheidungsprozessen, Theoretische Ansätze und ihre empirische Überprüfung, s. n, 1976.

[83]   Grover, V., Teng, J. T. C., Segars, A. H. and Fiedler, K. "The influence of information technology diffusion and business process change on perceived productivity: The IS executive's perspective", Information & Management, Vol.34, No.3, pp.141-159, 1998.

[84]   Gupta, R. K. "Genetic Algorithms-An Overview", impulse, Vol.1, 2006.

[85]   Hadidi, A. and Kazemzadeh, S. "Structural Optimization using artificial bee colony algorithm", 2nd International Conference on Engineering Optimization, Lisbon, Portugal, 2010.

[86]   Hamilton, J. "Towards Customer Targeting", International Journal of Electronic Business, Vol.7, No.2, pp.1-21, 2009.

[87]   Hamilton, J. and Selen, W. "A Multi Agent Intelligence Framework for Travel Sector", 8th International Conference on Electronic Business, Hawaii, pp.36-42, 2008.

[88]   Hanafizadeh, P., Gholami, R., Dadbin, S. and Standage, N. "The core critical success factors in implementation of enterprise resource planning systems", International Journalof Enterprise Information Systems, Vol.6, No.2, pp.82-111, 2010.

[89]   Hanafizadeh, P., Ravasan, A. Z. and Khaki, H. R. "An expert system for perfume election using artificial neural network", Expert Systems with Applications, Vol.37, No.12, pp.8879-8887, 2010.

[90]   Hannula, M. and Pirttimäki, V. "Business Intelligence – Empirical Study on the Top 50 Finnish Companies", Journal of American Academy of Business, Cambridge, Vol.2, No.2, pp.593-599, 2003.

[91]   Hartemink, A., Gifford, D., Jaakkola, T. and Young, R. Maxi mum likelihood estimation of optimal scaling factors for expression array normalization, In SPIE BIOS, 2001.

[92]   Hendtlass, T. "Preserving diversity in particle swarm optimisation", In: Chung,P.W.H., Hinde, C.J. and Ali, M. (Eds.), In: Proceedings of the 16th International Conference on Industrial & Engineering Applications of Artificial Intelligence & Expert Systems, Loughborough, UK, pp.31–40, 2003.

[93]   Heristev, R. M. The ANN Book GNU Public License, Available at: htttp://ftp.funet.fi/pub/sci/neural/books/, 1998.

[94]   Herring, J. Measuring the Value of Competitive Intelligence: Accessing & Communication CI's Value to Your Organization, SCIP Publications, 1996.

[95]   Hochbaum, D. "Polynomial Time Algorithms for Ratio Regions and a Variant of Normalized Cut", IEEE Transactions on Pattern Analysis and Machine Intelligence, Vol.32, No.5, pp.889-898, 2010.

[96]   Hocevar, B. and Jaklic, J. "Assessing Benefits of Business Intelligence Systems: A Case Study", Management: Journal of Contemporary Management Issues, Vo.15, No.1, pp.87-119, 2010.

[97]   Hodgkinson, G. P. and Healey, M. P. "Cognition in Organizations", Annual Review of Psychology, pp.387-417, 2008.

[98]   Holsapple, C. W. and Whinston, A. B. "Decision Support Systems: A Knowledge Based Approach", St. Paul, West Publishing, 1996.

[99]   Howson, C. "Successful Business Intelligence: Secrets to Making BI a Killer App, McGraw-Hill Professional Computers", pp.244, 2007.

[100]   Hsieh, N. C. "An integrated data mining and behavioral scoring model for analyzing bank customers", Expert Systems with Applications, Vol.27, pp.623-633, 2004.

[101]   Hu, T.L. and Sheu, J. B. "A fuzzy-based customer classification method for demand-responsive logistical distribution operations", Fuzzy Sets and Systems, Vol.139, pp.431-450, 2003.

[102]   Huang, J.J., Tzeng, G.H. and Ong, C.S. "Marketing segmentation using support vector clustering", Expert Systems with Applications, Vol.32, No.2, pp.313-317, 2007.

[103]   Huang, K. T., Lee, Y. W. and Wang, R. Y. "Quality information and Knowledge", Prentice Hall PTR Upper Saddle River, NJ, USA, 1999.

[104]   Hugh, J. W. and Barbara, H. W. "The Current State of Business Intelligence", Computer, Vol.40, No.9, pp.96, 2007.

[105]   Hung, C. and Tsai, C. F. "Market segmentation based on hierarchical self-organizing map for markets of multimedia on demand", Expert Systems with Applications, Vol.34, No.1, pp.780-787, 2008

[106]   Hwang, H., Jung, T. and Suh, E. "An LTV model and customer segmentation based on customer value: A case study on the wireless telecommunication industry", Expert Systems with Applications, Vol.26, pp.181–188,2004.

[107]   Inmon, B. and Nesavich, A. "Unstructured Textual Data in the Organization: Managing Unstructured data in the organization", Prentice Hall, 2008.

[108]   Jiao, J. and Zhang, Y. "Product portfolio identification based on association rule mining", Computer-Aided Design, Vol.37, No.2, pp.149-172, 2005.

[109]   Jonathan, Z. B. (2005) "Market Segmentation: A Neural Network Application", Annals of Tourism Research, Vol.32, No.1, pp.93-111.

[110]   Jones, J. L., Easley, R. F. and Koehler, G. J. "Market segmentation within consolidated E-markets: A generalized combinatorial auction approach", Journal of Management Information Systems, Vol.23, No.1, pp.161–182, 2006.

[111]   Jonker, J. J., Piersma, N. and Poel, D. V. "Joint optimization of customer segmentation and marketing policy to maximize long-term profitability", Expert Systems with Applications, Vol.27, pp.159–168, 2004.

[112]   Jung, S. H. "Queen-bee evolution for genetic algorithms", Electron Lett, Vol.39, No.6, pp. 575–576, 2003.

[113]   Kaefer F., Heilman C. M. and Ramenofsky S. D. "A neural network application to consumer classification to improve the timing of direct marketing activities", Computers & Operations Research, Vol.32, No.10, pp.2595-2615, 2005.

[114]   Kahn, B. K., Strong, D. M. and Wang, R. Y. "Information Quality Benchmarks: Product and Service Performance", Communications of the ACM, Vol.45, No. 4, pp.185, 2002.

[115]   Karaboga, D. "An idea based on honey bee swarm for numerical optimization, Technical Report-TR06", Erciyes University, Engineering Faculty, Computer Engineering Department, 2005.

[116]   Karaboga, D. and Basturk, B, "On the performance of artificial bee colony algorithm", Applied Soft Computing, Vol.8, No.1, pp.687–697, 2008.

[117]   Karaboga, D. and Basturk, B. "A powerful and efficient algorithm for numerical function optimization: artificial bee colony (ABC) algorithm", Journal of Global Optimization, Vol.39, No.3, pp. 459-471, 2007.

[118]   Kauko T., Hooimeijer P. and Hakfoort J. 'Capturing Housing Market Segmentation: An Alternative Approach based on Neural Network Modelling', Housing Studies, Vol.17, No.6, pp. 875 – 894, 2002.

[119]   Kaveh, A. and Talatahari, S. 'Hybrid charged system search and particle swarm optimization for engineering design problems', Engineering Computations, Vol.28, No.4, pp.423 – 440, 2011

[120]   Kaveh, A. and Talatahari, S. "A novel heuristic optimization method: Charged system search", Acta Mechanica, Vol.213, pp.267-286, 2010.

[121]   Kennedy, J. and Eberhart, R. "Particle Swarm Optimization, In: Proceedings of the Fourth IEEE International Conference, Neural Networks, Perth, Australia, IEEE Service Center, 1995.

[122]   Kennedy, J. and Mendes, R. "Population structure and particle swarm performance, In: Proceedings of the World Congress on Computational Intelligence, Honolulu, Hawaii, pp. 1671–1676, 2002.

[123]   Kennedy, J. and Mendess, R. (2002) Population structure and particle swarm performance, In: Proceedings of the World Congress on Computational Intelligence, Honolulu, Hawaii, pp. 1671–1676.

[124]   Khoo, L. P., Chen, C. H. and Yan, W. "An investigation on a prototype customer-oriented information system for product concept development", Comput Ind, Vol.49, No.2, pp.157-74. 2002.

[125]   Kiang, M. Y., Hu, M. Y. and Fisher, D. M. "An extended self-organizing map network for market segmentation—a telecommunication example", Decision Support Systems, Vol.42 No.1, pp. 36-47, 2006.

[126]   Kim, K.-J. and Ahn, H. "A recommender system using GA K-means clustering in an online shopping market', Expert Systems with Applications", Vol.34, pp. 1200-1209, 2008.

[127]   Kim, S. Y., Jung, T. S., Suh, E. H. and Hwang, H. S. "Customer segmentation andstrategy development based on customer lifetime value: A case study", Expert Systems with Applications, Vol.31, pp.101-107, 2006.

[128]   Kim, Y. S. and Street, W. N. "An intelligent system for customer targeting: A data mining approach", Decision Support Systems, Vol.37, pp.215–228, 2004.

[129]   Kim, Y. S., Street, W. N., Russell, G. J. and Menczer, F. "Customer Targeting: A Neural Network Approach Guided by Genetic Algorithms", Management Science, Vol.51 No.2, pp.264–276, 2005.

[130]   Kim, Y., Street, W. N., Russell, G. J., and Menczer, F. "Customer targeting: A neural network approach guided by genetic algorithms", Management Science, 2001.

[131]   Kim, E., Goraksha-Hicks, P. L. L., Neufeld, T. P. and Guan, K. L. "Regulation of TORC1 by Rag GT Pases in nutrient response", Nat. Cell Biol, Vol.10, pp. 935–945, 2008.

[132]   Kimball, R. "The Data Warehouse Toolkit: The Complete Guide to Dimensional Modeling", 2nd edn., Wiley, New York, Weinheim, 2002.

[133]   Kimball, R. "The Data Warehouse Lifecycle Toolkit, Practical Techniques for Building Data Warehouse and Business Intelligence Systems", 2nd edn,   John Wiley & Sons, 2008.

[134]   Kimball, R., Ross, M., Thornthwaite, W., Mundy, J. and Becker, B. "The Data Warehouse Lifecycle Toolkit", 2nd Edn, chapter 1, Wiley Publishing, Inc, 2008.

[135]   Kobielus, J. What's Not BI? Oh, Don't Get Me Started....Oops Too Late...Here Goes....,
         Available at: http://blogs.forrester.com/james_kobielus/10-04-30-what%E2%80%
         99s_not_bi_oh_don%E2%80%99t_get_me_startedoops_too_latehere_goes, 2010.

[136]   Kohonen, T. "Self-organized formation of topologically correct feature maps",
         Biological Cybernetics, Vol.43, No.1, pp.59–69, 1982.

[137]   Kotler, P. "Marketing management", Prentice Hall, 2000.

[138]   Koudil, M., Benatchba, K., Tarabet, A. and Sahraoui, E. B. 'Using artificial bees to solve
         partitioning and scheduling problems in codesign', Appl Math Comput, Vol.186, No.2,
         pp. 1710–1722, 2007.

[139]   Kumar, D. N. (n. d) Optimization Problem and Model Formulation, Available at:
         http://civil.iisc.ernet.in/~nagesh/stwree_docs/LN01_2_Optimization_Model_formulat
         ion.pdf

[140]   Kuo R. J., Chang K. and Chien S. Y. "Integration of Self-Organizing Feature Maps and
         Genetic Algorithm-Based Clustering Method for Market Segmentation", Journal of
         Organizational Computing and Electronic Commerce, Vol.14, No.1, pp. 43-60, 2004.

[141]   Kuo, R. J., An, Y. L., Wang, H. S. and Chung, W. J. "Integration of self-organizing feature
         maps neural net work and genetic K-means algorithm for market segmentation",
         Expert Systems with Applications, Vol.30, pp. 313–324, 2006.

[142]   Kuo, R. J., Ho, L. M. and Hu, C. M. "Integration of self-organizing feature map and K-
         means algorithm for market segmentation", Computers & Operations Research, Vol.29,
         No.11, pp. 475-1493, 2002a.

[143]   Kuo, R. J., Ho, L. M. and Hu, C. M. "Cluster analysis in industrial market segmentation
         through artificial neural network", Computers & Industrial Engineering, Vol.42,
         No.2/4, pp. 391-399, 2002b.

[144]   Lai, C. C. and Chang, C. Y. "A hierarchical genetic algorithm based approach for image
         segmentation", In: Proc. IEEE Int. Conf. on Networking, Sensing and Control, pp. 1284-
         1288, 2004.

[145]   Lawton, G. "Making Business Intelligence More Useful", Computer, pp.14-16, 2006.

[146]   Lee, J. H. and Park, S. C. "Intelligent profitable customers segmentation system based
         on business intelligence tools",   Expert Systems with Applications, Vol.29,
         pp.145–152, 2005.

[147]   Lee, S. C., Suh, Y. H., Kim, J. K. and Lee, K. J. "A cross-national market segmentation of
         online game industry using SOM", Expert Systems with Applications, Vol.27,
         pp.559-570, 2004.

[148] Lee, W. I., Shih, B. Y. and Chung, Y. S. "The exploration of consumers' behavior in choosing hospital by the application of neural network", Expert Systems with Applications, Vol.34, No.2, pp.806-816, 2008.

[149] Lesca, H. and Lesca, E. "Gestion de l'information, qualité de l'information et performances de l'entreprise, Paris: Litec. 1995.

[150] Lewis, G. A. "Optimization methods", In: Swarbrick, J. and Boylan, J. C. (Eds.), Encyclopedia of pharmaceutical technology, New York: Marcel Dekker, Inc., pp. 1922 – 1937, 2002.

[151] Lewis, K., Li, C., Perrin, M. H., Bount, A., Kunitake, K., Donaldson, C., Vaughan, J., Reyes, T. M., Gulyas, J., Fischer, W., Bilezikjian, L., Rivier, J., Sawchenko, P. E, and Vale, W. W. (2001) Proc Natl Acad Sci, USA.

[152] Lewis, O. M., Ware, J. A. and Jenkins, D. H. "Identification of Residential Property Sub Markets using Evolutionary and Neural Computing Techniques", Neural Computing and Applications, Vol.10, No.2, pp. 108-119, 2001.

[153] Li, M. and Ye, L. R. "Information technology and firm performance: Linking with environmental, strategic and managerial contexts", Information & Management, Vol.35 No.1, pp.43-51, 1999.

[154] Li, X. "Adaptively choosing neighbourhood bests using species", In: A particle swarm optimizer for multimodal function optimization, Lecture Notes in Computer Science 3102, pp.105–116, 2004.

[155] Lillrank, P. "The quality of information", International Journal of Quality & Reliability Management, Vol.20, No.6, pp. 691-703, 2003.

[156] Liu, D. S., Tan, K. C., Huang, S. Y., Goh, C. K., and Ho, W. K. "On solving multi objective bin packing problems using evolutionary particle swarm optimization", European Journal of Operational Research, Vol.190, No.2, pp. 357–382, 2008.

[157] Liu, G., Yuan, J.P. and Xu, Y.S. "Multi-Objective Optimal Trajectory Planning of Space Robot Using Particle Swarm Optimization", Proc. Int. Symp. on Neural Networks, p.171-179, 2008.

[158] Lonnqvist, A. and Pirttimaki, V. "The measurement of business intelligence', Information Systems Management", Vol.23, No.1, pp.32-40, 2006.Lope, H. S. and Coelho, L. S "Particle swarm optimization with fast local search for the blind travelling salesman problem", In: proceedings of the fifth Iinternational Conference on Hybrid Intelligent System, China, pp. 245-250, 2005.

[159]   Lu, X. and Zhou, Y. "A novel global convergence algorithm: bee collecting pollen algorithm", In: ICIC'08: proceedings of the 4th international conference on intelligent computing, Berlin, Heidelberg: Springer-Verlag, pp. 518–525, 2008b.

[160]   Lu, X. and Zhou, Y. "A genetic algorithm based on multi-bee population evolutionary for numerical optimization In intelligent control and automation", WCICA 2008 7th world congress, pp.1294–1298, 2008a.

[161]   MacQueen, J. "Some methods for classification and analysis of multivariate observations" In : LeCam, L.M. and Neyman, J. (Eds.), Proceedings of the Fifth Berkeley Symposium on Mathematical Statistics and Probability, Vol.1, pp. 281-297, 1967.

[162]   Marchand, D. A., Kettinger, W. J. and Rollins J. D. Information Orientation: The Link to Business Performance, Oxford University Press, 2002.

[163]   Marinakis, Y. and Marinaki, M. "A Hybrid Honey Bees Mating Optimization Algorithm for the Probabilistic Traveling Salesman Problem", IEEE Conf. Evol. Comput, pp. 1762-1769, 2009.

[164]   Mazanec, J. A. "Neural market structure analysis: Novel topology-sensitive methodology, European", Journal of Marketing, Vol.357, No.8, pp.894 – 916, 2001.

[165]   McCarty, J. A. and Hastak, M. "Segmentation approaches in data-mining: A comparison of RFM, CHAID, and logistic regression", Journal of Business Research, Vol.60, pp. 656–662, 2007.

[166]   Mccarty, J. A. and Hastak, M. "Segmentation approaches in data-mining: A comparison of RFM, CHAID, and logistic regression", Journal of Business Research,Vol.60, pp.656-662, 2007.

[167]   Medsker, L. Hybrid Intelligent Systems, Kluwer Academic Publishers, Boston, 1995.

[168]   Menhaj, M. B. Fundamental of Artificial Neural Networks, Amir Kabir University, Tehran, Iran, 1998.

[169]   Microsoft. Solutia Microsoft pentru Business Intelligence, Available at http://www.microsoft.com/Romania/Solutii/BI.mspx, 2004.

[170]   Miettinen , K. Nonlinear Multiobjective Optimization, Springer, 1999.

[171]   Miller Devens, R. Cyclopaedia of Commercial and Business Anecdotes; Comprising Interesting Reminiscences and Facts, Remarkable Traits and Humors of Merchants, Traders, Bankers Etc. in All Ages and Countrie, Appleton and Company, New York, 1865.

[172]   Mintzberg, H., Raisinghani, D. and Théorêt, A. "The structure of unstructured decision processes", Administrative Science Quarterly, Vol.21, pp.246 – 275, 1976.

[173]   Mo J., Kiang M. Y., Zou P. and Li Y. "A two-stage clustering approach for multi-region segmentation", Expert Systems with Applications, Vol.37,No.10, pp. 7120-7131, 2010.

[174]   Morris, H. "The Financial Impact of Business Analytics", Build vs. Buy. Journal, Vol.13, No.1, pp. 40-41, 2003.

[175]   Morris, S., Meed, J. and Svensen, N. The Intelligent Manager: Adding Value in the Information Age, Pitman Publishing, London, 1996.

[176]   Moss, L. T. and Atre, S. Business Intelligence Roadmap: The Complete Project Lifecycle for Decision-Support Applications, Addison-Wesley Professional, 2003.

[177]   Mundy, J., Thornthwaite, W. and Kimball, R. The Microsoft Data Warehouse Toolkit: With SQL Server 2005 and the Microsoft Business Intelligence Toolset, Wiley Publishing, 2006.

[178]   Nenortaite, J. and Simutis, R. "Development and Evaluation of Decision-Making Model for Stock Markets", Journal of Global Optimization, Vol. 36, pp. 1-1. 2006.

[179]   Ngai, E. W. T., Xiu, L.and Chau, D. C. K. "Application of data mining techniques in customer relationship management: A literature review and classification", Exp. Syst. Appl, Vol.36, pp. 2592-2602, 2009.

[180]   Nigel, P. Consolidations in the BI industry, The OLAP Report, 2008.

[181]   O'Leary, D. E. Enterprise Resource Planning Systems, Cambridge University Press, 2000.

[182]   Okkonen, J., Pirttimäki, V., Hannula, M. and Lönnqvist, A. Triangle of Business Intelligence, Performance Measurement and Knowledge Management, IInd Annual Conference on Innovative Research in Management, Stockholm, Sweden, 2002.

[183]   Oleskow, J. Fertsch, M. and Golinska, P. Business Intelligence, Activity Based Costing, Process Management As Promising Tools For Profitable Business, 19thInternational Conference on Production Research, Poland , n.d.

[184]   Olszak, C. and Ziemba, E. "Approach to Building and Implementing Business Intelligence Systems", Interdisciplinary Journal of Information, Knowledge and Management, Vol.2, pp.135-148, 2007.

[185]   Pang, W., Wang, K., Zhou, C. and Dong, L. Fuzzy discrete particle swarm optimization for solving traveling salesman problem, Paper presented at the Fourth International Conference on Computer and Information Technology, 2004.

[186] Pang, W., Wang, K., Zhou, C. and Dong, L. "Fuzzy discrete particle swarm optimization for solving traveling salesman problem", In: Proceedings of the Fourth International Conference on Computer and Information Technology, Wuhan, China, pp.796-800. 2004b.

[187] Piateksky-Shapiro, G. and Masand, B. "Estimating campaing benefits and modelling lift", In: Proc. Of 5th ACM SIGKDD Int'l Conf. on knowledge Discovery and Data mining (KDD-99), pp.185-193, 1999.

[188] Piersma, N. and Jonker, J. Determining the direct maili8ng frequency with dynamic stochastic programming, Technical Report EI2000-34A, Econometric Institute, 2000.

[189] Porter, M. E. Competitive strategy, The Free Press, New York, 1980.

[190] Porter, M. E. and Millar, V. E. "How information gives you competitive advantage", Harvard Business Review,Vol.63, No.4, pp.149-160, 1985.

[191] Power, D. J. Justifying a Data Warehouse Project: Part 1, Available at: http://www.hpcwire.com/dsstar/98/0203/100092.html, 1997.

[192] Quinn, R. Worst Practices in Business Intelligence, Why BI Applications Succeed Where BI Tools Fail Kevin, Available at: http://www.loria.fr/~ssidhom/UE909R/1_BI_strategy.pdf, 2009.

[193] Raisinghani, M. S. Business Intelligence in the Digital Economy: Opportunities, Limitations, and Risks, Idea Group Pub, 2004.

[194] Rajagopalan, S. and Shen, C. "A cross-layer decentralized bittorrent for mobile ad hoc networks", In Third Annual International Conference on Mobile and Ubiquitous Systems: Networking & Services, pp.1–10, 2006.

[195] Rajagopalan, s. and shen, C. C. "ANSI: A swarm intelligence-based unicast routing protocol for hybrid ad hoc networks", Journal of Systems Architecture, Vol.52, pp.485-504, 2006.

[196] Ranjan, J. "Business intelligence: Concepts, Components, techniques and benefits", Journal of theoretical and applied information technology, Available at: www.jatit.org, 2005 .

[197] Rao, R. "From unstructured data to actionable intelligence", IT Professional, Vol.5, No.6, pp. 29, 2003.

[198] Redman, T. C. "Improve data quality for competitive advantage", Sloan Management, Vol.36, No.2, pp.99-107, 1995.

[199]   Reutterer T., Mild A., Natter M. and Taudes A. "A dynamic segmentation approach for targeting and customizing direct marketing campaigns", Journal of Interactive Marketing, Vol.203, No.4, pp.43-57, 2006.

[200]   Rusaneanu, A. "Comparative Analysis is of Business Intelligence Solutions", Informatica Economica, Vol.17, No.2, pp.148-156, 2013.

[201]   Ruževičius, J. and Gedminaitė, A. "Business Information Quality and its Assessment", Engineering Economics, Vol.52, No.2, pp.18-25, 2007.

[202]   Rygielski, C.H., Wang, J. C. H. and Yen, D. C. "Data Mining Techniques for Customer Relationship Management", Journal of Technology in Society, Vol.24, No.1, pp.483-501, 2002.

[203]   Ryzebol, L. Building Business Intelligence Skills, Available at: http://www.ibm.com/developerworks/data/library/techarticle/dm-0401ryzebol/index.html, 2004.

[204]   Salaun, Y. and Flores, K. "Information quality: Meeting the needs of the Consumer", International Journal of Information Management, Vol.21, No.1, pp. 21-37, 2001.

[205]   Sauder School of Business. Glossary of Common IT Terms, Available at: www.sauder.ubc.ca/cgs/itm/itm_glossary.html, 2000.

[206]   Sawka, K. "The analyst's corner: Are we valuable?" Competitive Intelligence Magazine, Vol.3, No.2, pp. 53, 2000.

[207]   Schaffer, J., Caruana, D. R., Eshelman, L. J. Designing Neural Nets that Generalize Optimally with Genetic Algorithms, Los Alamos Conference on Emergent Computation, 1989.

[208]   Schadt, E., Li, C., Su, C. and Wong, W. H. "Analyzing highdensity oligonucleotide gene expression array data", J. Cell.Biochem, Vol. 80, pp.192–202, 2001.

[209]   Scheps, S. Business Intelligence for Dummies, Wiley Publishing, 2008.

[210]   Schiefer, J. Enhanced business intelligence - supporting business processes with real-time business analytics, conference Univ. of Appl. Sci., Ludwigshafen, German, 2005.

[211]   Schiff, C. Business Intelligence and Business Performance Management: A Marriage Made in Heaven?, Available at: http://www.b-eye-network.com/view/3737, 2006.

[212]   Schwartz, J. B. and Connor, R. E. "Optimization techniques in pharmaceutical formulation and processing", In: Banker, G. S. and Rhodes, C. T. (Eds.), Modern pharmaceutics, 3rd edn, New York: Marcel Dekker Inc, pp 727-752, 1996.

[213]   Seog, J., Dean, D., Rolauffs, B., Wu, T., Genzer, J., Plaas, A. H. K., Grodzinsky, A. J., and Ortiz, C. "Nanomechanics of opposing glycosaminoglycan macromolecules", Journal of Biomechanics, Vol.38,No.9, pp.1789-1797, 2005.

[214]   Sheu, J.-J., Su, Y.-H. And Chu, K.-T. "Segmenting online game customers – The perspective of experiential marketing", Expert Systems with Applications, Vol. 36, pp. 8487-8495, 2009.

[215]   Shin, H. W. and Sohn, S. Y. "Segmentation of stock trading customers according to potential value", Expert Systems with Applica tions,Vol.27, pp.27–33, 2004.

[216]   Shirazi, M. and Soroor, J. "An intelligent agent-based architecture for strategic information systems applications", Knowledge-Based Systems, Vol.20, No.8, pp.726-735, 2007.

[217]   Sid, M., Larissa, M. and Les, B. "I found several definitions of BI", DM Review, Available at: http//www.dmreview.com/article_sub.cfm?article Id=5700, 2002.

[218]   Simon, H. A. "Administrative behavior: A study of decision-making processes in administrative organization", Hospital health services administration, Vol.39, pp.259, 1947.

[219]   Simon, H. A. The New Science of Management Decision, 3rd edn, Prentice-Hall, 1977.

[220]   Singh, A. "An artificial bee colony algorithm for the leaf-constrained minimum spanning tree problem", Applied Soft Computing,Vol.9, No.2, pp.625–631, 2009.

[221]   Singh, B. and Ahuja, N. "Response surface optimization of drug delivery system", In: Jain, N. K. (Ed.) Progress in controlled and novel drug delivery systems, 1st edn, CBS Publishers & Distributors, New Delhi, pp.470-509, 2004.

[222]   Sprague Jr., R. H. and Carlson, E.D. Building effective decision supports systems, Prentice-Hall, Englewood Cliffs, New Jersey, 1982.

[223]   Stackowial, R., Rayman, J and Greenwald, R. Oracle data Warehousing and business intelligence solutions, Wiely Publishing, Inc, Indianapolis, 2007.

[224]   Stone, M., Woodcock, N. andWilson, M. "Managing the change from marketing planning to customer relationship management", Long Range Planning, Vol.29, pp.675-683, 1996.

[225]   Suganthan, P. N. "Particle swarm optimizer with neighborhood operator", In:Proceedings of the Congress on Evolutionary Computation, Washington, Districtof Columbia, pp. 1958–1961, 1999.

[226] Tasgetiren, M. F., Liang, Y. C., Sevkli, M. and Gencyilmaz, G. "A particle swarm optimization algorithm for makespan and total flowtime minimization in the permutation flowshop sequencing problem", European Journal of Operational Research, Vol.177, No.3, pp.1930–1947, 2007.

[227] Taylor, J. and Raden, N. Smart (enough) Systems: How to Deliver Competitive Advantage by Automating Hidden Decisions, Professional Technical Reference, Prentice Hall, 2007.

[228] TDWI. 2005 TDWI Poster: Business Intelligence Maturity Model, Available at: http://tdwi.org/Publications/display.aspx? ID=7288, 2005.

[229] Thompson, O. Business Intelligence Success, Lessons Learned, Process ERP Partners, LLC, Available at:http://www.sydmart.com/artic/bi_success.pdf, 2006.

[230] Tsai C.Y. and Chiu C. C. "A purchase-based market segmentation methodology", Expert Systems with Applications, Vol.27, No.2, pp.265-276, 2004.

[231] Tseng, C. T. and Liao, C. J. "A discrete particle swarm optimization for lot-streaming flowshop scheduling problem", European Journal of Operational Research, Vol.191, No.2, pp.360-373, 2008.

[232] Turban, E., Aronson, J. E., Liang, T. P., and Sharda, R. Decision support andbusiness intelligence systems, 8th edn, Pearson Education, 2007.

[233] Tvrdíková , M. Business Intelligence Applications and its Support by high-quality Data, Available at: http://www.sssi.sk/casopis/aktualcislo/clanky/Tvrdikova_1.pdf, n. d.

[234] Tye, H. "Application of statistical 'designs of experiments' methods in drug discovery", Drug Discovery Today, Vol.9, pp.485-491, 2004.

[235] Van den Bergh, F. and Engelbrecht, A. P. "A new locally convergent particle swarmoptimiser", In: Proceedings of the IEEE International Conference on Systems, Man and Cybernetics, pp.96–101, 2002.

[236] Vassiliadis V. and Dounias, G. Applications of Nature-Inspired Intelligence in Finance, In: Proc. 4th IFIP Conf. Artificial Intelligence Applications and Innovations AIAI-07, Athens, Greece, pp. 247, 2007.

[237] Vellido, A., Lisboa, P. J. G. and Vaughan, J. "Neural networks in business: a survey of applications", Expert Systems with Applications, Vol.17, No.1, pp.51–70, 1999.

[238] Viitanen, M. "Business intelligence for strategic management in a technology-oriented company", Int. J. of Technology Intelligence and Planning, Vol.2, No.4, pp.329- 343, 2006.

[239] Wang, C. H. "Outlier identification and market segmentation using kernel-based clustering techniques", Expert Systems with Applications, Vol.36, No.2, pp.3744-3750, 2009.

[240]   Watson, H. J. and Wixom, B. H. "The BI-Based Organization", International Journal of Business Intelligence Research, Vol.1, No.1, pp.13-28, 2010.

[241]   Watson, H. and Wixom, B. H. "The Current State of Business Intelligence", Computer, pp.96-99, 2007.

[242]   Watson, H. J. and Haley, B. J. "Managerial Considerations", Communications of the ACM,Vol.41, No.9, pp.33, 1998.

[243]   Watson, H. J., Goodhue, D. L. and Wixom, B. H. "The benefits of data warehousing: why some organizations realize exceptional payoffs", Information & Management,Vol. 39, No.6, pp.491-502, 2002.

[244]   Wells, D. Business analytics Getting the point, Available at: http://b-eye network.com/view/7133, 2008.

[245]   White, c. The Role of Business Intelligence in Knowledge Management, available at: http://www.b-eye-network.com/view/720, 2005.

[246]   Wickramasinghe, L., Amarasisi, R. and Alahakoon, L. "A hybrid intelligent multiagent system for e-business", Computational Intelligence, Vol. 20, No. 4, pp. 603-623,2004.

[247]   Williams, S. "Assessing BI Readiness: A Key to BI RO", Business Intelligence Journal, Vol.3, No.9, pp.15-23, 2004.

[248]   Williams, S. and Williams, N. The Profit Impact of Business Intelligence, Morgan Kaufmann, 2007.

[249]   Woo, J. Y., Bae, S. M. and Park, S. C. "Visualization method for customer targeting using customer map", Expert Systems with Applications, Vol 28, pp. 763–772, 2005.

[250]   Wu, J. Calculating the ROI for Business Intelligence Projects, Available at: http://www.ijcim.th.org/SpecialEditions/v13nSP2/pdf/p1.1-1.3 Data%20Warehousing.pdf, 2000.

[251]   Yang, Y. H., Dudoit, P. S., Luu, D. M., Lin, V., Peng, J., Ngai, H. and T. P. "Speed.'Normalization for cDNA microarray data: a robust composite method addressing Single and multiple slide systematic variation", Nucl, Acids Res, Vol. 30, No.4, pp. 15,

[252]   Zeng, L., Lida, X., Zhongzhi, S., Maoguang, W. and Wenjuan, W. "Techniques, Process, and Enterprise Solutions of Business Intelligence", IEEE Conference on Systems, Man, and Cybernetics, Taipei, Taiwan, 2006.

[253]   Zeng, L., Xu, L., Shi, Z., Wang, M. and Wu, W. Techniques, process and enterprise solution of business intelligence, IEEE conference on system, Man and cybernetics October 8 – 11, Taipei, Taiwan, pp. 4722, 2007.

www.ingramcontent.com/pod-product-compliance
Lightning Source LLC
LaVergne TN
LVHW050558200726

843508LV00010B/1678